In His Own Image

In His Own Image

We Are Wonderfully Made

Art Mathias

Wellspring Publishing
ANCHORAGE, ALASKA

Published by Wellspring Ministries of Alaska
P.O. Box 190084
Anchorage, Alaska 99519-0084
907-563-9033
e-mail: akwellspr@aol.com
Website: akwellspring.com

Cover by C. Ruby Designs

WARNING: MEDICAL DISCLAIMER:
I am not a medical doctor. I do not intend for anyone
to use this work as a diagnostic tool or in any other
way, to practice medicine. We do not, nor will we ever,
advise anyone to stop medications or stop seeing their
doctor. We strongly advise you to consult your medical
doctor on all medical decisions.

Contents

Foreword

As a physician, I have long believed that every illness has a physical, emotional, and spiritual component. . . even the "common cold." But the proportion of these three components can be strikingly different in patients with the same illness. Some patients with a cold stay in bed, expecting family members to rally and wait on them, while others bundle up and go to work. Another example—two of my patients had a broken arm. One pined and bemoaned the temporary loss of her limb, while the other gleefully had friends signing her cast. Same injury, but the emotional and spiritual components made the difference between gloom and cheerfulness.

Medical science has come a long way in diagnosing and treating a wide variety of illnesses, yet many patients have poor responses to treatment, especially those with chronic illnesses. Rarely does a physician investigate the spiritual and emotional contributions to an illness, so two-thirds of the cause of the illness remains unexplored.

In His Own Image goes beyond the physical roots of illness and exposes the underlying spiritual contributions that may have made the patient susceptible to the illness in the first place. This book does not take the place of competent medical evaluation and treatment. Rather, it details and documents the impact of sin on the body, especially the immune system and the nervous system. Longstanding negative emotions (or sins) alter a whole array of physiological parameters in the body, producing stress and illness. These negative emotions can prolong or even prevent recovery. To realize that Satan is the author of these negative emotions and uses them to fuel human misery is, I believe, the next breakthrough in medicine.

The age-old battle between good and evil is not a storybook drama but a realtime phenomenon with painful consequences if the patient is unaware of the emotional and spiritual components of illness. Once discernment (understanding the difference between good and evil) has been gained and repentance for sins has been made, dramatic and complete recoveries have been reported and witnessed. The healing power of Jesus Christ is present and accessible today.

The list of illnesses contained in this book, and the sins which the author has noted to be commonly associated with each illness, can give hope to the patient still in search of healing. However, recognizing and surrendering the broader areas of sin produce profound effects. The lifting of fear, shame, guilt, trauma, damaging soul ties, bitterness, addiction, etc. may be the final acts that will produce the healing when all else has failed. It has been my observation that thoroughness and persistence in this kind of spiritual deliverance can bring about true healing.

Adrienne Buffaloe, MD

Acknowledgments

I want to offer a special thank you to Adrienne Buffaloe, MD; Kris Gugel, RN; Nancy Smith, RN; Kay Hopka, LPN; Esther Gugel, medical student; and Ellen Frieder for their work in editing and proof-reading, as well as insights into Scripture and medicine.

Introduction

Disease is one of the strongest motivations to begin exploring the deeper meanings of life. When we become sick, we begin to seek an explanation for our suffering and ask ourselves, why? The most common response is to blame God, someone else, or something else for our suffering. We would like to suggest a paradigm shift in our thinking and consider the question, "Is there a connection between behavior, attitudes, thoughts, emotions and disease?" In Christian terms is there a connection between sin and disease? Instead of finding someone or something to blame, should we instead be looking inside ourselves? These are age-old arguments. The purpose of this book is to shed new light on this subject from the secular viewpoints of pyschoneuroimmunology, immunology and endocrinology, and also from Scripture.

The idea that thoughts are linked with disease and death has existed for over three thousand years. Hippocrates (500 BC) theorized that health was related to the balance of four bodily humors which contributed to specific temperaments. Galen (AD 131–201) took this idea further, proposing that a balance of the "passions" was essential for physical health. He believed that severe emotional reactions were considered causes of diseases such as stroke, birth defects, asthma, ulcers and, ultimately, even death (Sternberg 1997). These beliefs persisted through the medieval period and the early Renaissance. In *The Anatomy of Melancholy*, Robert Burton said, "the mind most effectively works upon the body, producing by his passions and perturbations miraculous alterations...cruel diseases and sometimes death itself."

Although this idea dominated medical practice for much of early civilization, in the modern era the science of the biologic basis of health and disease (pathophysiology) has far surpassed the science of emotions (psychology). Today, despite overwhelming evidence, medical science mostly ignores the mind-body connection. Today's drug-oriented medicine seeks to find the magic drug to miraculously cure all our diseases. Is this the true answer?

There is extensive evidence from medical science itself which demonstrates the connection between the mind and the body—how negative thoughts and emotions contribute to disease and death through immune dysfunction.

The endocrine system in our bodies serves as one central gateway for psychological influences and health. Stress, depression, and other negative emotions can provoke the release of hormones that have multiple effects on the immune system (Rabin 1999).

The central nervous system also responds to our thoughts and emotions. Fear or alarm causes the adrenal glands to secrete neurotransmitters that create an immediate fight-flight response which also can have multiple effects on the immune system (Felten 1991, Maier 1994).

There is also an interconnectedness between the spirit, soul, and body that is plainly experienced in psychology, medicine, and in our walk with God.

III John 1:2 says, "Beloved, I wish above all things that thou mayest prosper and be in health, even as thy soul prospereth."

I Thessalonians 5:23 says, "And the very God of peace sanctify you wholly; and I pray God your whole spirit and soul and body be preserved blameless unto the coming of our Lord Jesus Christ."

The "psyche" or "soul" which can be defined as our mind, will and emotions, cannot be separated from our spirit and body. As we will see in this book, the sciences of psychology and medicine clearly demonstrate the effects of negative emotions on our physical and mental health but they fail to understand the connection to the Spirit.

The use of terminology in Scripture plainly teaches the connection between the spirit, soul, and body. For example, the terms for salvation, *soteria* and the verb form *sozo*, are used over one hundred and fifty times to mean "to save, cure, heal, preserve, keep safe and sound, rescue from danger or destruction, deliver, to save from peril, injury or suffering, to make whole from physical death by healing, and from spiritual death by forgiving sin and its effects" (Matthew 21-22, Mark 6:56, Acts 4:9, James 5:15-16).

Rapha means "to cure, heal, repair, mend, and restore health" (Genesis 20:17). *Rophe* or doctor means "the one who heals (Exodus 15:26) diseases and sins (Psalms 103:1-3) and broken hearts" (Luke 4:18-20, Psalms 147:3). *Marpe* refers to the healing of the body, but is also used to promote the soundness of mind and moral character (Proverbs 4:22, 16:24). The word health comes from *hugiaina*, which denotes soundness in the body and good health (III John 2). *Therapeuo* means "to service and care for, to medically treat, heal, and restore" (Matthew 10:8, Luke 10:9). This is the root for the English word "therapy."

The redemptive plan of God has implications for spirit, soul, and body. His blessings cover the spiritual, emotional, and physical.

The purpose of this book is to expose the reader to the truth of God's Word. King Solomon wrote the following verses in the Book of Proverbs about 1000 BC:

> Proverbs 16:24: "Pleasant words are as a honeycomb, sweet to the soul, and health to the bones." Our immune system is formed in the marrow of our bones.

> Proverbs 12:25: "Heaviness in the heart of man maketh it stoop: but a good word maketh it glad."

> Proverbs 14:30: "A sound heart is the life of the flesh: but envy the rottenness of the bones."

Proverbs 15:30: "The light of the eyes rejoiceth the heart: and a good report maketh the bones fat."

Proverbs 17:22: "A merry heart doeth good like a medicine: but a broken spirit drieth the bones."

King David said in Psalms 31:10: "For my life is spent with grief, and my years with sighing: my strength faileth because of mine iniquity, and my bones are consumed."

In this book we will demonstrate how the sciences of psychoneuroimmunology, immunology, and endocrinology support the Word of God. There is a definite connection between our thoughts and our health. While the sciences can demonstrate the truth of God's Word, they do not provide the cure or answer to the problems. We will also demonstrate that the Word of God has the answer or cure for our sicknesses and diseases.

We Are Wonderfully Made

PSYCHONEUROIMMUNOLOGY

Psychoneuroimmunology (PNI) refers, most simply put, to the study of the inter-actions between behavior (stress, i.e., our thoughts, attitudes, and emotions), the brain (central nervous system), the endocrine system (hormones), and the immune system. Its central premise is that the regulation of the internal environment (homeostasis), is an integrated process, involving interactions between the nervous (brain), endocrine (hor-mones), and immune systems (which provides the ability to fight viruses, bacteria, etc.).

PNI is the study of interactions or interrelations of emotions and behaviors (the mind) and how they affect the endocrine and the immune systems. The term interrela-tions is used because the relations are bi-directional (Felton 1985, Maier 1994, Shavit 1984). In other words, these systems communicate with each other. It grew from the realization that the immune system does not operate autonomously. PNI is the study of how and why stressors alter the immune system and its functions.

Traditionally, the immune system has been considered to be an autonomous or closed defense mechanism of the body. But due to the volumes of research suggesting a connection between the brain, emotional states (stress), and the immune system, a new field of research began.

In this book I want to approach PNI in a simple manner to help all of us understand how negative and positive emotions affect our behavior and health. Our psychological state (i.e., the way we choose to respond to stress in our individual lives) creates a central nervous system response (electrical), an endocrine system response (hormonal), and a behavior change. This may result in an immune system change that causes disease susceptibility (Cohen 1996). Positive emotions can result in immune enhancement (Takahashi 2001, Berk 2001).

For the body to function properly, its various parts and organs must communicate with each other to ensure that a constant internal environment (i.e., homeostasis), is maintained.

A stressor can be defined as any sort of external or internal challenge, either visual, tactile, olfactory, or emotional, that disrupts the physiological equilibrium, or home-ostasis, of an individual (Friedman 1996). A stressor is in reality anything that we allow to change the internal balance in our bodies. As we will see as we study further, thoughts and emotions that may be the product of an experience are the number one stressor and thus the number one cause of an imbalance in our homeostasis.

Our choice in how we react to these experiences or stressors dictates the physiological response in our bodies. Two people can go through the same experience (stressor), with totally different responses, depending on how they view the stressor or experience. An inappropriate response will result in the activation of our sympathetic (autonomic or "automatic") nervous system, which causes the endocrine system to release catecholamine, norepinephrine (noradrenaline), and epinephrine (adrenaline), acetylcholine, and cortisol, all of which adversely affect the immune system (Friedman 1996).

It can also be said that if we are experiencing a physical response (i.e., fight-flight, rise in blood pressure, shortness of breath, headache, muscle tension, immune dysfunction, unexplained chronic pain, etc.), then there is very often first a psychological trigger. The triggers are usually negative emotions such as anger, resentment, jealousy, fear, rage, loneliness, rejection, hatred, violence, etc. We will study the results of these and other emotions in detail later.

Communication among various regions of the body causes the various organs to respond to any changes in the internal and external environments. Our bodies were created with two systems to help ensure communication: the nervous system and the hormone (neuroendocrine) system.

The nervous system generally allows rapid transmission — within fractions of seconds — of information between different body regions. The hormone system, which relies on the production and release of hormones from various glands and on the transport of those hormones through the bloodstream, is better suited for situations that require more widespread and longer lasting regulatory actions.

Thus, the two communication systems complement each other. In addition, both systems interact: stimuli from the nervous system can influence the release of certain hormones, and hormones from the endocrine system can influence the nervous system. Both systems influence the immune system. Generally speaking, hormones control the growth, development, and metabolism of the body, the electrolyte composition of bodily fluids, and reproduction (Hiller-Sturmhofel 1998).

To understand these reactions and communications, we will need a basic understanding of our brain or nervous, immune, and endocrine systems and stress. Let's take a brief look at each of these systems. As you read these basic descriptions, remember that it is our thoughts and emotions that trigger the responses. It is our thoughts and emotions that begin a chain reaction in our brain and endocrine systems that eventually have a consequence in our immune system.

As you read the following descriptions, please do not get lost in the big words and complicated processes, but marvel at how fearfully and wonderfully God made our bodies. Marvel at the complexity and beauty of His creation — you!

THE BRAIN/NERVOUS SYSTEM
The Structure of the Brain

Our brain functions much like a complicated computer that enables us to speak, solve difficult problems, and produce creative ideas. It is a complex system of interconnected parts. The "lower structures" include those circuits of the brainstem deep within the skull that mediate the basic elements of energy flow, such as states of arousal and alertness and the physiological state of the body (temperature, respiration, heart rate). At the top of the brainstem is the thalamus, an area that serves as a gateway for incoming sensory information and has extensive connections to other regions of the brain, including the neocortex.

The "higher structures," such as the neocortex at the top of the brain, mediate more complex information-processing functions such as perception, thinking, and reasoning. The centrally located "limbic system"—including regions called the orbitofrontal cortex, anterior cingulate, and amygdala—play a central role in coordinating the activity of the higher and lower brain structures. The limbic regions mediate emotion, motivation, and goal-directed behavior. Limbic structures permit the integration of a wide range of basic mental processes, such as the appraisal of meaning, the processing of social experience and the regulation of emotion. The limbic region also houses the medial temporal lobe (sides of the temples), including the hippocampus, which plays a central role in consciously accessible forms of memory.

The limbic system has extensive input and output pathways that link it to widely distributed areas in the brain and is primarily responsible for integrating brain activity. Just below the limbic system, and in direct connection with, are the hypothalamus and the pituitary (part of the endocrine system) which are responsible for physiological homeostasis, or the equilibrium of the body. The limbic system (brain) controls homeostasis through the regulation of neuroendocrine activity (neuronal firing and hormonal release). This is one of the ways an experience affects our health in a either a negative or positive way.

In stressful or traumatic situations the response of the brain and body are intricately intertwined. For example, stress is often responded to by the hypothalamic-pituitary-adrenocortical (HPA) axis (hormones), along with the autonomic nervous system (which regulates such things as the heart rate and respiration) and the immune system (which is responsible for defense against invaders).

As a whole the brain/nervous, endocrine and immune systems function as a system that is interconnected and dependent on its various parts (Siegel 1999).

The brain has an estimated one hundred billion neurons, which are collectively over two million miles long. Each neuron has an average of ten thousand connections that directly link it to other neurons (Siegel 1999, Kandel 1992). There are thought to be about one million billion of these connections, making it the most complex structure, natural or artificial, on earth (Siegel 1999, Green 1998). Because of the interconnectedness of the nerves, the activation of one neuron can influence an average of ten thousand neurons at the receiving ends.

The Structure of the Nervous System

The nervous system provides pathways by which information travels from a person's surroundings to the brain. The brain then sends instructions to various muscles and organs, via other pathways, so that the body can respond to the information. These pathways are called neural pathways.

The nervous system is made up of billions of special cells called neurons, or nerve cells. The nerves form a network of pathways that conduct information rapidly throughout our bodies. Our reaction to a stimulus may only take an instant, but it involves a highly complex process.

Specialized parts of neurons, or nerve cells called receptors, are located in every specific part of our bodies. For example, the eyes have specialized receptors that translate sight into nerve messages or impulses to the brain. The ears translate sounds into nerve messages to the brain. This same process occurs in every organ in the body. Thus, thousands of specific neurons or nerve cells are needed. They are very similar to our immune cells in that they also have specialized receptor cites that only allow them to respond to a specific stimulus. As we will learn later, this is also true of hormones.

The neuron (nerve cell) contains three basic parts: a cell body with dendrites, an axon, and an axon terminal, or end. The cell body is a microscopic cell. It is a center for receiving and sending nerve impulses.

The axon is the nerve fiber. It is a tube-like extension of a neuron, specialized to carry nerve messages and may have enough branches to make contact with as many as a thousand other neurons.

The dendrites of a neuron are branching tube-like extensions of the cell body that form a pattern, much like the limbs of tree. The dendrites receive the nerve impulses into the cell body, which initiates impulse transmission along the axon to its end or terminal. At the axon terminal the neuron doesn't quite touch the dendrites of the next neuron. They are separated by an extremely narrow space called the synaptic cleft or synapses, across which nerve impulses are transmitted by chemical and electrical conduction. The chemical conducting substances are hormones called neurotransmitters.

Communication is conducted by nerve impulses, which are simply electrical currents that flow along the nerve. Nerve cell membranes have pores or receptors that allow only certain substances or messages to pass through. The inside of the axon or nerve fiber is also filled with a solution that can conduct an electric charge. Some axons are covered and protected by insulation called the myelin sheath. The myelin sheath protects the nerve fiber and protects the nerve impulse from short circuiting.

As we mentioned, certain chemicals, or hormones called neurotransmitters, transmit the nerve impulses. When an impulse reaches the end of an axon (nerve), a neurotransmitter is released into the synaptic cleft (synapse). The neurotransmitter moves to the dendrites of the next nerve cell and causes certain pores or receptors to open, thus facilitating the conduction of the nerve impulse. This process happens thousands of times while transmitting a nerve impulse to the brain.

The Neurotransmitters

More than 30 substances are thought to be neurotransmitters, including norepinephrine (noradrenaline), epinephrine (adrenaline), acetylcholine, dopamine, histamine, and serotonin. Many of these neurotransmitters have more than one function. The neurotransmitters are divided into different types or categories such as acetycholine, monoamines, amino acids, and neuropeptides. Let's look at some of them and their functions in the body.

Acetylcholine (ACH): Aids in transmission of sensory information to the brain, control of muscles and many internal organs, including peristalsis, storage and recall of memory, improving motivation and slowing heartbeat. Alzheimer's disease is associated with a decrease in acetylcholine-secreting neurons.

MONOAMINES

Serotonin (5HTT): Influences mood and behavior; is a natural anti-anxiolytic, and vasoconstrictor (reduces blood vessel size); reduces appetite, impassivity and aggression, and is responsible for normal sleep.

Histamine: Found in mast cells and basophils; is released in allergic reactions, and results in increased blood flow to an injured part of the body, and releases gastric acid. It expands and dilates blood vessels.

CATECHOLAMINES

Epinephrine (adrenaline)/Norepinephrine (noradrenaline): These are produced in the adrenal glands and cause increased psychomotor activity and increase in respiratory and cardiac stimulation (i.e., a fight-flight response). Also function as vasoconstrictors (they reduce blood vessel size).

Dopamine: Found in basal ganglia, affects movement, emotional response, and pleasure and pain receptors; important for motivation and sexual arousal; and helps to regulate immune functions.

AMINO ACIDS

Aspartate and Glutamate: Involved in integrative function such as speech, memory, learning, planning and consciousness.

GABA: is an inhibitory neurotransmitter that puts the brakes on too much brain activity. People with epilepsy and seizure disorders are low on this brain chemical.

NEUROPEPTIDES

Gastrin and Secretin: Stimulates stomach to secrete gastric acid. Stimulates pancreas to secrete bicarbonate.

Angiotensin: A vasoconstrictor that stimulates the adrenal and pituitary glands to regulate blood pressure.

Bradykinin: Lowers blood pressure, and increases blood flow by dilating peripheral blood vessels.

Substance P: A vasodilator (increases blood vessel size), bronchoconstrictor, potent diuretic; pro-inflammatory and reduces pain sensitivity.

Enkephalins (endorphins): A natural opiate (painkiller).

Cholecystokinin: Secreted by the pancreas to act upon the gallbladder to release digestive enzymes.

GASES

Nitric Oxide: Signals the cardiovascular and nervous systems, affects blood pressure and penile erections. Important in the immune system to protect against infection because it kills bacteria and parasites.

Carbon Monoxide: Produced in hypothalamus and assists in nerve impulse transmission there.

We have listed just of few of the neurotransmitters and have given a very brief description of their function, just to let the reader see how they affect our everyday lives. Negative emotions have a significant impact on the under- or over-secretion of neurotransmitters (Kendall 2002, Cohen 2000).

The nervous system has three main parts: the central nervous system, the peripheral nervous system, and the autonomic nervous system.

The central nervous system functions as the main switchboard that controls and coordinates the activities of the entire nervous system. The central nervous system consists of the brain and the spinal cord.

The peripheral nervous system carries all the messages sent between the central nervous system and the rest of the body. It consists of twelve pairs of nerves that originate in the brain, and thirty-one pairs of nerves of the spinal cord. These cranial and spinal nerves serve as the telephone wires that carry messages to and from every receptor and effector cell in the body.

The autonomic nervous system is a special part of the peripheral nervous system that regulates such automatic bodily processes as breathing and digestion, without conscious control from the brain. This constant regulation enables the body to maintain a stable internal environment (homeostasis).

The autonomic nervous system has two distinct parts, the sympathetic and the parasympathetic system. The sympathetic system responds to the body's needs during increased activity and in emergencies. The actions of the sympathetic system include speeding up the heartbeat, sending additional blood to the muscles, and enlarging the pupils of the eyes, as well as other functions of the fight-flight response. The parasympathetic system in general opposes the actions of the sympathetic system. The parasympathetic system's functions include slowing down the heartbeat, diverting blood from the muscles to the stomach and intestines, and contraction of the pupils of the eyes. In other words, it stops the fight-flight response. The balance of activity between these two systems is controlled by the central nervous system (McCance 1998).

The Development of the Brain/Nervous System

Experts have long argued the question: "Is it heredity or experience that shapes who we are?" Daniel J. Siegel, M.D., in his book *The Developing Mind* teaches that the structure and function of the developing brain are determined by how experiences, especially interpersonal relationships, shape the genetically directed maturation of the nervous system (Siegel 1999).

Dr. Siegel received his medical degree from Harvard University and completed his postgraduate medical education at the University of California, Los Angeles, with training in pediatrics, general adult psychiatry, and child and adolescent psychiatry. He has served as a National Institute of Mental Health Research Fellow at UCLA. Dr. Siegel formerly directed the UCLA training program in child psychiatry and is currently the medical director of the Infant and Preschool Service at UCLA and associate clinical professor of psychiatry at the UCLA School of Medicine.

Dr. Seigel says, "recent findings of neural science show that interaction with the enviornment, especially relationships with other people, directly shape the development of the brain's structure and function" (Siegel 1999).

Our experiences alter both the activity and the structure of the connections between neurons and directly shape the circuits responsible for such processes as memory, emotion, and self-awareness. We can use an understanding of the impact of experience on the mind to deepen our grasp of how the past continues to shape present experience and influence future actions. In other words, human connections shape the neural connections from which the mind emerges (Siegel 1999). The mind is defined as the human soul, the psyche, the intellect, the will, and emotions.

Experience early in life may be especially crucial in organizing the way the basic structures of the brain develop. For example, traumatic experiences at the beginning of life may have more profound effects on the "deeper" structures of the brain, which are responsible for basic regulatory capacities and enable the mind to respond later to stress. Thus we see that abused children have elevated stress hormone levels (Siegel 1999).

More common everyday experiences also shape brain structure. The brain's development is an experience-dependent process, in which experience activates certain pathways in the brain, strengthening existing connections and creating new ones. Lack of experience can lead to cell death in a process called "pruning." In other words "we use it or lose it" (Siegel 1999).

An infant is born with genetically programmed excess in neurons. Both genes and experience determine the growth and development of these neurons and the synaptic connections. Genes contain the information for the general organization of the brain's structure, but experience determines which genes are expressed, and how, and when. Early in life, interpersonal relationships are a primary source of the experience that shapes how genes express themselves within the brain (Siegel 1999). This experience begins at conception. Experiences can shape not only what information enters the mind, but also the way in which the mind develops the ability to process that information, how we will react to situations containing similar triggers, and our concept of who we are, and what we expect from future relationships.

The misinterpretations of genetic studies have lead to beliefs such as "What parents do have no effect on their children's development." A wide range of studies have now clarified that human growth and development are products of the effects of experience on the genetic potential (Siegel 1999, Benedersky 1994, Coe 1992, Goldsmith 1997, Kendler 1986, Rosemblum 1994, Ruter 1997, Gunnar 1992, Teicher 1997, Rakic 1994).

Genes have two major functions. First, they act as templates for information that is to be passed on to the next generation. Second, they have a transcription function. Transcription is directly influenced by experience. In other words, experience determines which genes will express themselves via the process of protein synthesis (Kandel 1998, Siegel 1999). It is fascinating to learn that even our genes are not isolated from our experiences. In reality the first function of our genes, mentioned above, is the product of the experiences of our ancestors. So even what we inherit is affected by experiences.

I hope you are getting a picture of how important our experiences are. But we must always remember we are responsible for how we choose to react to the experiences of life. We have a choice to respond in anger or forgiveness. As adults we also have a choice in how we deal with our experiences in childhood. We can never blame our problems on others. The good news is that our genes are "plastic" and can be molded or changed through our lives (Siegel 1999). Positive responses to negative experiences can change genetics.

Our brains are living organisms or systems that are open and dynamic. In other words, how we choose to react to our experiences throughout our lives will influence our brain and our mind and thus our continued growth and development. How we choose to respond or react to an experience also affects our physical and mental health.

The brain is also functionally and physically linked to other systems in the body, thereby affecting, controlling or regulating many other systems, including the immune and endocrine systems.

**How does the brain (nervous system) control
or regulate the immune and endocrine systems?**

For this to be possible, two conditions would have to be demonstrated. First, the brain would have to make physical contact with the immune and endocine systems in some way. Second, this "connection" would have to affect how the immune system responds to antigens (i.e., pathogens or allergens) and how the endocrine system responds to stressors.

The first question is answered when we understand how the brain is able to connect with and control the peripheral organs and their processes. The brain has several ways to do this. One is through the autonomic nervous system. It is understood that its sympathetic and parasympathetic branches stimulate the nerve connections in organs like the stomach and heart. But research has also demonstrated that the sympathetic nervous system also stimulates immune system organs, such as the thymus, bone marrow, spleen, and lymph nodes (Feltman 1987).

Additionally, the brain and nervous systems are also directly connected to the glands of the endocrine system. Sympathetic nerve terminals cause endocrine glands to release norephinephrine and adrenaline, and immune organs have receptors for these neurotransmitters. Also, the terminals of sympathetic nerves in these immune system organs make contact with lymphocytes (B- and T-cells). Thus, the brain is physically connected to the immune system in several ways (Felten 1991, Maier 1994).

Another way in which the brain can communicate to peripheral organs is through releasing factors that cause endocrine glands to secrete hormones into the blood, thereby enabling the hormones to reach and affect the various organs of the body.

An example of this that we will consider later in this book is the hormones that are produced by stress. Stress causes many effects on our bodies, one of which is to produce a hormone called cortisol, which is released from the adrenal glands. The presence of stress is often defined by the presence of high levels of stress hormones in the blood (i.e., cortisol and adrenaline).

The brain also has direct contact with the immune and endocrine systems through the hypothalamus and limbic system. This process is started in the brain through physical and psychological stressors, which cause the hypothalamus to release corticotrophin into the blood. This hormone then reaches the pituitary gland (an endocrine gland), where it leads to the release of adrenocorticotrophic hormones into the blood. This pituitary hormone ultimately arrives at the adrenal gland (an endocrine gland) where it causes the release of glucocorticoids (cortisol) (Maier 1994). The reality is that the brain releases a chemical that leads to hormones from an endocrine system gland being released into the blood circulation. The immune T- and B-cells have receptors for many of these hormones including the stress hormones (Plaut 1987). Excess cortisol can, over time, destroy the cells of the immune system. Thus again, there is a physical and psychological connection between the brain and the immune and endocrine systems.

The stimulation of the sympathetic nervous system by stressors also leads to the release of catecholamines (i.e., epinephrine (adrenaline), and norepinephrine (noradrenaline), from the adrenal gland (an endocrine gland) into the blood. Lymphocytes (B- and T-cells) are affected because they also have receptors for these catecholamines, thus immune functions are altered by the action of these hormones.

If the brain participates in the regulation of the immune system, then it would follow that brain damage, lesions or stimulation of a brain site should change some aspect of the immune response. Indeed, this has been proven correct. Lesions of the hypothalamus alter the course of a variety of immune responses. This is true for measures of immune function such as antibody production, rejection of tissue transplants (Macris 1970), and lymphocyte production (Roszman 1985). Lesions in other areas of the brain have also altered immune function (Nance 1987). Electrical stimulation of the hypothalamus also augments several immune functions (Korneva 1967).

The point is that destruction or stimulation of nerves that are connected to the immune system does in fact alter the function of the immune system. Thus, the connection between the immune system and the central nervous system (brain) is important (Maier 1994).

In a later chapter we will study how psychological events (thoughts and emotions from experiences) also alter our immune and endocrine systems. This is the main point of this book. But before we study the effect of our emotions on our health, we need to understand our immune and endocrine systems and how they communicate with our nervous system and the resulting effects.

THE ENDOCRINE SYSTEM

Our Creator was very wise in the way He designed our bodies. He set in place a delicate system of checks and balances. For the body to function properly, its various parts and organs must communicate with each other to ensure that a constant, internal environment (i.e., homeostasis) is maintained.

For example, neither the body temperature, nor the levels of salts and minerals (i.e., electrolytes in the blood), must fluctuate beyond preset limits. Communication among various regions of the body also is essential for enabling the organism to respond appropriately to any changes in the internal and external environments.

Two systems help ensure communication: the nervous system, which we have just studied, and the hormonal (neuroendocrine) system. The nervous system generally allows rapid transmission (within fractions of seconds) of information between different body regions. The nervous system sends electrical messages to control and coordinate the body.

Hormonal communication, which relies on the production and release of hormones from various glands, and on the transport of those hormones through the bloodstream, is much slower, and thus better suited for situations that require more widespread and longer lasting regulatory actions. Generally speaking, hormones control the growth, development, and metabolism of the body, the electrolyte composition of bodily fluids, and reproduction.

Thus, the two communication systems complement each other. In addition, both systems interact: stimuli from the nervous system can influence the release of certain hormones, and hormones affect the nervous system (Hiller-Sturmhofel 1998). Additionally, psychological factors (thoughts and emotions) affect both our nervous and endocrine systems, which in turn modulate, alter, or regulate our immune system. The effects on our immune system can be positive or negative, depending on the emotion (Solvason 1988). We will study this in detail in the chapters on classical conditioning and stress.

To maintain proper homeostasis, our endocrine system, a complex network of glands and chemical messengers (hormones), transfers information and instructions from one set of cells to another. These hormonal messages are sent to essentially all cells in our bodies. Thus, our mood, growth and development, sleep, appetite, tissue function, metabolism, blood pressure, respiration, sexual function and brain chemistry are regulated.

The endocrine system also alters and affects or regulates the autonomic nervous system by way of the hypothalamus (a gland located in the brain). The communication is bi-directional. In other words, the nervous and endocrine systems regulate each other by communicating with each other. Endocrinology is the study of the endocrine glands and their hormones and their effects on our bodies.

What Are Hormones?

Hormones are molecules or chemicals that are produced by endocrine glands, including the hypothalamus, pituitary, adrenals, gonads (testes and ovaries), thyroid, parathyroid, and pancreas (see Figure 1, following page). They are sometimes called "messenger molecules."

The term "endocrine" implies that in response to specific stimuli, the products of those glands are released into the bloodstream. Conversely, exocrine glands (sweat glands and salivary glands) release their secretions to the outside of the body (sweat), inside the mouth (saliva), or into the gastrointestinal tract (digestive hormones).

The hormones then are carried via the blood to their target cells. Some hormones have only a few specific target cells, whereas other hormones affect numerous cell types throughout the body. In other words, a specific hormone is designed to affect only specific cells or organs.

The target cells for each hormone are characterized by the presence of certain docking molecules (receptors) for that hormone, which are located either on the cell

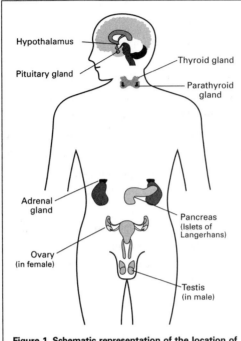

Figure 1. Schematic representation of the location of the major hormone-producing (i.e., endocrine) organs in the body. For the purposes of illustration, both male and female endocrine organs are presented here.

surface or inside the cell. The interaction between the hormone and its receptor triggers a reaction in the target cells that eventually modifies the cell's function or activity.

Mechanisms of Action

Several classes of hormones exist including steroids, amino acids, polypeptides and proteins. These hormone classes differ in their size and chemical properties. As a result of the structural differences, their mechanisms of action (whether they can enter their target cells and how they change or regulate the activity of those cells) also differ.

Just as we learned in our study of the immune and nervous systems, different types of cells have different and specific functions that cannot be accomplished by any other cell. We will also learn that different emotions affect specific cells in specific ways. This is why different emotions make unique contributions to some diseases (Leventhal 1998, Kiecolt-Glaser 2002).

Regulation of Hormone Activity

To maintain the body's homeostasis and respond appropriately to changes in the environment, hormone production and secretion must be tightly controlled. To achieve this control, many bodily functions are regulated not by a single hormone, but by several hormones that regulate each other.

For example, the hypothalamus secretes what are called "releasing hormones," which are transported via the blood to the pituitary gland. There the releasing hormones cause the production and secretion of pituitary hormones, which in turn are transported by the blood to their target glands (the adrenal glands, gonads, or thyroid). Thus, this results in a complicated multi-step process to modulate or change the function of the adrenal, gonads or thyroid glands. This is true in many bodily functions (Hiller-Sturmhofel 1998, McCance 1998).

Additionally, there is constant feedback from the target glands to the initiating gland. In this example, the hypothalamus initiated an adjustment to the adrenal glands through the pituitary. Then the glands "talk" to each other through "feedback loops."

Thus, feedback from the adrenal glands can affect the initiating glands, the pituitary and/or hypothalamus (Hiller-Sturmhofel 1998, McCance 1998).

When certain predetermined blood levels of those hormones are reached, the hypothalamus and/or the pituitary cease hormone release, thereby turning off their production (negative feedback loop or inhibiting hormones).

Although negative feedback is more common, some hormone systems are controlled by positive feedback (stimulating) mechanisms in which a target gland's hormone acts back on the hypothalamus and/or pituitary to increase the release of hormones that stimulate the secretion of the target gland's hormone.

One example occurs during a woman's menstrual period, increasing estrogen levels in the blood temporarily to stimulate rather than inhibit hormone release from the pituitary and hypothalamus, thereby further increasing estrogen levels and eventually leading to ovulation. Such a mechanism requires a specific threshold level at which the positive feedback loop is turned off, in order to maintain a stable system.

Our bodies are truly fearfully and wonderfully made.

Individual Endocrine Glands and Their Function

As we look at individual endocrine glands, and the hormones that they produce, pay attention to what these glands and their hormones do in our bodies. Remember that your thoughts and emotions control the function of each gland, and the increase or decrease in the secretion of each hormone. Negative emotions, such as depression or anxiety, can also directly and adversely affect the cells of the immune system (Kendall 2002, Cohen 2000).

The distinct or classical endocrine organs include the hypothalamus, pituitary, adrenals, ovaries and testes (gonads), thyroid, parathyroid, pancreas and pineal glands.

In addition to these classical endocrine organs, many other cells in the body secrete hormones. For example, myocytes in the heart and epithelial cells in the stomach and small intestine secrete hormones. This is part of what is sometimes called the "diffuse" endocrine system. If the term hormone is defined broadly to include all secreted chemical messengers, then virtually all cells can be considered part of the endocrine system.

This further emphasizes the fact that all bodily functions are influenced by the endocrine system. There are no cell types, organs or processes that are not influenced—often profoundly—by hormones.

Let's study each of these organs and their hormones.

THE HYPOTHALAMUS AND ITS HORMONES

The hypothalamus is the supervisory center of the brain. It is a small region located in the lower central part of the brain that controls many bodily functions, including hunger and thirst, sexual functions and behaviors, blood pressure and heart rate, body temperature maintenance, and the sleep-wake cycle.

Hypothalamic hormones play pivotal roles in the regulation of many of those functions. Because the hypothalamus is part of the central nervous system, the hypothalamic hormones actually are produced by nerve cells (neurons). These nerve cells also regulate the catecholamines (the fight-flight hormones) and are affected by emotional stimuli.

In addition, because signals from other neurons can affect the release of hypothalamic hormones, the hypothalamus serves as the major link between the nervous and endocrine systems. For example, the hypothalamus receives information from higher brain centers that respond to various environmental signals. Consequently, hypothalamic function is influenced by both the external and internal environments as well as by hormone feedback.

Stimuli from the external environment that indirectly influence hypothalamic function include the light-dark cycle, temperature, communication from other people, our own thoughts and emotions, and a wide variety of other sensory stimuli such as sights, sounds, smells, and touch (Hiller-Sturmhofel 1998). Once again, it is important to remember that the way we choose to respond or react to these stimuli dictates the response of the endocrine system.

The communication between other brain areas and the hypothalamus, which conveys information about the internal environment, involves communication through molecules called neurotransmitters (aspartate, dopamine, gamma aminobutyric acid, glutamate, norepinephrine, and serotonin).

The complex actions and reactions of the various neurotransmitters regulate the production and release of hormones from the hypothalamus. The hypothalamic hormones are released into blood vessels that connect the hypothalamus and the pituitary gland. Because they generally promote or inhibit the release of hormones from the pituitary gland, hypothalamic hormones are commonly called releasing (positive feedback or stimulating) or inhibiting (negative feedback) hormones.

The major hypothalamic (releasing and inhibiting) hormones include the following:

Corticotrophin-releasing hormone (CRH): Regulates carbohydrate, protein, and fat metabolism, as well as sodium and water balance in the body. CRH, also stimulates the pituitary to release ACTH, which stimulates the adrenal glands to produce cortisol.

Gonadotropin-releasing hormone (GnRH): Helps to control sexual and reproductive functions, including pregnancy and lactation (i.e., milk production).

Thyrotropin-releasing hormone (TRH): Controls the metabolic processes of all cells via the thyroid gland and contributes to the hormonal regulation of lactation.

Growth hormone-releasing factor (GRF): Is an essential component of the system promoting the growth of our bodies.

Somatostatin: Affects bone and muscle growth but also has the opposite effect by inhibiting the release of growth hormone-factor (GHF).

Dopamine: Functions primarily as a neurotransmitter but also has some hormonal effects, such as repressing lactation until it is needed after childbirth. Dopamine also sends messages of pleasure, alertness and motor control (Hiller-Sturmhofel 1998, McCance 1998).

THE PITUITARY AND ITS MAJOR HORMONES

The pituitary is a gland about the size of a small marble or pea and is located in the brain directly below the hypothalamus. It receives its stimulation directly from the hypothalamus by nerves and hormones. In turn, it controls the functioning of many other glands. The pituitary gland consists of two major parts: the anterior pituitary and the posterior pituitary.

The Anterior Pituitary

The anterior pituitary produces several important hormones that either stimulate target glands (e.g., the adrenal glands, gonads, or thyroid gland) to produce their hormones or directly affect target organs.

The first three pituitary hormones act on other glands to create a response:

Adrenocorticotrophic hormone (ACTH): Stimulates the adrenal glands to produce corticosteroid hormones—primarily cortisol—as well as small amounts of female and male sex hormones.

Gonadotropins: The Gonadotropins comprise two molecules, luteinizing hormone (LH), and follicle-stimulating hormone (FSH). These two hormones regulate the production of female and male sex hormones in the ovaries and testes, as well as the production of the germ cells, that is, the egg cells (ova) and sperm cells (spermatozoa).

Thyroid Stimulating Hormone (TSH), *also called Thyrotropin*: Stimulates the thyroid gland to produce and release thyroid hormone.

The remaining two pituitary hormones, growth hormone and prolactin, directly affect their target organs.

Growth Hormone (GH): GH is the most abundant of the pituitary hormones. As the name implies, it plays a pivotal role in controlling the body's growth and development. For example, it stimulates the growth of the bones, promotes the growth of internal organs, fat tissue, connective tissue, endocrine glands, and muscle, and controls the development of the reproductive organs.

As you would expect, GH levels in the blood are highest during early childhood and puberty. Nevertheless, even relatively low GH levels still may be important later in life and GH deficiency may contribute to some symptoms of aging.

In addition to its growth-promoting role, GH affects carbohydrate, protein, and fat metabolism. GH increases the levels of the simple sugar, glucose, in the blood and fatty tissues. (These actions are opposite to those of the hormone insulin which is produced in the pancreas.)

GH also enhances the uptake of amino acids from the blood into cells, as well as their incorporation into proteins, and stimulates the breakdown of lipids in fatty tissue.

To cause these various effects, GH alters or changes the activities of numerous target organs, including the liver, kidneys, bone, cartilage, skeletal muscle, and fat cells. For some of these effects, GH acts directly on the target cells. In other cases, however, GH acts indirectly, by stimulating the production of a molecule called insulin-like growth factor 1 (IGF-1), in the liver and kidneys.

Two hypothalamic hormones control GH release: (1) GHF, which stimulates GH release, and (2) somatostatin which inhibits GH release. This regulatory mechanism also involves a feedback component by which GH acts on the hypothalamus to stimulate somatostatin release.

Stressors such as low blood sugar levels, or alcohol use, can have severe affects on the production of GH.

Prolactin: Together with other hormones, prolactin plays a central role in the development of the female breast and in the initiation and maintenance of lactation after childbirth. Prolactin's function in men, however, is not well understood, although excessive prolactin release can lead to reduced sex drive and impotence.

Several factors control prolactin release from the anterior pituitary. For example, prolactin is released in increasing amounts in response to the rise in estrogen levels in the blood that occur during pregnancy. In nursing women, prolactin is released in response to suckling by the infant.

Several releasing and inhibitory factors from the hypothalamus also control prolactin release. The most important of those factors is dopamine, which has an inhibitory effect (Hiller-Sturmhofel 1998, McCance 1998).

The Posterior Pituitary

The posterior pituitary does not produce its own hormones. Instead, it stores two hormones, vasopressin and oxytocin, which are produced by neurons in the hypothalamus. Both hormones collect at the ends of the neurons that are located in the hypothalamus and extend to the posterior pituitary.

Vasopressin, also called arginine vasopressin (AVP): AVP plays an important role in the body's water and electrolyte economy. Thus AVP release promotes the re-absorption of water from the urine in the kidneys. Through this mechanism, the body reduces urine volume and conserves water. This hormone is sometimes called antidiuretic hormone (ADH).

AVP release from the pituitary is controlled by the concentration of sodium in the blood, as well as by blood volume and blood pressure. For example, high blood pressure or increased blood volume results in the inhibition of AVP release. Consequently, more water is released with the urine, and both blood pressure and blood volume are reduced.

Alcohol also has been shown to inhibit AVP release. Conversely, certain other drugs (nicotine and morphine) increase AVP release, as do severe pain, fear, nausea, and general anesthesia, thereby resulting in lower urine production, water retention, and an increase in blood pressure.

Oxytocin: This is the second hormone stored in the posterior pituitary. It stimulates the contractions of the uterus during childbirth. In nursing women, the hormone activates milk ejection, in response to suckling by the infant (the so-called "let down reflex") (Hiller-Sturmhofel 1998, McCance 1998).

THE ADRENAL GLANDS AND THEIR HORMONES

There are two adrenal glands, which are located on top of the kidneys. Structurally, they consist of an outer layer (the cortex), and an inner layer (the medulla).

The Adrenal Cortex

The adrenal cortex produces numerous hormones, primarily corticosteroids (gluco-corticoids and mineralocorticoids). The cortex is also the source of small amounts of sex hormones; however, those amounts are insignificant compared with the amounts normally produced by the ovaries and testes but adequate for a menopausal female if the adrenal cortex is functioning normally.

The primary glucocorticoid in humans is cortisol (also called hydrocortisone).

Cortisol: Cortisol has many functions including several metabolic activities. It helps control carbohydrate, protein, and lipid metabolism. Cortisol also reduces glucose uptake into muscle and fat tissue, thereby opposing the effects of insulin. Cortisol promotes protein and lipid breakdown into usable products (amino acids and glycerol, respectively).

In addition to those metabolic activities, cortisol appears to protect the body against the effects of various stress factors including acute trauma, major surgery, severe infections, pain, blood loss, hypoglycemia, and emotional stress. All of these stress factors lead to drastic increases in the cortisol levels in the blood. For people in whom cortisol levels cannot increase (e.g., because they had their adrenal glands removed), even mild stress can be fatal.

Finally, high doses of cortisol and other corticosteroids can be used medically to suppress tissue inflammation in response to injuries and to reduce the immune response to foreign molecules.

The primary mineral corticoid in humans is aldosterone.

Aldosterone: Helps regulate the body's water and electrolyte balance. Its principal functions are to conserve sodium and to excrete potassium from the body. For example, aldosterone promotes the re-absorption of sodium in the kidney, thereby reducing water excretion and increasing blood volume, thus regulating blood pressure.

Aldosterone decreases the ratio of sodium to potassium concentrations in sweat and saliva, thereby preventing sodium loss via those routes. The effect can be highly beneficial in hot climates where much sweating occurs.

The Adrenal Medulla

The major products secreted by the adrenal medulla are epinephrine (adrenaline) and norepinepherine (noradrenaline). Adrenaline and noradrenaline are released as part of the fight-or-flight response to various stress factors.

Epinephrine (adrenaline): This hormone is a powerful vasoconstrictor; it increases heart rate, breathing, muscle strength and increases blood sugar levels, and other functions to increase strength in response to a real or perceived need for fight-flight.

Norepinepherine (noradrenaline): A vasoconstrictor used in treating low blood pressure and shock (Hiller-Sturmhofel 1998, McCance 1998). When blood vessels are constricted or made smaller, blood pressure increases.

THE GONADS AND THEIR HORMONES

The gonads serve two major functions. First, they produce the germination cells (ova in the ovaries and spermatozoa in the testes), without which egg and sperm reproduction could not happen. Second, the gonads produce steroid sex hormones that are necessary for the development and function of both female and male reproductive organs and secondary sex characteristics (e.g., the adult distribution of body hair, such as facial hair in men) as well as for pregnancy, childbirth, and lactation.

Three types of sex hormones exist, each with different functions: (1) estrogen (estriol, estrone, estradiol), which exerts feminizing effects; (2) progestin (progesterone), which affects the uterus in preparation for and during pregnancy; and (3) androgen (testosterone), which exerts masculinizing effects. In addition to the reproductive functions, sex hormones play numerous essential roles throughout the body. For example, they affect the metabolism of carbohydrates and lipids, the cardiovascular system, and bone growth and development.

Estrogens (a group of three hormones: estradiol, estrone, estriol): The main role of estrogen is to coordinate the normal development and functioning of the female genitalia and breasts. During puberty, estrogen promotes the growth of the uterus, breasts and vagina, determines the typical female shape, regulates growth and cessation of growth at adult height, and controls the development of secondary sexual characteristics.

In adult women, the primary function of estrogen includes regulating the menstrual cycle, contributing to the hormonal regulation of pregnancy and lactation, and maintaining female sex drive.

Progestins: The ovaries produce progestin during a certain phase of the menstrual cycle and in the placenta during pregnancy. Progestin causes changes in the uterine lining in preparation for pregnancy and, together with estrogen, stimulates the development of the mammary glands in the breasts.

Androgens: The principal androgenic steroid is testosterone. It is secreted primarily from the testes, but also in small amounts from the adrenal glands (both in men and women), and from the ovaries. Its main function is to stimulate the development and growth of the male genital tract.

In addition, testosterone has strong protein anabolic activities, that is, it promotes protein generation, which leads to increased muscle mass. The specific functions of testosterone vary during different developmental stages.

In the fetus, testosterone primarily ensures the development of the internal and external male genitalia. During puberty, testosterone promotes the growth of the male sex organs and is responsible for other male developmental characteristics, growth and eventual cessation of growth at adult height, deepening of the voice, growth of facial, pubic, and body hair; and increase in muscularity and strength. In the adult male, testosterone primarily serves to maintain masculinity, sex drive and sexual potency, as well as regulate sperm production.

Testosterone levels decline slightly with age, although the drop is not as drastic as the reduction in estrogen levels in women during menopause (Hiller-Sturmhofel 1998, McCance 1998).

THE THYROID AND ITS HORMONES

The thyroid gland, which consists of two lobes, is located on either side of the windpipe. The gland produces two structurally related hormones, thyroxin (T4) and triiodothyronine (T3). Both hormones are collectively referred to as "thyroid hormone." Additionally, the thyroid produces calcitonin.

Thyroid hormone: In general, thyroid hormone serves to increase the metabolism of almost all body tissues. For example, thyroid hormone stimulates the production of certain proteins involved in heat generation in the body, a function that is essential for maintaining body temperature in cold climates.

Moreover, thyroid hormone promotes several other metabolic processes, involving carbohydrates, proteins, and lipids that help generate the energy required for the body's functions.

In addition to those metabolic effects, thyroid hormone plays an essential role in the development of the central nervous system during late fetal and early postnatal developmental stages. Thyroid hormone exerts an effect similar to that of GH on normal bone growth and maturation.

Finally, thyroid hormone is required for the normal development of teeth, skin, and hair follicles as well as for the functioning of the nervous, cardiovascular, and gastrointestinal systems.

Calcitonin: Calcitonin is a hormone that helps maintain normal calcium levels in the blood. Specifically, calcitonin lowers calcium levels in the blood by reducing the release of calcium from the bones. The effect is opposite to those of parathyroid hormone (PTH), which is discussed in the following section (Hiller-Sturmhofel 1998, McCance 1998).

THE PARATHYROID GLANDS AND THEIR HORMONES

The parathyroid glands are four pea-sized bodies located behind the thyroid gland that produce PTH.

Parathyroid Hormone (PTH): This hormone increases calcium levels in the blood, helping to maintain bone quality and an adequate supply of calcium, which is needed for numerous functions throughout the body (e.g., muscle movement and signal transmission within cells).

Specifically, PTH causes re-absorption of calcium from, and excretion of, phosphate in the urine. PTH also promotes the release of stored calcium from the bones, both of which increase calcium levels in the blood.

Finally, PTH stimulates the absorption of calcium from the food in the gastrointestinal tract. Consistent with PTH's central role in calcium metabolism, the release of this hormone is not controlled by pituitary hormones but by the calcium levels in the blood. Thus, low calcium levels stimulate PTH release whereas high calcium levels suppress it (Hiller-Sturmhofel 1998, McCance 1998).

THE PANCREAS AND ITS HORMONES

The pancreas is located in the abdomen, behind the stomach, and serves two distinctly different functions. First, it acts as an exocrine organ because the majority of pancreatic cells produce various digestive enzymes that are secreted into the gut, and are essential for the effective digestion of food and cleansing of the body, by digesting waste from cells.

Second, the pancreas serves as an endocrine organ, because certain cells (the islets of langerhans) produce two hormones, insulin and glucagon, that are released into the blood to regulate glucose (sugar) in the blood.

Insulin: Its primary purpose is to lower blood glucose levels. In fact, insulin is the only blood sugar-lowering hormone in the body. To this end, insulin promotes the storage of energy (e.g., glycogen, proteins, and lipids), and suppresses the breakdown of those stored nutrients. Accordingly, the target organs of insulin are primarily those that are specialized for energy storage, such as the liver, muscles, and fatty tissue.

Insulin has the following metabolic effects: promotes glucose uptake into cells and its conversion into glycogen; stimulates the breakdown of glucose and inhibits gluconeogenesis; stimulates the transport of amino acids into cells and protein synthesis in muscle cells, thereby lowering the levels of amino acids available for gluconeogenesis in the liver; increases fat synthesis in the liver and adipose tissue, thereby lowering the levels of glycerol, which also can serve as a starting material for gluconeogenesis.

Glucagon: Glucagon increases blood glucose levels. Accordingly, its main actions generally are opposite those of insulin. For example, glucagon increases glycogen breakdown and gluconeogenesis in the liver, as well as the breakdown of lipids and proteins.

A finely tuned balance between the activities of insulin and glucagon is essential for maintaining blood sugar levels. Accordingly, disturbances of that balance, such as an insulin deficiency or an inability of the body to respond adequately to insulin, result in serious disorders such as diabetes.

THE THYMUS GLAND

The thymus is a small gland located behind the sternum of the chest. It stops growing at puberty and then begins to atrophy. T-cells are born in the bone marrow and migrate to the thymus to mature and be educated. They play an important role in the immune system and are needed to fight infection. One of the important processes the T-cells go through during their "education" in the thymus gland is learning to distinguish "self" from "nonself." After the T-cells are educated, they are released into the circulation to live peaceably among the other immune cells, and have "self tolerance." When we do not tolerate ourselves it affects the T-cells ability to function properly, resulting in autoimmune diseases. Thymosin is the major hormone from the thymus.

Thymosin: Stimulates the maturation of T-cells (Hiller-Sturmhofel 1998, McCance 1998).

THE PINEAL GLAND

The Pineal gland is located in the same area of the brain as the hypothalamus. It is responsible for two important roles in human functioning. The pineal gland produces melatonin, which is important in regulating the body's circadian rhythms (body clock). It also contains a complete map of the visual field of the eyes. There is a neural pathway from the hypothalamus to the pineal gland and when stimulated by the sympathetic nervous system, melatonin is secreted.

Melatonin: Melatonin regulates daily body rhythms which aid in normal sleep. Inhibits the growth of some cancers by stimulating the production of interleukin 2 and natural killer cells in the immune system. Low melatonin is found to be connected to depression. Melatonin is also a powerful antioxidant, protecting the body from stress and infection, and resists cancer (Hiller-Sturmhofel 1998, McCance 1998).

As you can see the endocrine system is complicated and affects our bodies in many ways. Both the brain and the endocrince system also have a direct connection and thus effect on the immune system. Now, let's take a brief look at the immune system.

THE IMMUNE SYSTEM

The immune system is designed to protect the body from damage by invading microorganisms such as bacteria, viruses, fungi, tumors, parasites, and cancerous cells. These foreign materials are called antigens. It is also an important component in the tissue repair process after an injury.

Our immune system could be compared to an army or armed forces. When we were born, our "immune army" was small, untrained and unspecialized. This is called the innate or initial immune system. Our immature or innate "immune army," was unskilled and untrained thus it was what is referred to as non-specific. In other words, it reacted to or resisted all antigens (viruses, bacteria, etc.) in a non-specific, general way, without regard to the exact pathogen or antigen. Our innate immunity reacted to all antigens or pathogens in the same manner.

But this immature "immune army" was not as effective as it needed to be, to protect us from all the foreign invaders (i.e., antigens, viruses, bacteria, tumors, etc.). So our "immune army" was designed to become more specific and specialized, through training. In other words, God designed our immune system to become educated, trained and specialized. He designed each of us with a highly adaptable, "homeland security system." Our "immune army" is designed to mature and grow, as we encounter different invaders. This is called specific or acquired immunity.

Specific immunity is acquired rather than innate (inborn). It involves two separate but related processes: recognition of specific foreign invaders, or "nonself" substances called antigens, and then the destruction of these specific antigens. T and B-lymphocytes (white blood cells) are critical to these processes. Let's take a quick look at these cells and how they function.

T-cells are produced in the bone marrow and migrate to the thymus where they mature. After maturation, the T-cells circulate through the blood and lymph and often reside in secondary immune organs, such as the spleen, lymph nodes, tonsils, appendix and thymus.

Each T-cell has a very selective receptor on its surface that can recognize only one kind of antigen (bacteria, virus, etc.). A given T-cell may have many receptor sites, but they are all specific for the same antigen. In other words, our bodies must recognize specific invaders and then develop and mature specific T- cells to fight every different antigen or pathogen. This is a process that can extend over many days and requires complex coordination between many different types of cells that have to interact with each other.

For example, T-cells cannot recognize antigens by themselves. Instead, the antigen must be presented to T-cells in a processed form. Immune cells called macrophages most often accomplish antigen processing and presentation. Macrophages engulf and digest the antigens. They then excrete chunks of the digested antigen and these antigen fragments bind onto the exterior surface of the macrophages. It is this processed, macrophage-bound form of the antigen that the T-cells can recognize and then attack.

Thus, the macrophages bearing the antigen must contact those few T-cells that happen to have the receptor for that antigen. Because there are on the order of 10 to the 15th power different T-cell receptors in the human body, and each T-cell has only one type of receptor, it follows that there cannot be very many T-cells with a receptor for the antigen that has now invaded the body. Thus, it can take many days to build specific immunity to the invader. Additionally, T-cells circulate in the blood in an inactive form, so the first task is to activate them. To do this, the macrophages release cytokines (hormones) called interleukin-1, which activate T-cells. Interleukins are hormones that the body uses to communicate between leukocytes (white blood cells).

There are also several different types of T-cells. The T-helper cell becomes activated and secretes other cytokines that control the progress of the immune response. The activated T-helper cell releases interleukin-2, which promotes the multiplication and maturation of T-cells that are specialized to fight the antigen (invader) that began the process. The cytokines released by the T-helper cells also help cytotoxic T-cells to multiply, if they are specialized for killing the invading antigen (i.e., they have the proper receptor site). This is called cellular immunity.

As you can see, the immune process is complicated. It involves many complex functions that can take several days from the first detection of an invader, to creating an army of cells to fight it. Thankfully, our T-cells develop a memory and become "trained," so they can rapidly recognize the invader and respond if it is encountered in the future.

The immune system or "immune army" also consists of B-cells. B-cells mature in the bone marrow. They also have specific receptors on their surfaces. But, they have a different structure than the T-cell and produce antibodies. When a B-cell encounters the antigen (invader) that matches its receptors, it begins to divide and multiply for the purpose of attacking and destroying the invader before giving off antibodies. Also, as our body encounters different antigens or invaders, B-cells create specific antibodies to attack the new invader.

This process is aided by a large number of different cytokines (hormones called interleukins) secreted by activated T-helper cells. This is a complex process that is orchestrated by the interleukins secreted by the T-helper cells and takes several days. The T-helper cells release the different interleukins in a very specific sequence, over many days, which control the maturation of memory and plasma B-cells.

As the B-cells develop and mature, they are secreted into the blood. These antigen-specific B-cells secrete antibodies. They will only attack or bind to a specific invader or antigen. Each antibody is designed to destroy only a specific invader or antigen.

The process of generating antibodies takes roughly five days. Like the T-cells, B-cells are also given a memory. If the invader is encountered again, the antigen-specific cells can evoke a much more rapid and potent reaction from the immune system. This is why vaccinations are developed to create these antibodies.

In summary, our innate or inborn "immune army" is designed to grow and mature. It is designed to become highly trained and specialized, to protect us from any invader.

There are several types of immune cells that grow in number, become trained to attack specific invaders, and communicate and cooperate with each other in a highly complex and wonderful process.

Unfortunately, because of the extreme number of invaders or antigens that require a specific response from our immune system, the response takes time. This means that a far greater number of lymphocytes (the T- and B-cells), specific to the antigen, must be developed and then multiplied before a defensive response can occur (Maier 1994).

Also as we study further, you will learn many ways that this complex immune system and its response can be interfered with, thus delaying and weakening its response.

Organs of the Immune System

Thymus: T-cells mature and are "educated" in the thymus.

Spleen: A fist-shaped organ lying beneath the left diaphragm. The spleen contains T-cells and B-cells which monitor the blood for non-self invaders.

Bone Marrow: All cells of the immune system are produced in the marrow.

Lymph nodes: Filters of the lymphatic system designed to trap viruses, bacteria, cancer cells and other pathogens.

White Blood Cells of the Immune System

So far, we have discussed only two of the many immune cells. Let's take a brief look at some of the other cells or components of our "immune army."

T-cells: They are formed in the bone marrow and migrate to the thymus gland, where they mature and are educated. In the education process they become specific, or learn to attack specific antigens. They are important in defending the body against viruses, bacteria, and cancer cells. They activate B-cells, NK cells and macrophages. T-cells also secrete cytokines.

B-cells: B-cells make specific responses to antigens, which are called antibodies. Each specific antibody hooks up with or attacks a specific antigen or pathogen, (i.e., virus, bacteria, cancer cells, tumor, etc.). Thousands of different B-cells producing antibodies are needed to counteract the different invaders that can attack us. The good and bad news is that our bodies cannot create an antibody unless, and until, we are exposed to the antigen.

Macrophages: A large white blood cell that engulfs and ingests antigens and releases processed portions of them, so the T-cell can recognize them. They also initiate autoimmune and inflammatory responses.

Natural Killer (NK) Cells: An aggressive white blood cell that kills on contact. It releases lethal chemicals that put holes in cancer and viral cell membranes.

Dendritic Cells: A white blood cell that presents antigens to the B- and T-cells. They are found in the lymph, spleen and blood.

Granulocytes: A white blood cell filled with granules containing potent chemicals, which digest pathogens or produce inflammation. Neutrophils, eosinophils, and basophils are granulocytes.

Cytokines (hormonal component): Are chemical mediators produced by cells in the body. Interleukins are one type of cytokine. There are more than one hundred cytokines or interleukins that serve many different functions in the body. Cytokines act by binding to specific receptors at the cell membrane, setting off a cascade that leads to the enhancement or inhibition of a number of cytokine-related genes in the nucleus of the affected cell. Cytokines can best be defined as small proteins that play a central role in positive and negative regulation of the innate and acquired immune response, and in integrating the immune response with other components of our physiology such as the endocrine system. Cytokines also activate cytotoxic, inflammatory and delayed hyper-sensitivity reactions (Berk 2001).

There is excellent evidence that negative emotions such as depression and anxiety enhance the production of proinflammatory cytokines, including interleukin-6 (Dentino 1999, Lutgendorf 1999, Maes 1995, 1998, 1999).

Other studies also show that negative emotions such as depression or anxiety can directly affect the cells of the immune system with either up or down regulation of the secretion of proinflammatory cytokines. Proinflammatory cytokines create inflammation (swelling) in many parts of the body. Inflammation has recently been linked to several conditions or diseases including cardiovascular disease, osteoporosis, arthritis, type 2 diabetes, certain cancers (including multiple myeloma, non-Hodgkin's lymphoma, chronic lymphocytic leukemia), Alzheimer's disease, and periodontal disease (Cohen 2000, Ershler 2000, Kendall 2002).

Our immune system is a beautiful and complicated system that is designed to protect and keep us healthy and safe. Now, let's begin to study how it is affected by other systems in our bodies.

Why We Get Sick

STRESS

Can psychological factors (thoughts and emotions) influence or change our immune system? The connections or communications between the nervous (brain) and endocrine (hormones) systems and the immune system suggest that psychological events should also be capable of altering the immune system for two reasons. First, psychological events alter brain and hormonal activities. Second, the brain and endocrine systems have physical contact with each other and with the immune system (Felten 1991; Maier 1994). We have seen several examples in the prior chapter.

Research concerning how the effects of psychological events (thoughts and emotions), affect the immune system has centered on two topics, classical conditioning, and the impact of stress.

First, let's define stress from the viewpoints of psychology, medicine, and Scripture.

Psychology and medicine define stress as anything that causes a stress response. This can vary from person to person depending on their coping skills (i.e., choosing to forgive). Generally speaking, stress is anything that causes a fight-flight response. Fight-flight response is a set of changes that mobilize the body for energy production. This involves sending energy toward muscular exertion, and high levels of brain energy (Sapolsky 1992).

A stressor can also be defined as any sort of external or internal challenge — visual, tactile, olfactory or emotional — that disrupts the physiological equilibrium or home-ostasis of an individual (Ramsey 1982).

Hans Selye, known as the "doctor of stress," defines stress as anything that creates an "alarm reaction." An alarm reaction results in nerve impulses being sent from the brain that stimulate the adrenal glands to release adrenaline and noradrenaline which are neurotransmitters for the sympathetic nervous system. When the sympathetic nervous system is stimulated, blood sugar is raised to make it readily available for fuel. In addition, the heart beats faster, the lungs breathe more rapidly, the eyes dilate, and blood is sent to organs such as the brain and muscles that are essential for fight or flight. Organs that are not needed in such an emergency are essentially shut down (Jacobson 2000).

Now, let's look at a Christian definition of stress. What creates an alarm reaction in our bodies? Here are a few possibilities: unforgiveness, resentment, retaliation, anger, hatred, violence, guilt, shame, sorrow, regret, loneliness, fears, grief, performance, self-hatred, being rejected, rejecting others, fear of rejection, jealousy, envy, covetousness, gossip, slander, etc. Can you think of other negative emotions or actions? These negative emotions are stress, but in Christian terms they are also called sins. They are sins because they violate God's principles of forgiveness and repentance.

When you think about a situation where you were hurt or abused, is there emotional pain? Doesn't this pain cause your heart to beat a little faster? You bet it does. That is stress! And it is also a sin, because behind that pain, there is unforgiveness and other negative emotions or sins such as fear, anxiety, worry, anger, resentment, bitterness, etc. When we have forgiven from our hearts (Matthew 18:35), then the emotional pain is gone (Mathias 2000). Forgiveness is our armor that prevents or stops a fight-flight response. In other words, nothing can be a stressor to us unless we somehow allow it to be. As we study further, we will learn how important this concept is.

Stress begins in the mind but ends in the body. There is no such thing as stress only being in the mind (Hart 1986). In other words, there can be consequences in our physical bodies, because of our negative thoughts or emotions (i.e., our sins). We will also see that there is a positive consequence to positive thoughts and emotions.

History of Stress Research

Hans Selye was born in Vienna in 1907. As early as his second year of medical school (1926), he began his landmark work on the influence of stress on people's ability to cope with and adapt to the pressures of injury and disease. He discovered that patients with a variety of ailments manifested many similar symptoms which he called the General Adaptation Syndrome (GAS).

Hans Selye did not set out to discover stress. His "discovery" happened while doing other medical research. In his animal experiments, he noticed that animals injected with "noxious chemicals" consistently demonstrated similar responses.

First, the animals developed stomach ulcers.

Second, the adrenal glands became swollen. As we have studied, the adrenal glands play many very important roles in our bodies, one of which is to release adrenaline and cortisol, which trigger the fight-flight response. Without adrenaline and cortisol we could not live, but excessive amounts are life-threatening.

Third, the thymus gland and lymph nodes atrophied. The thymus gland and lymph nodes are very important parts of the immune system. They are primarily involved in fighting infection and inflammation. When subjected to stress, the lymph nodes and thymus shrink, causing a suppression of the immune system.

Selye continued to experiment and learned that it did not matter what the stress was, the above three-fold response was always the same (Selye 1998). But he did not know why or how the changes were produced. He continued his experiments by removing the thymus gland in laboratory rats, and then repeated the experiment. But the response was the same. Thus, he knew that the thymus was not the cause.

Next, he removed the adrenal glands and then exposed the rats to the stressor. This time the three reactions listed above did not happen. It became obvious that the stress reaction began in the adrenals. He continued his work and learned that adrenal over-activity was caused by a hormone released from the pituitary gland, called ACTH, in response to stress (Selye 1956).

When external stressors (such as exercise, other people, jobs, temperature, etc.) or internal stressors (such as disease, pain or negative emotions) are perceived by the brain, a stress response is triggered. Selye's work demonstrated that there are two pathways where stress affects our bodies.

The first pathway is through our endocrine system. As we have discussed earlier, the endocrine glands secrete many different hormones or neurotransmitters. ACTH, adrenaline, and cortisol are only three of many.

The second pathway is the sympathetic nervous system. Stressors activate our autonomic or "automatic" nervous system in ways that we do not know, recognize or perceive. We can be thankful that our "automatic" nervous system controls such things as heartbeat and breathing, without us having to think about it. But this "automatic" response can have negative effects also.

Stress dramatically increases the activity of the sympathetic nervous system, creating a fight-flight response. Selye called this the alarm reaction. An alarm reaction, results in nerve impulses being sent from the brain that stimulate the adrenal glands to release adrenaline and cortisol, which are neurotransmitters for the sympathetic nervous system. When the sympathetic nervous system is stimulated, blood sugar is raised to make it readily available for fuel. In addition, the heart beats faster, the lungs breathe more rapidly, the eyes dilate, and blood is sent to organs such as the brain and muscles that are essential for fight or flight. Organs that are not needed in such an emergency are essentially shut down (Jacobson 2000).

As we will learn, the prolonged stimulation of our endocrine and nervous systems has numerous negative effects on many organs of our bodies. Thus stress (i.e., anxiety and fears) is responsible for many serious diseases.

Selye's General Adaptation Syndrome

How stress affects each of us individually depends upon the strength of our individual bodies, and on our personal ability to cope. The body is like a chain; it may have a weak link, and the weakest link breaks down under stress, although all parts are equally exposed to it (Selye 1974).

Selye taught that despite the fact that there is a great deal of individual variation, everyone under prolonged stress follows the same general pattern of response. He called this the General Adaptation Syndrome (GAS). This syndrome describes the overall health and resistance to disease of the individual under stress, and has three phases.

The Alarm Reaction: This is the reaction that we discussed above. This fight-flight response creates the second phase.

The Stage of Resistance: As the stress continues, we begin to adapt, and resist the stressor. In this stage, we see the immune system begin its response, with increased activity in the T- and B-cell response to invaders or antigens. Our bodies begin to work overtime, to combat emotional, physical, or disease stressors.

The Stage of Exhaustion: Eventually, our bodies simply wear out and give up. Our ability to resist is gone. When we are exhausted, even mild levels of stress are beyond our ability to handle and produce exaggerated increases of cortisol and adrenaline. In the exhaustion stage, almost anything triggers an alarm reaction.

CLASSICAL CONDITIONING

In our lives and experiences, we have adapted to our environment and situations by what psychology calls the associative process. Ivan Pavlov's work is a classical example. For thirty years Pavlov studied brain functions and found that repeated association created a reaction that he called a "conditioned reflex." He believed that all acquired habits and even higher mental activity depended on chains of conditioned reflexes.

This leads us to the question: Is it possible to condition the immune system responses through behavior, attitudes or thoughts? In one of the initial studies using animals, an immunosuppressive drug was associated with a taste in a Pavlovian manner. This study demonstrated that the animal's immune system could be suppressed by association with a specific taste. After conditioning to the taste occurred, the taste by itself suppressed the immune system (Ader 1975).

Since this initial study a large amount of additional research has confirmed the results (Ader 1993). Other studies have also confirmed that human immune systems can be suppressed or enhanced through conditioning (Smith 1983, Solvason 1988).

This raises two very important questions. First, how does this conditioning take place? Are the immune changes "directly" conditioned, or is something else, such as fear, anxiety, or other negative emotions, responsible for the immune changes? This leads to the second question. Could a conditioned immune response occur in real-life settings, and affect or cause disease in our bodies?

As we will see, negative emotions do suppress the immune system while positive emotions, such as laughter and peace, enhance the immune system. It is also obvious that these do occur in real-life settings.

Numerous animal studies have linked to immune suppression many internal and external stressors such as electric shock, maternal separation, rotation, odor, immersion in cold water, and crowding. Divorce, Alzheimer's caregiving, final exams, sleep deprivation, battle task vigilance, loneliness, anger, anxiety, depression, and virtually every other negative emotion, suppresses the immune system in humans. Immune enhancement has been associated with positive emotions, such as laughter, and healthy family relationships. We will study the effects of specific positive and negative emotions in the next chapter.

Conditioned immune suppression might be expected to occur whenever a person repeatedly encounters an immune suppressant in a similar environment. Chemotherapy treatment for cancer would be an example. The chemotherapy drug suppresses the immune system, as it is hopefully killing the cancer, and the therapy is usually repeatedly given in the same setting (i.e., the hospital or clinic). A recent study found that women who had undergone a number of chemotherapy treatments for ovarian cancer displayed immune suppression after simply being brought to the hospital, prior to chemotherapy (Bovjberg 1990). The conditioned response, which resulted from the fear and anxiety of entering the hospital setting, suppressed their immune systems.

Thinking about or encountering a learned signal from an unpleasant event can activate the autonomic nervous system and the release of hormones that impact the immune system. For example, we often associate a neutral stimulus such as a light, a sound, a smell, a feeling, or a familiar setting with an adverse event. Thus, exposure to just the light, sound, smell, feeling, or setting suppresses the immune system (Lysle 1990). The negative thoughts and emotions from the physical and emotional traumas of life can be devastating to our health. These thoughts and emotions can be triggered by even an unconscious exposure to sights, sounds, smells or feelings from a past experience.

Conditioning plays a role in each of these situations and you can demonstrate this in your own life. What happens to your heart rate when you think about a person who has hurt you in the past? What happens when you see someone face to face, who has rejected you? What happens when you think about an abuse experience? In these situations, the immediate response is the fear that it will happen again, and probably the emotions of anger, betrayal or shame. The feelings or emotions of fear, anger, betrayal, and shame create an immediate alarm reaction, or fight-flight response.

In my life, I used to be allergic to more than a hundred different allergens. I was on the fast track to becoming a universal reactor (i.e., allergic to everything). In my mind, I had made associations with different foods, lights, magnetic fields, fabrics, etc., that I believed caused a reaction in my body. The list of allergies grew as I formed more associations or became further conditioned. The list grew as I became afraid of more things that I thought hurt or produced an allergic reaction. The reaction could occur if I was simply thinking about the allergen, even if it was not present. In the "thinking about" the allergen, I was really expressing a fear of it. At other times I could have a reaction, without any cognitive recognition of any fear, because the fears usually are so "conditioned," that there is not a cognitive recognition of the fear.

I will always remember one trip to a doctor. While I was sitting in his office, he asked me about the watch that I was wearing. It had a battery in it. He told me that most people with my disease (i.e., environmental illness) could not wear a watch with a battery because of the magnetic field that it created. The next morning, the watch made my wrist cramp, and I could no longer wear it.

This type of story is common, especially among those who suffer with environmental illness. I have seen in others and experienced in myself, severe allergic reactions just from the thought or fear of an allergen. Fear is a powerful emotion that conditions our responses resulting in an alarm reaction, thus conditioning our immune system. Scripture calls this kind of fear an evil spirit (II Timothy 1:7).

Many of the current studies in psychoneuroimmunology explore our exposure to internal and external environmental stressors, and their effects on the immune system, thus providing a link between stress (anxiety and fears) and physical disease. Because stressors activate both the sympathetic nervous system and the endocrine system (Stanford 1993), it is not surprising that stressors can impact immunity.

Many different studies have demonstrated that stress impacts every part of the immune system such as the reaction of T-cells to antigens, humoral immunity, innate and specific immunity, function of macrophages and interleukins, and the reaction of B-cells to antigens (Zwilling 1990, Weiss 1989, Fleshner 1992). Virtually every aspect of immunity can be altered by some stressor (thought or emotion).

A recent article in *Newsweek* magazine explains fear conditioning very well. The author Geoffrey Cowley reports:

> The psychological state of fear affects us biologically. People who are anxious drink and eat more. They have more accidents. They are more likely to get colds or suffer heart attacks. Fear and anxiety shackle us, diminishes our lives, and may even kill us.

> Until recently, no one knew how the brain generated such feelings or why they were so hard to will away. When you consider that nineteen million Americans suffer from fear-related disorders, even in the best of times, the value of such insights is hard to exaggerate.

> Fear and anxiety are on a continuum and are rooted in the same physiology and have similar consequences. The brain is not just a thinking machine. Its biological adaptation is designed to promote survival by responding to a threat. The brain is a web of circuitry that is highly attuned to signs of potential danger. And through a process known as "fear conditioning," it can readily learn to perceive a mundane stimulus as a warning sign.

> Twenty years ago no one knew how fear conditioning worked. Science has learned that the fear system's command center is the amygdala, a small structure in the center of the brain that is tied to many other regions through nerve fibers. Even a threat perceived for just a split second activates the

amygdala in a normal brain. An activated amygdala doesn't wait around for instructions from the conscious mind. Once it perceives a threat, it can trigger a body-wide emergency response within milliseconds.

Jolted by impulses from the amygdala, the nearby hypothalamus produces a hormone called corticotropin releasing factor, or CRF, which signals the pituitary and adrenal glands to flood the bloodstream with epinephrine (adrenaline), norepinephrine and cortisol. These stress hormones then shut down nonemergency services such as digestion and immunity, and direct the body's resources to fighting or fleeing. The heart pounds, the lungs pump and the muscles get an energizing blast of glucose. The stress hormones also act on the brain, creating a state of heightened alertness and supercharging the circuitry involved in memory formation. The amygdala tells the rest of the brain, "hey, whatever happened, make a strong memory of it." It makes a strong correlation between whatever the experience was and the remembrance of it ("Our Bodies, Our Fears," *Newsweek,* February 24, 2003).

This article explains how we are conditioned to a fear without even consciously knowing or understand the trigger or experience that set us off. This is why we have learned to trust our bodies and not our conscious mind to let us know what is really happening in our thoughts and emotions.

Memory

Another factor in the conditioning process that we need to explore further is memory. We often think of memory as what we can consciously recall about what happened in the past. If you think about what you did last weekend or last year, for example, you may begin to visualize some event or interaction with other people. But how are experiences remembered? How does recollection actually happen?

There are several common misconceptions about memory which include the following: that we are always aware of what we have experienced; that when we remember something, we have the feeling of recollection; and that the mind is somehow able to make a sort of a photograph of the experience, which is stored without modification. Thus recollection is often seen as the presentation of bits of information, independent of elements present at the time of recall or of bias from prior experiences (Siegel 1999).

In reality memory is sensitive to both external and internal factors as it constructs the past, the present and anticipates the future (Siegel 1999, Johnson-Laird 1983, Ingvar 1985, Bechara 1994).

Memory is more than what we can consciously recall about events from the past. A broader and more accurate definition is that memory is the way past events affect future function. Memory is the way the brain is affected by experience and then subsequently alters the brain's future responses. The brain experiences the world and encodes this interaction in a manner that alters future ways of responding (Siegel 1999).

Understanding memory in this manner allows us to see how past events can directly shape how and what we learn, even though we may have no conscious recollection of those events. Our earliest experiences also shape our ways of behaving, including patterns of relating to others, without our ability to consciously recall the experience, or when it occurred (Siegel 1999). This further explains how we can become "conditioned" without a consciousness knowledge of the events or experiences in our lives.

Furthermore, our initial memory or engram is influenced by many experiences such as: our knowledge of the subject of the memory (semantic); our sense of self or who we are (autobiographical); what we felt like at the time (somatic); what things looked like, or how they smelled (perceptual); what our mood was (emotional); and even what we were doing with our body at the time (behavioral) (Siegel 1999).

Additionally, in the process of remembering, or retrieving, the initial memory is influenced by our current semantic, autobiographical, somatic, perceptual, emotional and behavioral state of mind. Remembering is not merely the reactivation of an old engram; it is the construction of a new memory with features of the old engram and elements of memory from other experiences, as well as influences from the present state of mind (Siegel 1999). Memory is not static. It changes with our experiences and our coping skills.

This is why Scripture warns us that our hearts (minds) are deceitful and instructs us not to trust them. Jeremiah 17:9 says that "the heart is deceitful above all things, and desperately wicked: who can know it?" In Scripture the word heart is also used very widely for the feelings, the will and even the intellect.

Scientists have grouped memories into two categories, explicit and implicit. Explicit memories are those we consciously know that we are remembering. We might express them as "I am remembering...." Implicit memories are those that are not cognitive. They are not in our awareness. We do not feel that we are recalling anything. Implicit memories are from traumas and experiences of the past that can flood us with feelings without any recollection or perception of where they come from.

Memories usually involve the associations of explicit and implicit elements. Dr. Siegel gives this case history as an example: "a thirty-five-year-old woman began to recount her experiences of being raised by a violent, alcoholic father. When she began to tell her story, her eyes became filled with tears, her hands began to tremble, and she turned away from her therapist. She stopped speaking and seemed to become frozen, with a look of terror on her face. For the therapist, the feeling in the room was intense and consuming. The patient began to speak again, but this time spoke of her father's positive attributes. Her nonverbal communication remained, though she wiped away her tears and tried to compose herself and not worry so much about the past. In this case, the patient was being flooded by implicit elements of early experiences, evoked in part by her recounting (explicit memory) the story of father's rages" (Siegel 1999).

This case history also demonstrates that our memories are context dependent. This means that conditions in the physical world (sights, sounds or smells) and our state of mind (emotions, anger, fear, mental models, or states of arousal) that were present at the time of initial encoding of a memory affect how we remember and also how we recall a memory. When a similar context occurs (sight, sound, smell, fear, etc.), a memory or even just a feeling can be triggered (Siegel 1999). This explains how we can be upset, agitated, angry or even happy and not understand why.

We do not remember everything that has occurred. Forgetting is a normal and essential part of explicit memories. We tend to easily forget the events that we have categorized as not important or having little emotional intensity. And we remember events that have greater emotional intensity. If an event is filled with terror and is over-whelming, explicit memories can be blocked or buried, but a sight, sound, smell, feeling or emotion from the context of the memory can still trigger the implicit memory.

Memory is also an anticipatory process. In other words we anticipate our experiences from the past to repeat in the future. An example of this is found in relationships with our parents. An infant who has a healthy, secure attachment (relationship) has had the repeated experience of nurturing, perceptive, sensitive, and predictable caregiving from the parents. The infant has developed a generalized representation of that relationship, which helps him/her to know what to expect from mom and dad in the future. Thus, this infant has been able to develop a secure and organized mental image or model of their emotional relationship and is therefore secure and happy.

An infant with an insecure attachment (relationship) may have experienced their parents to be less predictable, emotionally distant, or perhaps even frightening. These experiences, too, become encoded in the infant's mind as a generalized representation of the relationship with the parents. This child perceives the relationship as being filled with uncertainty, distance or fear. Thus just being with the parent can stimulate confusion, fear and even terror. These implicit representations can become reactivated and create a very unpleasant, disorganizing, and frightening internal world for the infant.

This state of mind, a part of the infant's emotional memory has been implicitly learned by a child's first birthday, and these repeated patterns of implicit learning are deeply encoded in the brain (Siegel 1999).

We can become conditioned by our experiences before we can even talk, walk, and even while we are still in the womb. This conditioning may produce anger, colic, fears, weak immune systems, asthma and allergies even in newborn babies. We can also be conditioned to be happy and well adjusted.

Dr. Thomas Verny in his book, *The Secret Life of the Unborn Child*, says that the unborn child can see, hear, taste, feel and even learn in the womb. He teaches that the messages the child receives about itself in the womb determine how they see themselves as children and adults, and therefore how they act as happy or sad, aggressive or meek, secure or anxiety ridden. He further explains that the chief source of those shaping messages is the child's parents. What matters are deep persistent patterns of feelings. Chronic anxiety or ambivalence about motherhood can leave a deep scar on an unborn child's personality. His research and that of many others also shows that how a man feels about his wife and unborn child is one of the single most important factors in determining the wellbeing of the unborn child (Verny 1981).

Entry points for these negative messages include any way that the child might perceive rejection, abandonment or fear. Some of the most common entry points include: being conceived or born out of wedlock; parents that are not excited about the coming baby; fighting and turmoil in the family during pregnancy; drug, alcohol or tobacco use; or wanting the opposite sex. It is equally true that being excited about the coming baby and blessing the baby in the womb will result in positive messages that result in a happy, well baby.

Early child maltreatment may directly affect the circuits that link the bodily response to brain function: the autonomic nervous system, the HPA axis, and the immune process (Siegel 1999, van der Kolk 1996, Perry 1997). These ingrained (implicit) ways in which negative child experiences are remembered, and directly affect the development of regulatory brain structure that govern basic brain-body process, may explain the markedly increased risk for medical illness in adults with histories of childhood abuse and dysfunctional home environments (Siegel 1999, Felitti 1998).

God created the fight-flight response to give us more strength and energy in the rare emergency. He did not design our bodies to be in a constant state of fight-flight. But many of us end up in an almost constant fight-flight response because negative emotions that are in memories, such as fear and anger, that are unchecked in our lives. God's plan is for us to forgive others and be freed of the anger, resentment, fear and bitterness that are in the old memories and cause the physical response. God's plan is for us to repent, so we can be freed of all the shame, regret, sorrow and guilt in our memories, thus setting ourselves free from the anger and bitterness.

Since most diseases are caused by our thoughts and emotions (sins), we have learned that our bodies are excellent barometers for what is going on spiritually in our lives. Most emotions that cause a fight-flight response are really sins. Proverbs 26:2 says that the curse does not come without a cause. These negative emotions are sins that bring with them a curse.

At Wellspring Ministries, we teach that when we learn that we have a sin, it is time to shout "Hallelujah!" Learning about the sin is the same as learning the answer to a problem. We can now deal with the sin, get free, and draw closer to our Lord and Savior (James 4:7-8).

PLACEBO EFFECT

The discussion of classical conditioning would be incomplete if we did not consider placebos. The word placebo comes from the Latin meaning, "I will please," and by the nineteenth century, it had come to mean "a medicine given more to please than to benefit the patient" (Amaral 1999).

When a medicine is prescribed or administered to a patient, it can have several effects. Some of them depend directly on the medicine's pharmacological action. But there is also another effect that is not linked to the medicine's pharmacology, and that can also appear when a pharmacologically inactive substance (placebo) is given. It is called the placebo effect. The placebo is the treatment or medicine, and the placebo effect is the result obtained by the use of the placebo. It is one of the most common phenomena observed in medicine, but also a very mysterious one.

The placebo effect is powerful. In a study carried out at Harvard University, its effectiveness was tested in a wide range of circumstances including pain, high blood pressure and asthma. The result was impressive: thirty to forty percent of the patients obtained relief with the use of a placebo. Furthermore, the placebo effect is not limited to medicines but it can appear with any kind of medical procedure (Amaral 1999).

In a trial to test the value of the recognized surgical procedure of ligating (i.e., binding or tying) the internal mammary artery for angina (heart pain), the surgery was shown to be ineffective. The placebo procedure consisted of anesthetizing the patient and only cutting his skin. The fictitiously treated patients showed an eighty percent improvement, while those actually operated upon showed only forty percent. In other words, the placebo gave better results than surgery (Amaral 1999, Beecher 1961).

A recent Discovery Channel program, "Placebo: Cracking the Code," stated:

> Although it's not fully understood how placebo works, three major reasons may explain the effect. For many patients, taking a placebo causes the release of endorphins, opiate-like substances naturally produced by the brain in times of stress.
>
> There's also the conditioning response to medical treatment, the belief that a drug administered by a doctor will do you good. Irving Kirsch, a psychologist at the University of Connecticut, believes the effectiveness of drugs, such as Prozac, may be attributed to the placebo effect. He analyzed nineteen clinical trials of antidepressants and concluded that the expectation of improvement accounted for seventy-five percent of the drugs' effectiveness.
>
> And lastly, there is the expectancy that taking a drug will have a powerful effect on your body. In one study, subjects given sugar water were told that it was an emetic. Over eighty percent of patients in the study responded by vomiting. As Asbjorn Hrobartsson, author of the study, The Uncontrollable Placebo

Effect, puts it, "Any therapeutic meeting between a conscious patient and a doctor has the potential of initiating a placebo effect" (Discovery Channel 2003).

This program reveals that our minds have a very powerful effect on our bodies, first, by the releasing of endorphins to ease the pain in painful situations. Second, our minds become conditioned by events such as fear, bitterness and other negative or positive emotions. This conditioning creates an autonomic nervous system response that specifically affects our bodies. And third, when we expect something to happen, either positive or negative, it will usually happen. Our expectations create a response in our bodies that can even alter the effects of powerful medications. Modifying reactions to medicines through conditioning is a very important topic to help us understand the placebo effect. Pavlov demonstrated this in many of his experiments. Here is one example in an animal.

After a sound stimulus, acetylcholine is injected in a dog. Hypotension (lowering of arterial blood pressure) is the dog's response to acetylcholine. After several combinations of the sound with the injection, the dog will still show hypotension at the sound, even if adrenaline is used instead of acetylcholine. Adrenaline would normally cause hypertension (high blood pressure); this indicates that conditioning completely modified the response to the second medication. The pharmacological action of adrenaline is actually reversed, since an increase in the dog's blood pressure would be the expected reaction to an adrenaline injection. The dog's body simply ignores the pharmacological action of adrenaline and obeys the hypotension signal engraved in its central nervous system.

What would happen in a human being? The same thing. There are many experiments showing that man's functions are as conditionable as those of animals. This was demonstrated earlier in the study of women with ovarian cancer, but let's look at a couple of additional studies. For instance, patients suffering intense pain caused by a disease called arachnoiditis were relieved and slept after they received intravenous injections of novocaine (an anesthetic). After some time, the patients still experienced pain relief and slept, although weak saline injections, instead of novocaine, were used.

In man there is something more important to be considered. According to Pavlov, in animals there exists only what he called the first system of signals of reality. It is made up of the brain systems that receive and analyze stimuli that come both from within and without the organism (for instance, sounds, lights, CO_2 levels in the blood, bowel movements, etc.).

In human beings there exists, besides the first system of signals, a second one: language. Language increases the possibilities of conditioning. For human beings, words can function as stimuli so real and effective that they can mobilize us just like an actual stimulus and even more sometimes, because words are symbols and abstractions.

For example, if we condition a man by applying electric shocks to his hand after he hears the word "bell," a defensive reaction results, and he withdraws his hand. After some time, hearing the word "bell," or even seeing a bell (or a picture of one), will cause this man to withdraw his hand. Why? Because this man was not conditioned to a group of sounds, as in the dog's case, but to an abstraction, the idea of a bell.

Additionally, our minds make associations with other words or pictures. In another example, electric shocks are applied to a subject's hand after he hears the word "path." After some time, just hearing the word path is enough to cause the defensive reaction of withdrawing the hand. Additionally, the defensive reaction is also produced by synonyms, like road, way, route, etc.

Thus, the placebo effect is also an organic effect that occurs in people due to Pavlovian conditioning on the level of abstract and symbolic stimuli. According to this explanation, what counts is the reality present in the brain, not the pharmacological one (Amaral 1999).

This helps us to understand how many of our physical responses occur. This is part of the reason why we teach that our bodies are true barometers of our thoughts and emotions. In Christian terms, our bodies are the true barometers for the spiritual. Later we will study Hypersensitivity Reactions that include allergies, autoimmune and alloimmune responses, and an understanding of conditioning will explain these and many other bodily responses.

Job said in Job 3:25, "For the thing which I greatly feared is come upon me, and that which I was afraid of is come unto me." The things that we fear will usually come to pass. The reverse is also true.

Proverbs 17:22 says, "A merry heart doeth good like a medicine: but a broken spirit drieth the bones."

Specific Effects of Specific Stressors

Different stressors also have different effects on the immune system and are often a predictor of certain diseases. This is a fascinating reality that requires special attention. The effects of different stressors are subtle and selective. Stressors do not produce generic events that have identical outcomes. Different stressors produce different mixes of autonomic nervous system and hormonal (endocrine) responses (Mason 1971). For example, one stressor might lead to intense autonomic nervous system activation, and the corresponding release of catecholamines, but a relatively small activation of the pituitary and adrenal glands and their hormones (adrenaline and cortisol). Another stressor might produce the opposite pattern. In addition, the activation or response time changes for different stressors, emotions or thoughts (Maier 1994).

Also, different aspects of the immune response are affected differently by autonomic nervous system function and hormones. Thus, the effects of a particular stressor on the immune system might be very selective, impacting one kind of immunity or immune response and not another (Maier 1988, 1994). In other words, different attitudes, thoughts and emotions affect our different immune cells in different ways, thus affecting how we respond to different antigens or invaders.

The effects on our immune system and the resulting diseases will depend on the precise blend, duration, and timing of the hormonal and sympathetic nervous system responses (Croiset 1987, Lysle 1987, Rinner 1992). Different emotions make unique contributions to some disease processes (Leventhal 1998, Kiecolt-Glaser 2002).

As we have seen in the above studies, and as we study further, we will continue to see that negative emotions hinder our immune response while positive emotions enhance our immune response. We have also been able to demonstrate that different stressors (emotions) can produce different diseases. As you study the chapter on specific diseases, you will see that we have made associations with different attitudes, emotions, or thoughts with different diseases.

Over years of working with people, we found that specific patterns of thought and behavior are associated with specific diseases. We have been able to demonstrate that one specific emotion can be found in a specific disease. For example, in some types of cancer or Premenstrual Syndrome (PMS), we have found a specific bitterness always present.

Another example is the association of autoimmune diseases and self-hatred. As we attack ourselves with our own words, thoughts or actions, we see a corresponding conditioned autoimmune response resulting in an autoimmune disease. Our research also shows that specific negative emotions are involved in the formation of autoantibodies (autoimmune disease). The negative emotions involved in the many facets of self-bitterness cause the body to produce autoantibodies, sometimes very specifically. Autoantibodies can be organ-specific (Singh 1997). In other words, certain negative emotions cause the body to produce specific autoantibodies that will only attack a specific organ or cell in our body. This further explains why, at times, we have been able to associate a specific self-bitterness with a specific disease. In the section on specific diseases, this connection is demonstrated from many different clinical studies as well as our research.

As we have learned, the normal immune system is composed of several different forms of white blood cells, which normally circulate in the bloodstream and take up residence in such organs as the spleen and lymph nodes. Their normal function is to recognize and destroy foreign invaders such as bacteria, which are constantly attempting to gain access. A complex identification system exists that allows these cells to recognize the difference between the body's normal cells, called "self," from those foreign invaders, called "non-self." "Self-tissues" are not normally attacked because they are recognized as belonging there.

The problem in autoimmune diseases is that the fail-safe mechanism is bypassed. The guardians of the body's internal peace and safety, the white blood cells, get their identification signals confused and turn their destructive powers on the body's own tissues, because they see them as being foreign. It is as if the National Guard were to become confused in scattered parts of our country and begin to attack our own citizens, as if they were all agents of the enemy (Russell 1996). Our research shows that the negative emotions of self-bitterness are the root cause for this failure in our immune response called autoimmunity.

Another interesting point to ponder is that specific antibodies, and the amount of those antibodies, can be identified and measured in our blood. As we have learned and will demonstrate further, certain antibodies can only be in our blood if certain exposures have taken place. In other words we must be exposed to a specific foreign invader, for our immune system to create a specific antibody. It is almost as if our bodies have their own "black box" that tracks where we have been and what we have been exposed to or involved in. God tells us that we will answer for every idle word (Matthew 12:36). Could this be part of His record keeping system?

Moreover, personality and coping ability change the autonomic nervous system and hormonal (endocrine) consequences of the stressors (Ursin 1993, Maier 1994). Conditioning (anxiety, worry, fear, bitterness etc.) can even reverse the effect of medications (Amaral 1999). Thus, our coping ability increases or decreases the effect stressors have on our immune system. Our ability to cope or deal with the stresses of life predicts the effect stressors have on our bodies. This is why some thrive in stressful situations and others get sick.

We usually cannot control the stressor or the circumstance, but we can control how we respond or react. We cannot control the words or actions of others that may hurt us, but we can control our reaction or response. In fact, we have total control of our response or reaction. We can choose to get angry and suffer the corresponding effect on our body and immune system, or we can choose to forgive. If we forgive immediately, the fight-flight response will not happen and the positive emotions associated with the victory over the situation will actually enhance our immune system.

Thus, there are conditions where stressors will interfere with our immune system, have no effect on it, or even enhance it (Croiset 1987, Lysle 1987, Rinner 1992).

PHYSICAL EFFECTS OF STRESS (ANXIETY AND FEAR)

Now that we have defined stress, I want to study how the stress of negative emotions affects our bodies. As we mentioned, the endocrine system is one of the two pathways or gateways for psychological influences on our health. Stressors such as negative emotions and depression can provoke the release of pituitary and adrenal hormones that have multiple effects on immune function (Rabin 1999).

Negative emotions can substantially elevate key stress hormones such as adrenaline and cortisol from the adrenal glands into the blood. These hormones have multiple effects on immune function (Glaser 1994).

Let's study the effect of these two hormones, adrenaline and cortisol, on our immune system and other bodily functions.

Dr. Michael D. Jacobson, in his book, *The Word on Health*, explains the negative consequences of excessive adrenaline and cortisol by listing and describing various diseases they cause. The following section is drawn from his work.

Detrimental Effects of Excessive Adrenaline

Gastric Ulcers: Stress induces increased secretion of stomach acid, leading to an increased risk of ulcers (Seyle 1996). In a recent example the occurrence of gastric ulcers was noted to increase dramatically in Japanese residents who survived the devastating Hanshin-Awaji earthquake (Aoyama 1998). The presence of another significant disease further increases the likelihood that stress will cause gastric ulcers (Suzuki 1989).

Skin Disorders: Stress may also play a role in some skin diseases. For example, vitiligo is a disease in which cells lose their pigmentation, causing white blotches to form on the skin. Dr. Morrone and colleagues demonstrated that the onset and progression of vitiligo correlates with increased levels of adrenaline (Morrone 1992).

High Blood Pressure: A growing body of evidence seems to support the potential connection between stress and high blood pressure. In one study patients who had borderline hypertension or a family history of high blood pressure were more likely to have stress-related behavior patterns (Nassaro 1986). In a long-term study involving nearly three thousand patients, those who had high anxiety or high depression were nearly twice as likely to develop high blood pressure over time (Jonas 1997).

Heart and Circulatory System Damage: According to the doctors who discovered the link between personality types and heart disease, "the most serious effect of elevated adrenaline, when persistent and unrelenting, is its damage to the heart and arteries" (Hart 1996). Adrenaline's detrimental effects include the following:

Constriction of Blood Vessels: This can result in spasm of the coronary arteries reducing blood flow to the heart.

Increased Cholesterol Production: Especially LDL, the "bad" cholesterol, and decreased cholesterol clearance. This results in increased formation of plaque on artery walls (Hart 1996).

The evidence that stress raises cholesterol levels is abundant. Accountants' cholesterol levels have been found to be highest at tax time; medical students registered ten percent higher during examination time; employees fired from their jobs showed a ten percent drop in cholesterol when they finally secured new work (Van Doornen 1982).

But cholesterol may not be so deserving of all the bad press it has been receiving. Archibald Hart cites evidence that elevated cholesterol does not increase the risk of heart disease unless it is combined with stress.

Simply put, if blood cholesterol levels are high, stress will much more likely contribute to heart disease. On the other hand, if stress levels are kept low, even high cholesterol will probably not result in heart disease (Hart 1996).

Plaque Disruption: Two-thirds of all acute coronary events tend to occur when there is only mild to moderate obstructive plaque. The culprit does not appear to be the plaque itself, but the adrenaline surge that precipitates the crisis, which can result from anger and rage (Shah 1997).

Arterial Spasm and Increased Clotting: Stress depletes magnesium, which results in increased arterial spasm and an increased clotting of platelets (Leary 1983).

Heart Dysrhythmias: Adrenaline stimulates the heart to beat faster and more erratically. For example, when given intravenously in amounts to match stressful situations, adrenaline induced episodes of PSVT (a condition in which the heart spontaneously beats extremely rapidly) in patients that were being medicated for this condition (Morady 1989). Healthy physicians, when paged while on call in the hospital, showed derangement in their EKG similar to those seen preceding fatal dysrhythmias (Toivonen 1997). Likewise, when rats and dogs were subjected to acute stress, there was a corresponding destabilization in their ventricular rhythm, as the heart showed signs of increasing injury (Sun 1995).

Sudden Death: Most episodes of stress-related sudden death appear to be due to the direct effect of stress upon the heart. For example (in a recent study by Dr. Jacobson), thirty-eight out of forty-three cases of stress-related sudden death were determined to be due to heart problems. This was despite the fact that ninety percent who died from an underlying heart condition during this stress episode had no known prior history of heart disease. Two died of stroke. All of these episodes of stress-related sudden death were witnessed. Fear and anger were the stressful triggers in forty out of forty-three cases, and death occurred without warning in all of them (Lecomte 1996). This is exactly what happened to Nabal when he heard from his wife that David had come to take his life: "But it came to pass in the morning when the wine was gone out of Nabal, and his wife had told him these things, that his heart died within him and he became as a stone" (I Samuel 25:37).

Mitral Valve Prolapse: Mitral Valve Prolapse (MVP) is a relatively common diagnosis, given to patients who have chest pain that is not due to coronary artery disease. Such patients are more than twice as likely to suffer from panic disorder or major depression than are patients who have chest pain due to coronary artery disease (Carney 1990). Similarly, another study demonstrated that forty percent of patients with non-cardiac chest pain met the diagnostic criteria for panic disorder compared to none of the patients with typical angina (Basha 1989).

Panic Disorder: This stress-related disorder is especially common in middle-aged women, and is characterized by rapid heart rate, pressure or burning sensation in the chest, neck or head, shortness of breath, and a sense of impending doom.

Detrimental Effects of Excessive Cortisol

The adrenal cortex produces two of the most critical stress hormones, cortisol and DHEA. Cortisol is a steroid hormone, with effects very similar to those of the medication prednisone. It powerfully blocks inflammation, and it suppresses the immune system. On the other hand, DHEA serves to balance out the effects of cortisol. It is believed to have anti-aging effects, to be an immune system booster, and to have important effects on the sex hormones and fertility.

With the onset of stress, the adrenal cortex normally increases production of cortisol by about fifty percent. At the same time, DHEA levels fall off. Once the stress is removed, cortisol and DHEA levels will typically return to the normal range.

However, with prolonged stress, these changes become even more exaggerated. Cortisol rises to nearly two hundred forty percent of normal, and DHEA production drops to near zero. The elevated cortisol with its prednisone-like effects, along with virtually no DHEA to counteract it, eventually wreaks havoc on a variety of the body's organ systems (Diagnostechs 1991).

The adrenal glands always produce cortisol, even at the expense of other hormones.

Effects on Hormones: First of all, cortisol stimulates the conversion of noradrenaline to adrenaline, resulting in increased levels of adrenaline in the blood. This puts the individual at increased risk for all of the problems related to adrenaline excess noted above. Cortisol also blocks the conversion of T4 thyroid hormone to the more active T3 form, so that individuals under stress may develop symptoms of hypothyroidism (even though the thyroid function tests may appear normal).

Infection: Cortisol suppresses antibody production and T-cell activity. This puts the stressed individual at much greater risk for infection (Sheridan 1994). For example, the risk of the common cold has been found to correlate directly with the level of stress one is experiencing (Cohen 1991). Selye said, "If a microbe is in or around us all of the time, and yet it causes no disease until we are exposed to stress, what is the "cause" of our illness, the microbe or the stress? I think both are — and equally so" (Selye 1956).

Increased risk of infection is of particular concern with surgical patients, since in addition to the exposure of the inner sanctum to germs, surgery itself has been demonstrated to be a potent stressor, depressing the immune system, through dramatically stimulating increased cortisol production (Dahanukar 1996).

Louis Pasteur, the first great microbiologist, was constantly challenged by Claude Bernard, who insisted on the body's own homeostasis being more important than the microbe. Upon his deathbed, Pasteur said, "Bernard is right. The microbe is nothing, the soul is everything" (Selye 1956).

Protein Breakdown Increase: Under the influence of cortisol, protein breakdown increases thirty-eight percent (Selye 1956), while the manufacturing of protein drops twenty-eight percent. Together, this translates into a sixty-six percent drop in protein production. Thus, lean muscle is converted to fat, so that individuals with chronically elevated cortisol may develop a "buffalo hump" between their shoulders (Goldberg 1980). A lack of protein also leads to poor wound healing.

Arthritis: Selye claimed that gout is related to stress (Selye 1956). In addition, researchers have indicated that rheumatoid arthritis activity correlates with the degree of emotional stress (Crosby 1988).

Heavy Metal Chelation: Today especially in alternative medicine, there is a growing interest in the treatment of heavy metal toxicity with chelation. "Chelation" comes from the Greek root word *chele*, meaning "claw" and refers to the manner in which protein molecules or other substances grab and bind heavy metals in the body. The human body is already designed with an inherent, powerful chelation system, for binding and removing toxic heavy metals. But stress, through elevated levels of cortisol, blocks this process, rendering the stressed individual more vulnerable to heavy metal toxicity and related illness (Diagnostechs 1991).

Cancer: Elevated cortisol also suppresses natural killer cells, which are critical in the destruction of tumor cells (Diagnostechs 1991). Giving cortisol to rats with cancer caused their cancer to spread in direct proportion to the amount of cortisol administered (Kida 1988). Incidentally, stress also triggers a release of endogenous opiates (morphine-like compounds that are found naturally in the body). Studies show these appear to block immune responses and interfere with the body's ability to reject tumor cells (Dunn 1988).

The association of stress with cancer has led investigators to identify the personality or behavioral profile of the typical individual who is at an increased risk for cancer. Now referred to as "type C," such an individual is characterized by denial and suppression of emotions (especially anger), "pathological niceness," avoidance of conflicts, exaggerated social desirability, harmonizing behavior, over-compliance, over-patience, high rationality, and a rigid control of emotional expression. Christians understand that love, joy, patience, kindness and self-control are fruits of the Holy Spirit (Galatians 5:22). The point here is that these characteristics must not be "put on," but come from a sincere, pure heart.

This pattern, usually concealed behind a facade of pleasantness, appears to be effective as long as environmental and psychological homeostasis is maintained, but collapses in the course of time, under the impact of accumulated strains and stressors, especially those evoking feelings of depression and reactions of helplessness and hopelessness. As a prominent feature of this particular coping style, excessive denial, avoidance, suppression and repression of emotions and one's own basic needs, appears to weaken the organism's natural resistance to carcinogenic influences (Baltrusch 1991).

These and other findings have led researchers to recommend that, "more attention should be paid to the manipulation of the psyche, in the prevention and management of cancer" (Miller 1977).

Diabetes: Laboratory animals that are genetically susceptible to insulin-dependent diabetes mellitus develop this dreaded disease more commonly when they are subjected to stress (Lehman 1991). And, since cortisol blocks insulin, patients who already have diabetes have a more difficult time controlling their blood sugars, when they are under stress (Diagnostechs 1991).

George, the leader of a large Christian ministry, has struggled for several years with adult-onset diabetes. Although he has some degree of success controlling his blood sugar with proper diet, it has become clear over the last year or so that the level of his blood sugar is more related to stress than to anything else. He can get up in the morning, have normal blood sugar and eat a healthy breakfast with no sugar or starches. But if he has a stressful morning at work, his blood sugar can easily shoot up a hundred points or more. On the other hand, when he is out of a stressful environment, he tends to have little difficulty keeping his blood sugar under control.

Adverse Effect on Sex Hormones, Infertility, Miscarriage: Cortisol stimulates the conversion of DHEA to estrogen in fat cells (especially abdominal fat). Therefore, a woman who is obese and under stress can have blood estrogen levels equivalent to that of a woman in her thirties. This estrogen-dominance picture is consistent with an increased risk of estrogen-related disorders such as cancer, especially of the breast and uterus (Diagnostechs 1991).

Years ago, Selye reported that stress had a definite negative effect on the reproductive system. "During stress, the sex glands shrink and become less active," and nursing mothers stop producing milk. In addition, monthly cycles become irregular or may even stop altogether. Likewise, in men who are under stress, sperm cell formation is reduced (Selye 1956, Tache 1974, Cui 1996, Llonso-Uriarte 1991).

In addition, stress increases miscarriages by blocking protective mechanisms and promoting an increased release of the natural inflammatory chemicals that can cause miscarriage (Arck 1995).

Memory Loss: In order for us to recall stored information, our brains must be able to make connections at nerve endings called dendrites. Cortisol "fries" the delicate dendrites in the brain that are necessary for the transfer of information. Therefore, stress can lead to learning disabilities and memory loss problems similar to what Alzheimer's disease patients experience (Magarinos 1997).

Emotional and Mental Illness: Selye noted that certain breakdown products of adrenaline can cause hallucination, and he proposed that it might therefore play a role in some mental illness (Selye 1956). Certainly stress has been implicated as a cause of depression (Hart 1996). As Dr. Jacobsen put it, "and no wonder, I'd be depressed, too, if I were suffering from infections, protein loss, arthritis, cancer, diabetes, infertility, miscarriages, mental illness, and — what was the other one? — oh yes, memory loss!" (Jacobson 2000).

What an amazing effect just two hormones can have on our bodies. But stressors such as worry, fear and anxiety have effects on virtually every part of our body. The following section is based on information from a medical textbook, *Pathophysiology: The Biological Basis for Disease in Adults and Children*, which teaches that the following disorders are anxiety and stress related (the words in small caps and italics are from the textbook).

CARDIOVASCULAR SYSTEM

Coronary Artery Disease: The Bible says, "In the last days men's hearts shall fail them because of fear" (Luke 21:26). Fear, anxiety and stress are synonyms.

Hypertension (High Blood Pressure): Fear and anxiety are the root causes of high blood pressure. The Bible and medical science agree. What we teach is not opposed to medical science. In fact, what I see in the Bible only proves medical science and medical science only proves the Bible.

Stroke and Aneurysms: Strokes and aneurysms are the result of rage and anger, but behind the rage and anger is also fear. Do you know why people go into rage and anger? First of all, they have a root of bitterness. They are really afraid to deal with issues. Rather than being confronted on an issue and having to deal with it, they just blow up because that is their defense mechanism. They don't want to be confronted on an issue because they are afraid of men and they are afraid of rejection.

Disturbances of Heart Rhythm: Irregular heart beat and mitral valve prolapse may be the result of anxiety and stress.

MUSCLES

Tension headaches: We rub the back of our neck when we are under stress and tension to relieve the pain. Why not turn to God and deal with the fear and anxiety?

Muscle contraction backache: Again anxiety and stress is the issue. I have witnessed many healings when people have repented of the lack of faith in God that is manifested in worry, anxiety and fears, and then learned to trust Him.

CONNECTIVE TISSUES

Rheumatoid Arthritis: We have found that there is a direct relationship between the tremendous stress of self-hatred and all autoimmune disease. The negative emotion and action of degrading or putting ourselves down in any way has a severe consequence in our body. Intuitively, we know that it is wrong to condemn what God said was very good (Genesis 1:31). Thus these negative emotions expressed against ourselves, and the resulting guilt, have a consequence in our bodies. This internal conflict causes the immune system to form antibodies to our own flesh. This is called an autoimmune response which leads to autoimmune diseases.

Related inflammatory diseases of the connective tissues.

PULMONARY SYSTEM

Asthma and Hay fever: According to the medical textbook mentioned above, hay fever and asthma are caused by anxiety and stress, not by airborne allergens. We have learned and demonstrated hundreds of times that fear of abandonment and rejection are the two most common causes of asthma. It has nothing to do with breathing, dander, dust, pollen, etc.

IMMUNE SYSTEM

Immunosuppression or Immune Deficiency: As we have already studied, the over-secretion of cortisol and adrenaline damages the immune system. When the immune system is weak, almost any disease can invade our bodies.

Autoimmune Disease: In this type of disease the immune system has become over-active and has formed antibodies to parts of our own body (autoantibodies). It has been discovered that antibodies can be formed to almost any body tissue. We have learned that the body attacks the body as a person attacks himself spiritually in self-rejection, self-hatred, and self-bitterness. Guilt, regret, sorrow, and shame are negative emotions that are evidence of self-hatred. The body agrees with the mind, and starts attacking itself. This is a high price to pay for not loving yourself, as Scripture requires (Matthew 22:37-40). Lupus, Crohn's, diabetes, rheumatoid arthritis, and multiple sclerosis (MS) are examples.

GASTROINTESTINAL SYSTEM

Ulcers: For years the medical community believed that stress and anxiety caused an irritation in the stomach, which eventually caused the ulceration. Recently they have begun to prescribe antibiotics and are telling us that bacteria or viruses cause ulcers. People who have ulcers also have compromised immune systems because of anxiety and stress. When you have a compromised immune system, you don't have the ability to defeat bacteria and viruses. The fear and anxiety come first and the bacteria and viruses show up after the immune system is compromised.

Irritable Bowl Syndrome (IBS), Diarrhea, Nausea/vomiting, Ulcerative colitis: Many ulcerative malfunctions in the gastrointestinal tract are caused by anxiety and stress. The peace of God in your heart regarding issues of your life is the cure.

GENITAL AND URINARY SYSTEMS

Diuresis, Impotence, Frigidity: Are all caused by anxiety and fear.

SKIN

Eczema, Acne, Dermatitis: Adolescent acne is caused by fear, which usually is the result of peer pressure. It is not a genetic or biologic problem by itself, but in most cases the children are afraid of other children. That level of fear and anxiety triggers increased histamine secretion. It also increases white corpuscle activity in the epidermis, thus causing acne.

ENDOCRINE SYSTEM
Diabetes, Amenorrhea

CENTRAL NERVOUS SYSTEM

Fatigue and lethargy, Type A Behavior, Overeating, Depression, Insomnia: It is fascinating and convicting to look through this list of diseases and realize that they are all caused by anxiety and fear. In Biblical terms, anxiety, worry, and fear are synonyms and fear is equated in scripture with unbelief or faithlessness. Thus fear is the opposite of faith, and faith is the opposite of fear. If we are in fear, we are not in faith. If we are in faith, we cannot be in fear. Almost all things that we might call stress or stressors are sins because they represent something that we have chosen not to trust God in.

Stress and Psychosomatic Disease

Some teach that there are two kinds of stress: the stress of action and the stress of entrapment. In reality, the difference is found in our choice of how to respond.

In the stress of action, a situation may cause us to become upset, but prompts us to be aware of the need for action, allowing us to act and resolve it. We feel relieved, satisfied, pleased, happy, and proud after its resolution. This type of stress is often referred to as "resolved stress." In this example we have learned to properly cope with the situation.

In the other type of situation, we feel entrapped and helpless. It does not readily offer us an opportunity to resolve it, and it leaves us feeling helpless, frustrated, angry, and depressed. The stress that does not get resolved is called the "stress of entrapment" or "unresolved stress." It is this second kind of stress that has become a silent killer. Unresolved stress is the leading cause of cardiovascular, neurological, digestive, and psychological problems. In this example, we have not learned to properly cope (i.e., forgive or repent). Some symptoms include:

Cardiac: High blood pressure, Heart attacks due to coronary artery disease, Strokes, Sudden death from the injured heart muscle, Death from increased blood clotting

Neurological: Depression that may lead to suicide, Permanent neurosis, Compulsive behavior such as smoking, alcoholism, and eating disorders, Decreased intellectual capacity, Tics, Nervous stomach and dyspepsia (heartburn), Spastic colon

This list is very similar to other lists of anxiety and fear disorders. In fact, many teach that at least eighty percent of all diseases are caused by our thoughts and emotions (psychosomatic). I believe that the percentage is much higher. Psychosomatic diseases are those that are caused by psychologic factors (Merck 1990). In other words, our thoughts and emotions are the cause of the majority of our diseases.

A STUDY OF NEGATIVE EMOTIONS AND EXPERIENCES FROM PSYCHOLOGY

Have you ever noticed that you usually get cold a few days after being stressed out, overwhelmed or having had a bad experience? A recent experiment reported in the New

England Journal of Medicine (Cohen 1991) confirmed that this is no mere illusion. The researcher gave psychological stress questionnaires, designed to measure helplessness and negative emotions, to 394 healthy subjects. He then gave them nose drops containing several types of cold viruses. Cold symptoms were twice as high in subjects with negative emotions.

A similar experiment (Cohen 1997), published in the *Journal of the American Medical Association*, found that people with poor social connections were four times as likely to come down with cold symptoms after intentional exposure to a cold virus than people with a wide variety of close friends. Major diseases, cancer and even accidents have been similarly linked to emotional reactions.

Chemical messengers in your bloodstream, called peptides, mediate emotional reactions. Many of these, such as endorphins, are directly associated with and are affected by emotions. Each of your immune cells has receptors for all of these chemical messengers, as do virtually all of your internal organs. They are in two-way communications with your brain, but in particular with your limbic system where eighty-five to ninety-five percent of the receptors are concentrated.

The Limbic System

As we have mentioned before the limbic system is an important part of the brain that is connected to endocrine and immune function. The limbic system is made up of a group of structures, namely the hypothalamus (also part of the endocrine system), the amygdala, hippocampus, cingulate gyrus and olfactory lobe. The limbic system is known as the "emotional center" of the brain where neural circuits for emotions are processed.

It is important to note that emotion is not limited to some specifically designed circuits of the brain. Instead, these same limbic regions appear to have wide-ranging effect on most aspects of brain functioning and mental processes (Siegel 1999, Watt 1998, Stein and Trabasso 1992).

Emotions are everywhere in the processes of the mind. They can be regulated and emotions also perform regulatory functions. Emotions involve complex layers of processes that interact with our environment. At a minimum, these interactions involve cognitive process (such as appraisal or perception and evaluation of meaning) and physical changes (such as endocrine, autonomic, and cardiovascular changes) and usually fall into patterns that repeat over time (Siegel 1999).

Emotions are primarily nonconscious mental processes. Most people have very little awareness of their emotional responses to a stimuli or stressor. Emotions also create a state of readiness for action, disposing or causing us to behave in a particular way by nonconsciously assigning significance to a stimuli or stressor (Siegel 1999). This is another reason why we have learned to trust our physical response instead of our cognitive recognition.

An example of this can be found in the study of fear. The amygdala has been studied more than any other part of the limbic system in how we appraise or perceive situations and has been found to play a crucial part in the fight-flight response. The amygdala can rapidly bias the perception or interpretation of a situation as being dangerous. All this occurs within seconds and does not depend on conscious awareness. Nonconsciously, the brain is wired, at least with regard to the fear response, to create a "self-fulfilling prophecy" (see Job 3:25). If the amygdala fires off a danger signal, it will automatically alter ongoing perceptions to appear to the individual as threatening (Siegel 1999). This automatic, nonconscious reaction to a stimulus or stressor can create the fight-flight response that we have discussed earlier.

Other negative emotions or experiences such as divorce, abandonment (physical and emotional), lack of bonding, abuse (sexual, physical, mental), death of loved ones, trauma, betrayal, rage, anger, hatred, depression, jealousy and envy, to name a few, also have a negative effect on the chemical messengers or hormones controlled by this system.

Conversely, positive emotions release endorphins, the "natural morphine" produced by the body. Endorphins enhance our immune systems and have anti-aging effects.

Just as a positive mindset influences our immune system to become stronger, conversely, helplessness, hopelessness, passivity, apathy, depression and the inability to express emotions can weaken our immune system.

We need to realize that our responses and reactions to a stressor are initiated during the first few seconds of a stress encounter (negative emotions or negative people). What we choose to do during the first sixty seconds determines how our body will deal with that encounter and whether or not we succeed in developing habits (i.e., forgiveness and repentance) that help us manage the stressor, in a way that minimizes illness and disease (Jacobson 2000, Goliszek).

Other research has demonstrated that just a six-minute stressor suppressed the B-cells, helper T-cells, and T-cell helper/suppressor ratios significantly (Berk 2001). Similar research has shown that natural killer cell activity did not normalize to baseline even after twenty-one hours of recovery (Berk 2001).

Natural Killer Cells

There is a large body of research that demonstrates that our state of mind directly affects our immune system's natural killer cells. These amazing fighting units have the ability to recognize and selectively kill both cancer cells and virus-infected cells. Experimenters have actually measured variations in natural killer cell activity, based on interactions between stress and attitude.

Dr. Steven Locke of Harvard Medical School questioned subjects about stressful events in their lives and also about their attitudes and emotions. He then took blood samples and used them to measure their natural killer cell activity. The subjects were sorted into four equal-sized groups, according to the level of their stress and the degree of their symptoms. The median killer cell activities measured for the four groups were as follows:

GROUP	NATURAL KILLER CELL ACTIVITY
Good coping (high stress/low symptoms)	22.5
Lucky (low stress/low symptoms)	15.1
Neurotic (low stress/high symptoms)	10.6
Bad coping (high stress/high symptoms)	7.5

As you see by the above results, the killer cell activity level of the group with high stress and low symptoms was three times higher than those with high stress and high symptoms (Locke 1984).

This brings out a very interesting point that people under stress who know how to deal with it emotionally appear to have more positive immune activity than even un-stressed people with poor mental habits.

Feelings of pleasure and well-being indicate that you are thriving, and your immune system responds by working at peak efficiency so that you can fight disease and remain healthy. The feeling of exultation that follows successfully dealing with a challenge actually energizes your immune system. Stress dealt with in this manner actually helps you to maintain good health (Croiset 1987, Lysle 1987, Rinner 1992).

Maybe this is why the Apostle James taught us to count it all joy when trial and tribulations come (James 1:2). He knew that through Jesus there was victory.

II Corinthians 10:5 teaches to examine each thought or attitude to see if it lines up with Scripture. Philippians 4:8 teaches us to think or meditate only on things of good report. These "coping" skills from Scripture teach us how to handle the negative situations in this life. There are many studies that have explored the effect of specific emotions or attitudes on our health. Negative emotions often activate the disease process (Leventhal 1998).

Let's take a look at some of these feelings, attitudes or life situations from the viewpoints found in psychological studies.

Feelings of Hopelessness or Helplessness

The opposite of feeling peace and well-being is hopelessness or feeling helpless. Just as animals separated from the herd often quickly die from disease, humans who feel chronic hopelessness are extremely vulnerable to disease and even cancer. Experiments have shown that the immune system is significantly weakened by helpless reactions to stress, yet can actually be strengthened by stress that is dealt with successfully.

This effect can be demonstrated experimentally on rats using an ingenious apparatus to induce the feelings of helplessness. Yes, rats can feel helpless just like we do when they are given an unpleasant stress that they have no power to control. The apparatus used consists of special pairs of cages wired to give the rat in each cage identical random shocks through its feet. One of the rats has control of the shocks, because he has a bar in his cage that stops the shocks in both cages when he presses it. The helpless rat receives exactly the same shocks, but the bar in his cage does nothing to stop them. When a cancerous tumor is implanted under the rats' skins, only twenty-seven percent of the helpless rats can reject it, compared to sixty-three percent of the rats with control. Rats receiving no shocks at all reject the tumor fifty-four percent of the time.

Experiments on humans are necessarily much less direct, but they confirm that we have the same tendency for our immune response to give up when we experience feelings of helplessness. Helplessness even slows the healing of wounds. Kiecolt-Glaser compared the rate of healing of wounds of long-term caregivers with normal controls. The caregivers were people who had spent years of their lives caring for relatives with Alzheimer's. The feeling of helplessness resulting from their situation showed its effects in significantly slower healing of their wounds. After six weeks fifty-five percent of the wounds of the control subjects were healed, versus only seventeen percent for the caregivers (Kiecolt-Glaser 1987).

In one Finnish study (Everson 1996) 2,428 men aged 42 to 60 were tested for helplessness. When the health status was checked six years later, the men with high helplessness scores were 3.4 times more likely to have died than those with low scores.

Death of a Spouse

Everson also studied the health records of 96,000 widowed people and found that their probability of dying actually doubled in the week after losing their spouse.

Depression

Depression is the most common and most studied negative emotion. Depression is clinically defined as a shortage of the neurotransmitter serotonin. Serotonin facilitates the transfer of nerve impulses across the synapse and brings with it a feeling of well-being. The *Journal of Consulting and Clinical Psychology* (Kendall 2000) refers to depression as a "negative emotion" that carries many substantial health risks.

A number of well-controlled prospective studies have linked depressive symptoms with coronary heart disease (CHD), the leading cause of death in the United States. For example, a 13-year prospective study suggested that individuals with major depression had a 4.5-times greater risk of a heart attack, compared with those with no history of depression (Pratt 1996).

Not surprisingly, patients who had pre-existing cardiovascular disease also had poorer outcomes if they were depressed (Glassman 1998); mortality among patients who had suffered a heart attack was four times higher among the depressed than the non-depressed (Frasure-Smith 1993).

One recent, well-controlled study, found that a chronically depressed mood was linked to cancer risk. This study showed that the risk almost doubled (Penninx 1998b).

It is also very interesting that some cancers may show stronger relationships with negative emotions than others (Ershler 2000). We see this connection in certain female cancers, lymphomas, and prostate cancer.

Depressed mood was an independent risk factor for mortality in medical inpatients regardless of the disease (Herrmann 1998). Among 1,286 persons who were 71 years or older, depressive symptoms predicted greater physical decline over the subsequent four years (Penninx 1998a).

Depression heightens the risk for osteoporosis; either past or current depression in women was associated with lower bone mineral density (Michelson 1996).

Among older men, depressed mood was associated with an increased risk for declines in muscle strength over a three-year period; important as an indication of current physical functioning, grip strength is also a powerful predictor of future functional limitations and disability (Rantanen 2000). Depression has also been associated with reduced rehabilitation effectiveness in a spectrum of diseases (e.g., stroke, fractures and pulmonary disease) (Katz 1996).

Dr. Nichols' research shows that depression is found twice as often in people who are diabetics. His research also shows that depression may even be the cause of diabetes (see the diabetes profile, Nichols 2003). Additionally, depressed diabetics are less likely to follow recommendations for dietary management and glycemic control (Katon 1998).

Pain, a pervasive medical problem, accounts for substantial levels of disability and contributes greatly to the overall burden of illness (Turk 1992). Depression and other negative moods have a great effect on pain. Pain can increase disease severity and mortality (Staats 1999, Wells 1989). Pain can provoke increases in heart rate and blood pressure, and enhance secretion of stress-related hormones including catecholamines and cortisol, which adversely affect the immune system. (Kiecolt-Glaser 1998, Liebeskind 1991). Additionally, pain may disrupt many aspects of physical, mental, and social functioning (Leventhal 1998). Thus, depression can increase the risk of death by magnifying pain and disability across a range of acute and chronic health problems.

How large are the effects? One study says that depression is as dangerous to our health as "hypertension, cigarette smoking, hyperlipidemia, obesity, and diabetes" (Whooley 1998).

In another study, depression increased the risk of developing a disability over the next six years by seventy-three percent (Penninx 1999). Thus, the increased disease and death risk associated with the negative emotion of depression is substantial.

Anxiety, Worry, and Fear

Anxiety has adverse effects particularly in the cardiovascular system, where it plays a role in the development of coronary heart disease (CHD) and contributes to poorer prognosis after coronary events.

People with phobic or panic-like anxiety had three times the risk of fatal CHD, at a seven-year follow-up, compared with no anxiety (Haines 1987). In data from the Normative Aging Study, higher levels of anxiety were associated with almost double the risk of fatal CHD (Kawachi 1994b). Similarly, men in the "Health Professionals Follow-up Study" who reported the highest levels of anxiety had more than double the risk for fatal CHD and non-fatal heart attacks (Kawachi 1994a). Anxiety symptoms were associated with significantly increased risk of heart attacks and coronary-related death over a twenty-year period in women who were homemakers (Eaker 1992). Anxiety also has negative consequences for recovery from surgery (Kiecolt-Glaser 1998).

There is excellent evidence that depression and anxiety enhance the production of proinflammatory cytokines, including interleukin-6 (Dentino 1999, Lutgendorf 1999, Maes 1995, 1999, 1998). Women who were care giving for a relative with Alzheimer's disease had increased levels of interleukin-6 (Lutgendorf 1999). Chronic fatigue patients also show increases in interleukin-6 (Costello 1998).

Other studies also show that negative emotions such as depression or anxiety can directly affect the cells of the immune system with either up or down regulation of the secretion of proinflammatory cytokines. Proinflammatory cytokines create inflammation (swelling) in many parts of the body. Inflammation has recently been linked to several conditions or diseases including cardiovascular disease, osteoporosis, arthritis, type 2 diabetes, certain cancers (including multiple myeloma, non-Hodgkin's lymphoma, chronic lymphocytic leukemia), Alzheimer's disease, and periodontal disease (Cohen 2000, Ershler 2000, Kendall 2002).

Hostility/Anger

Chronic anger and hostility also negatively impact health. One nine-year study found that men high in hostility had more than twice the risk of cardiovascular mortality compared with men low in hostility (Everson 1997). Similarly, a large study of employees found that hostility predicted the total number of long-term medically certified absences over a four-year period among men (Vahtera 1997). Indeed, a rigorous meta-analysis concluded that hostility was a robust risk factor for CHD, as well as for all mortality (Miller 1996).

Hostility has also been associated with Coronary Artery Calcification (a marker for atherosclerosis) in young adults. The CARDIA study involved 374 white and black men and women, age eighteen to thirty at the beginning of the study. The Cook-Medley hostility assessment data was collected from 1985 to 1986. Re-exams were done at five- and ten-year intervals. After the ten-year examinations in 1995-96, electron-beam computed tomographic scans were performed. This study showed that those with high hostility scores were at greater risk for coronary artery calcification (Iribarren 2000).

Stress and Marriage

Another recent clinical trial explores the impact of marriage on health. A study in APA's *Journal of Clinical and Consulting Psychology*, by Ohio State University's J.K.

Kiecolt-Glaser, Cynthia Bane, Ph.D., Ronald Glaser, Ph.D., and William Malarkey, MD, took blood samples of married couples to test stress factors at the beginning of the study, then examined them relative to marital status ten years later. They found that couples who divorced at ten years had already displayed a thirty-four percent higher rate of the stress hormone norepinephrine at the beginning of the study than couples who stayed married.

The fact that the stress hormones were higher in the conflicted couples at the beginning of the study, even when they weren't arguing, suggests a chronic pattern of stress in their lives. "These findings show us in a microcosm how close personal relationships can get translated into health outcomes. They show that marital quality is as good a predictor of subsequent health as any of the usual major prognostic indicators" (Kiecolt-Glaser 1987).

Other Stressors: Thoughts, Emotions or Events

Researchers in the field of psychoneuroimmunology have researched many other acute stressors such as final examinations (Dorian 1982), battle task vigilance (Palmblad 1976), sleep deprivation (Palmblad 1979), and chronic stressors, such as divorce (Kiecolt-Glaser 1987), bereavement (Schleifer 1983), and Alzheimer's caregiving (Kiecolt-Glaser 1987). In each of these and many other studies, psychology and medicine have found that our response to these "stressors" alters our immune systems.

Summary

There are literally thousands of studies and research articles that could be quoted or cited. There are enough to fill several books. Our news programs and newspapers are constantly reporting new findings in someone's research about a specific disease. This is ongoing and always will be.

The point is that no one has all the answers, but there is more than ample evidence from medical and psychological research to confirm that our attitudes, emotions and behavior do have either a positive or negative effect on our immune system and our health. Without a strong immune system, our physical health will suffer. As we have seen, almost any disease can invade our bodies if our immune system is suppressed.

Now I want to switch gears and look at emotions and behavior from a Scriptural standpoint.

A STUDY OF SPECIFIC NEGATIVE EMOTIONS AND EXPERIENCES FROM SCRIPTURE We have just studied many emotions that psychology and medicine call "negative emotions." Now let's look at this issue from a Scriptural view.

Proverbs 16:24: "Pleasant words are as an honeycomb, sweet to the soul, and health to the bones."

Psalms 38:3: "There is no soundness in my flesh because of thine anger; neither is there any rest in my bones because of my sin."

Proverbs 12:25: "Heaviness in the heart of man maketh it stoop: but a good word maketh it glad. When I kept silence, my bones waxed old through my roaring all the day long."

Proverbs 15:30: "The light of the eyes rejoiceth the heart: and a good report maketh the bones fat."

Proverbs 17:22: "A merry heart doeth good like a medicine: but a broken spirit drieth the bones."

What is located in the bones? The bone marrow is where most of the cells of our immune system originate.

When God created the earth and mankind, there was no disease, sorrow, suffering or death. There were also, no "negative" emotions. The book of Genesis tells us that Adam and Eve walked with God in the cool of the day enjoying each others' company. But somehow all this has changed. Let's take a look at what happened.

Romans 5:12 says, "By one man sin entered into this world." "One man" is Adam.

Genesis 2:16-17 says, "And the LORD God commanded the man saying, of every tree of the garden thou mayest freely eat: But of the tree of the knowledge of good and evil, thou shalt not eat of it: for in the day that thou eatest thereof thou shalt surely die."

Genesis 3:4-5 says, "And the serpent said unto the woman, ye shall not surely die: For God doth know that in the day ye eat thereof, then your eyes shall be opened, and ye shall be as gods, knowing good and evil." Satan tempted Eve by asserting that God is a liar and that He is only withholding something good from her. Satan implied that she could be like God if she just ate of the forbidden tree.

Verse 6 says that Eve yielded to temptation, ate the fruit and gave some to Adam. He also ate. That act of disobedience to God was the event that allowed Satan and sin to enter into this world. Through Adam sin entered into the world.

Adam had the responsibility before God to set aside or correct Eve's sin, as the spiritual head of the home (Numbers 30:6-8). He did not fulfill his duty and additionally, he partook of the fruit (sin) himself.

Next, let's explore what changed in Adam and Eve's lives.

When Adam and Eve sinned, they became double-minded, developing a sort of split personality (James 1:8). They were still drawn to God but something was wrong, something separated them from Him that had not been present before eating the fruit

What entered into Adam and Eve that had not been there before they sinned? What entered into their lives that God did not create in them?

They showed doubt, doubting God's Word; unbelief, not believing God's Word; and rebellion, disobeying or rebelling against God's Word. Satan lied to Eve telling her that she would not die, but rather she would be a god like her Father, able to discern both good and evil. This new mindset created double-mindedness, sometimes believing God, and other times believing Satan.

What was the first thing Adam and Eve did after they sinned? They discovered their nakedness and became ashamed, so they took leaves and covered themselves. Then they hid from God. Before they sinned, God would walk and talk with Adam in the cool of the evening, just like we talk to each other (Genesis 3:8). After sinning Adam was afraid of God. Satan wins a victory when we become afraid of God so that we hide from Him.

Adam and Eve experienced condemnation for the first time. How many of us have had to fight off condemnation after we have sinned? Romans 8:1 says that if we are following after the spirit of God there is no condemnation. Condemnation comes from following after the devil.

Adam and Eve felt shame. They had been created naked, but now felt unclean and had to put on clothes.

What did Adam do when God asked, "Why did you do this?" Adam said, "...the woman whom thou gavest to be with me, she gave me of the tree, and I did eat" (Genesis 3:12). Adam refused to take personal responsibility, adding to his sin. The first man quickly learned to blame others and his wife. We had a good teacher who taught us the same behavior. We often blame others even when we know that we are at fault. To become the spiritual leaders of our homes as men means taking responsibility for our actions, thoughts, and emotions.

The garden is also the first incidence where man blamed God for what went wrong. Adam implied that his sin was God's fault. God gave the woman to him. He reasoned that if God had not given him the woman, the sin would not have happened.

When we blame God we are trying to rid ourselves from all responsibility and accountability. The truth was that Adam used his free will to choose to disobey God. Each of us does the same thing when we sin. We should not blame others. We should accept the responsibility and be accountable for our actions.

Some of the most powerful negative emotions from the devil show up in the behavior of Adam and Eve after they sinned. We see lying, shame, condemnation, doubt, false accusations, and unbelief. For the first time lust of the flesh, lust of the eyes, and the pride of life are evident (Genesis 3:6, I John 2:15-17). These are the same root problems that we still fight today.

This was just the start of what Adam's sin allowed Satan to bring into this world.

Eve gave birth to Cain and Abel. Years later, Cain killed Abel, the first murder. Why? God regarded Abel's sacrifice as more excellent than Cain's and Cain's soul filled with bitterness and jealously, driving him to commit murder (Hebrews 11:4, Genesis 4:8).

God did not reject Cain. He rejected his sacrifice. God required a blood sacrifice as a sin offering, and the best animal was to be sacrificed. God had demonstrated this act of sacrifice, when He killed an animal to provide clothing for Adam and Eve. Cain chose instead to bring crops from his fields.

Cain perceived God's reaction to his sacrifice as a personal rejection. It was a lie from Satan, and he meditated on it. Satan's evil nature started to bubble inside him, and Cain might have said, "I hate Abel. I wish I could just get even with him." Jealousy, resentment, unforgiveness, hatred, violence, and murder rose up within Cain — all elements of bitterness. Overwhelmed by them, he killed his brother.

In chapters 3 and 4 of Genesis we find that through Adam's sin, most of the negative emotions (sins) that we all still struggle with came into this world. Let's study these negative emotions or sins individually.

Bitterness

When Cain killed Abel there was a progression of emotions that led to the murder. We teach that this progression of emotions is all part of bitterness. Thus if we are bitter at least one of the following emotions will be present in us: unforgiveness, resentment, retaliation, anger, hatred, violence, and murder.

Let's look at these individually.

Bitterness gains its entrance to us through unforgiveness, the first piece of the armor surrounding bitterness. Unforgiveness whispers in our ear, "No, you're not going to forgive them, you don't need to forgive them, there's no way you need to forgive them." Unforgiveness keeps a "record of wrongs" against another person. Satan banks on the spirit of unforgiveness to remind us of the bitterness that somebody else has toward us. Unforgiveness reminds, rehashes, projects and torments us with past negative events. It reminds us of what others have done to us, and what we have done to others.

Unforgiveness causes us to constantly accuse others and ourselves. But unforgiveness is just the beginning. After unforgiveness has done its work, resentment is next.

Resentment builds on the foundation laid by unforgiveness. The record of wrongs ferments and resentment begins to grow. Resentment generates a feeling of ill will toward a person who has wronged us. Resentment says, "I don't like Mary," or "I will never forgive Alex," or "I don't trust my neighbors." Resentment constantly reminds us of past events, seeking to stir up negative sentiments that stew and ferment within us.

Unforgiveness formed the first piece of armor to provide protection for bitterness. Resentment feeds off of unforgiveness. Resentment is stronger because unforgiveness supports it. Thus, it is more dangerous than unforgiveness.

Because of the work of resentment, families and churches become dysfunctional. They maintain their own records of wrongs that generate stronger resentment. One person shares his or her resentment, and soon everybody is doing the same. Then the church splits or the family ends up in divorce, and the devil has won a battle in his war against good.

Unforgiveness is like instant replay, replaying the words, voices, sights, and sounds of wrong events from our past. Unforgiveness flashes negative thoughts and images of everything someone ever said or did to us. Have you ever had that happen? The accusing spirit continuously replays a record of the evil music of our lives to reinforce itself, so this strong man of bitterness can find a home in us. Resentment adds fuel to the fire.

After unforgiveness and resentment have gained a foothold in our minds, retaliation is next. Now it's time to get even.

I remember a bumper sticker I saw a few years ago that said, "I don't forgive, I just get even." Retaliation projects these kinds of sentiments: "Bill should pay for what he did to me," or "I am going to make Jane pay for what she said," "I am going to make sure Bob gets what he deserves, if it is the last thing that I do!"

Retaliation is much more dangerous than unforgiveness or resentment, because the emotion is stronger and is leading to a negative action. When we see someone who wants to "get even," or says "they're gonna pay," we know that an act is soon to follow.

After retaliation comes anger, which could also be defined as hostility or wrath. Anger and hostility are outward expressions that remind others that we are not going to forgive them, that we resent them, and that we plan to get even. With anger, we have crossed a line. Anger gives a voice to unforgiveness, resentment, and retaliation.

Once this line is crossed to anger and hostility, there are outward physical manifestations. Have you ever seen anger in a person's eyes? It is very real and very observable. This is anger caused by the root of bitterness, because of unforgiveness, resentment and retaliation. Maybe you have experienced this yourself. We all have.

We get angry when a trust has been breached, resulting in hurt. We feel victimized. Then unforgiveness, resentment, and retaliation well up and overflow with anger and hostility.

After anger and hostility has gained its foothold, hatred moves in. Bitterness gains fuel from unforgiveness, resentment, retaliation, and anger and hostility. Now hatred starts a process of elimination. Hatred says, "I live on this planet and so do you. And one of us has to go and it ain't going to be me." Maybe hatred says, "This church ain't big enough for both of us. I think you'd better leave." Hatred seeks to eliminate the other person.

Retaliation ferments anger on behalf of bitterness. Anger vocalizes bitterness, and next comes hatred, to act out of bitterness. Hatred reveals your feelings toward an offender, tells them that they don't belong in your world, and you absolutely hate their guts. Hatred says, "I will do what it takes to get even."

The sixth level of bitterness is violence. Violence is anger and hatred set into motion. Our emotions erupt into physical or sometimes hate-filled verbal attacks. At this point, we see pots and pans thrown across the room, wrenches flying and punches being thrown. Fights erupt, physical, sexual and verbal abuse result.

The seventh and worst spirit in the principality of bitterness, is murder. Just as Cain slew Abel because of his bitterness, so we see others murder their children, spouses or friends in a fit of rage.

Murder includes more than taking someone's physical life. God's Word teaches how we can "murder" someone with our words. Murder starts in the heart, because the ultimate level of bitterness is the elimination of someone's personhood. I John 3:15 says, "Whosoever hateth his brother is a murderer: and ye know that no murderer hath eternal life abiding in him."

Murderous, hate-filled speech, driven by bitterness, kills a person's spirit. Whether it is the person who is doing the screaming, and his speech crucifies his own sense of decency, or a person who receives a verbal attack, whose spirit shrinks in fear, the end result is the death of a godly, peaceful spirit.

Hebrews 12:14-15 says that we are to "Follow peace with all men, and holiness, without which no man shall see the Lord: Looking diligently lest any man fail of the grace of God; lest any root of bitterness springing up trouble you, and thereby many be defiled."

Bitterness not only defiles us spiritually but also physically. Each thought of bitterness causes an alarm reaction, or fight-flight response, and we have seen the tremendous damage that happens to our immune system.

Self-Bitterness

In self-bitterness, instead of being bitter toward others, we are bitter toward ourselves. Self-bitterness produces an inability to forgive ourselves. Have you ever struggled with unforgiveness toward yourself? I have. My experience is that many people cannot say, "I forgive myself."

Unforgiveness of ourselves leads to self-resentment. It says, "I can never do anything right. The harder I try, the worse things get. I never have been any good, never will be any good. I'm just a nobody. I don't like the way I look. Daddy was right—I'll never amount to anything." This kind of self-talk buffets and bruises us, leaving us too weak to withstand Satan's onslaught.

Self-resentment leads to self-retaliation. This will cause us to react strongly and negatively to someone who accuses us. Our negativity results in their rejection of us, which is what we expected in the first place. We go into these situations with our eyes wide open, because we have a need to be rejected. Then the unloving spirit (self-bitterness) starts accusing us, telling us that we're not loved, causing a spiraling down. The worse we are, the worse we get. Before long, we have developed a continual pattern of victimization.

Self-resentment leads to self-anger. "I just can't stand myself!" "See, here's more proof how stupid I am. I should just kill myself!" Where does this behavior come from? It is the result of a successful attack by an unloving spirit.

In self-anger, we will find perfectionism, self-accusation, and self-condemnation. When these three come together, they will trigger anger like a flash fire. When self-anger wells up, we are wise to keep our distance from others because we are heading for territory where even angels fear to tread.

Self-anger is no respecter of persons. We see how it affects us well enough, but if we're not careful this anger will spill over onto somebody else. The evil "fruit" of this attack is to include others as victims, not just us. The devil is an equal opportunity oppressor.

Self-hatred is next. We don't get to self-hatred without self-bitterness accusing us. Self-hatred is the result of a process of working through self-unforgiveness, self-resentment, and self-retaliation and self-anger, each stage being more dangerous than its predecessor. Self-hatred results from something that simmers and festers below the surface often for days, weeks, months or years.

The next stage is self-violence. Self-anger spills over into committing some type of hurtful act against oneself. At this stage people may start hurting, cutting, or mutilating themselves out of extreme shame or guilt. Usually the self-violence is much less severe and manifests in choices of not taking care of oneself.

The ultimate expression of self-violence is self-murder or suicide. When we entertain thoughts of suicide, we have clear evidence of self-bitterness with its entire evil armor in full battle array getting close to celebrating final victory over us.

Self-murder happens most often in our thought life. It is characteristic of people who have reached the point of suicide to constantly entertain thoughts like, "I need to eliminate myself, I don't belong here." "Nobody would care if I died. In fact, the world would be better off." "The only way I can make Jane happy is to kill myself!" These are sick, irrational thoughts, but quite common.

Self-murder is an anti-Christ mentality that comes from the armor of an unloving spirit. Self-murder is also any way that we put ourselves down in our thoughts, words or deeds. When we experience such thoughts, it is necessary to turn them around, by saying, "I do belong here." "God made me. I'm precious to Him." "I am the child of the Most High God!" We must repent for believing the lies of the devil; then, in the name of Jesus command the lying spirit to go, command the spirit of death to go, and then ask the Holy Spirit to heal us and make us whole.

In the business world we determine the value of something by what someone is willing to pay for it. What did God the Father pay for you? What did Jesus pay for you? The Father gave His only Son to pay the penalty of our sins. Jesus willingly chose to lay down His life for you. What greater price could be paid for you? Please accept your worth in God's eyes and then act upon it.

Self-bitterness includes self-pity, self-abuse, self-rejection, self-hatred, competition, self-pride, self-enthronement, false piety. It thrives on the "I will" self-exaltation, attention-getting, excessive talkativeness, insecurity, self-mutilation, excessive eating and bingeing. It fires self-comparison, self-idolatry, perfectionism and self-torment at us. It pushes us to be defensive and filled with self-doubt, unbelief, self-bitterness, self-resentment, self-unforgiveness, self-retaliation, self-anger, self-violence and self-murder.

Next to God, we should be our own best friend, enjoying and accepting ourselves. We should love ourselves. Perhaps self-love is a novel concept to you.

Pastors, teachers and parents often teach us to consider ourselves "as nothing." Most of our "Christian" schools and colleges teach that we are depraved and to count ourselves as nothing. Sadly, many of us were even told as children that we were "stupid" or "ugly" or "garbage," or that we would "never amount to anything," or "never be as good as Billy Smith." We often see God as unreachable and ourselves as insignificant.

Self-love though, is an important Biblical principle. Jesus taught that we are to love our neighbors as ourselves (Matthew 22:39). If we condemn, hate, and belittle ourselves, and we are to love our neighbors as ourselves, does this mean that we should treat our neighbors, spouses and families just as negatively? Of course not.

Matthew 22:36-40 says, "Master, which is the great commandment in the law? Jesus said unto him, Thou shalt love the Lord thy God with all thy heart, and with all thy soul, and with all thy mind. This is the first and great commandment. And the second is like unto it, Thou shalt love thy neighbour as thyself. On these two commandments hang all the law and the prophets."

A lawyer in this passage asked Jesus a trick question. "Master, which is the greatest commandment in the law?" The Jews had over six hundred man-made laws (the curse of the law), and he was positive that he would cause offense through his question. But Jesus understood his intent and surprised everyone with His answer. We are to love God the Father with all our heart, soul and mind. We are to love our neighbors as ourselves. This means that we must love ourselves or we cannot love our neighbors.

These two commandments are so important that Jesus said all the law and the prophets hang on them. These two commandments are the sum of all divine revelation and responsibility. We have learned that if we do not love ourselves we cannot love others or God. In ministry we explore our relationships with others, with ourselves and with God the Father. In these broken relationships we find the cause of our problems in life. If the Bible is not working for you, you will find the answer in the healing of these relationships.

In contrast, being "stuck on ourselves" is prideful. Pride means having an unrealistically high opinion of one's own worth—conceit. Scripture warns us often about pride. Proverbs 16:18 says, that "Pride goeth before destruction, and an haughty spirit before a fall."

Praise God, there is balance between pride and self-hatred. The Bible lays out this balance, and God desires us to grasp hold of it and apply it in our daily lives.

If there are any feelings of shame, guilt, regret or sorrow in any memory of something that you have done, there is self-bitterness. If you are putting yourself down in any way there is self-bitterness.

Jealousy and Envy

First, let's define jealousy and envy. There are two types of jealousy and envy mentioned in Scripture. One is the "righteous" jealousy or zeal that God has for each of His sons and daughters, and the other is Satan's counterfeit.

The dictionary defines jealousy as "envy, grudging, resentment, or suspicion;" envy as "discontent or ill will at the good fortune of another, because one wishes it had been his." In both the Greek and Hebrew languages as used in Scripture, the words for jealousy and envy are interchangeable. In addition, they describe covetousness. Jealousy and envy lead to bitterness.

There are two major routes jealousy and envy use to enter our lives. One is through comparison and the other is through competition with others. Either route results in bitterness at another, or ourselves.

Competition drives us to say, "I don't care if Jodie has a new diamond ring. I'm worth at least as much as she is, so I think you should get me that diamond earring and necklace. That'll make Jodie take notice." Competition doesn't care that the other person has something; we just want more. This usually results in anger and bitterness directed at another. We become angry with others because they have something that we don't.

Comparison takes a different approach to jealousy and envy. Comparison says, "Oh that Jodie thinks she's really something with her fancy clothes and all. Now she's got this big ring. I can't stand her haughty attitude." Or we might compare our figure, intelligence, speaking abilities or other talents with others. Comparison results in bitterness toward ourselves. In comparing to others we degrade or belittle ourselves. We become angry with ourselves because we do not measure up to others in some way.

Here are some examples from Scripture of jealousy and envy:

Cain, of Abel (Genesis 4:4-8): Cain hated Abel because God accepted Abel's offering and not his. Cain's envy fueled anger and murder.

Sarah, of Hagar (Genesis 16:5-6, 21:9-10): Sarah hated Hagar because Hagar gave Abraham a son and she could not. Sarah's envy led to harsh treatment and expulsion of Hagar.

Philistines, of Isaac (Genesis 26:15): The Philistines hated Isaac because of Isaac's riches. Their envy led to filling Isaac's wells and asking him to leave the country.

Joseph's brothers, of Joseph (Genesis 37:4, Acts 7:9): Joseph's brothers hated Joseph because of his favored position with their father. Their envy led to plots to murder Joseph and they sold him into slavery.

Saul, of David (I Samuel 18:8-11): Saul became angry with and hated David because David was more popular and God was with him. His envy led to many attempts to kill David.

Korah, Dathan, and Abiram, of Moses (Numbers 16:3-10, Psalms 106:16-18): These men hated Moses and Aaron because they wanted the leadership position for themselves. Their envy led to evil speaking and rebellion against Moses and Aaron.

Haman, of Mordecai (Esther 5:9-13): Haman was indignant toward Mordecai out of pride because Mordecai did not consider Haman to be as important as Haman considered himself to be. Haman could not bear Mordecai being honored. His envy led to his plot to have Mordecai hanged.

Chief Priest, of Jesus (Mark 15:10, Matthew 27:18): The chief priest hated Jesus because Jesus performed miracles from God that he could not. He feared losing his position to Him. His envy led to Jesus' crucifixion.

Proverbs 14:30 says, "A sound heart is the life of the flesh: but envy the rottenness of the bones." The bitterness resulting from jealously and envy play a special role in the rottenness of our bones (osteoporosis).

Rejection

The dictionary defines reject as "to cast off, to rebuff or repulse. To throw away, as useless, or unsatisfactory. To put aside, to disapprove." This is the way of the world and Satan. But God tells us that He will never leave us or forsake us.

Rejection consists of several major aspects.

Rejection tells us we are unwanted, put aside and refused. It's a feeling of being unloved and not accepted either as a member of a group, by a friend, or sometimes even by the human race. Rejection places a wall around us that repels acceptance even when it is offered.

Rejection reminds us of our desperate need to be loved, while at the same time we're convinced we're unloved and unlovable. This causes emotional torment. Rejection drives love from us, and drives us from love. Even when someone does love us, we still feel rejected. "You're just saying that. I know better. You don't really love me. You only like what I can do for you."

Rejection tells us that no one can ever really love us—we're unlovable. Any time someone begins to open love's door to us, rejection slams it shut with accusations that we're unworthy of being loved.

As someone starts to show love toward us, rejection starts picking his or her affection apart. "Oh, you say you love me, but you won't go to my ball games." "I saw you looking at my dress. You think I dress stupid!" "See, you said it. You can't stand detail. You've never been able to tolerate someone who talks as much as me. This'll never work out." Rejection judges facial expressions and body language, or evaluates nuances, looking for a reason to feel more rejected.

Rejection drives us to pick a fight with the person who wants to love us. The result will be another sure rejection. Rejection says, "You're like everyone else. You're avoiding me. Well, I understand. I can't imagine anyone who'd want to be with me anyway." We speak our own words of rejection to others, and play a game of verbal Ping-Pong.

Rejection blocks our ability to reconcile differences with others over misunderstandings. It carries us into bitterness. We debate with ourselves about the rejection rather than going to the other person to resolve the misunderstanding. The hope of reconciliation rapidly disintegrates.

The fear of being rejected is fueled by the fear of man and by the fear of failure. Rejection, self-hatred and fear work together. Rejection says, "I'm not accepted." Self-hatred agrees, saying, "There's a good reason for you not being accepted, because you're not worthy of being loved." Then fear says, "If he ever knew what I was really like, he'd hate me." We're afraid that no one loves us, not even God. Yet, as these spirits are talking to us, and we're under attack, it's time to go to God. He is the only one who knows the real truth about us and is big enough to forgive us. God accepts us as we are, provided we come to Him in faith.

Rejection drives us to reject love from others. Even if people offer love and acceptance to us, we're unable to believe them and receive it. Giving and receiving love forms the foundation for our relationship with God, others and ourselves. The cause of all spiritually-rooted disease is the inability to give and receive love. Love has the power to break rejection and fear.

Rejection tells us that we will never belong. Even though we desire to "be a part of something," we never feel like we belong. We attempt to become involved in family, church, a group of friends, or some organization, or we strive to fit in at work. Yet, we just can't accept the fact that we belong. This sense of "not belonging" is rejection. Shame and guilt result from rejection, making us feel uncomfortable, so we don't "fit in." We're not "good enough." "I've been working at the same job for sixteen years, but no one really likes me down there. They still won't let me sing at the picnic. Julie won't even talk to me. Well, I talk too much. I understand. Why would anyone want to be my friend?"

A person who is plagued by rejection is given to irrational and continual self-introspection. They walk around with their head hanging down, are unable to "look you in the eye," but seem to always be looking for approval and acceptance from others. They're constantly on guard watching to see if someone notices them.

Rejection produces double-mindedness. "I know God said He loves me, but I don't feel His love, and He certainly never answers my prayers. I want to believe His promises, but why should I?" We constantly argue with God's eternal truth, bolstered by Satan's eternal lies. Rejection robs us of our true identity in Christ Jesus, preventing us from becoming the special person that God created us to be. It creates internal instability and restlessness. James 1:8 says, "A double-minded man is unstable in all his ways."

Rejection causes us to run and hide, or to search for our identity in all the wrong places. It prevents us from really facing our problems. Ironically, rejection drives us to seek some level of intimate contact with others—through a job, church, groups and individuals—but continuously drives us away from establishing intimate contact.

What began as our own irrational fear of rejection evolves into real rejection. "I can't stand being around Bob. He's so negative about himself. I don't want to hear any more of it!"

Do you see the many ways that these negative emotions can create an alarm reaction? Do you see how rejection can destroy your health? The good news is that we do not have to receive rejection. We can choose how we respond.

Receiving the hurt and pain from rejection is idolatry. We cannot prevent people from rejecting us but we can control how we respond. If we have responded by receiving the hurt and pain, we have fallen into idolatry. It is idolatry because we have given more importance to their words or actions than we have to God's. Anything that we allow to come between God and us is idolatry or a form of occultism. Picture the moon coming between the sun and the earth, thus blocking the sun from view. This is called an occult moon. We do the same thing when we allow another person's actions or words to "block" us from His truth.

Receiving the pain from rejection is therefore a sin. This is an important principle to deeply understand. It will set you free, as you work through it. This means that we do not have to receive the pain. We must learn to remember who we are in the eyes of God, not man. When we are whole and secure in who we are in God, we will be able to minister to others, instead of being hurt and offended.

Fear

First, let's define fear. Satan is the master counterfeiter. He will always take what God has meant for good and distort it for his purposes. The dictionary defines fear as "the emotion of being afraid, of feeling danger or that evil is near, an uneasy or anxious thought." Synonyms are dread or alarm. Dread is defined as "great fear."

Fear can warn us of danger so that we can protect ourselves. If we are standing next to a cliff it warns us to be careful. In times of danger, fear also creates a fight-flight response in our bodies. This fight-flight response causes the adrenal glands to secrete large amounts of adrenaline and cortisol, which causes several different physiological responses in our bodies. The primary one is an increase in strength to provide protection. But many live in a constant state of fight-flight as they think about the things that have happened to them. The oversecretion of adrenaline and cortisol will destroy your immune system and damage many other parts of your body.

Scripture teaches us that we are to fear God. This does not mean that we are to be afraid of Him. The Hebrew word used for this kind of fear is *yir'ah* (Strong's, 3374). It means "to have reverence" for God. He is the giver of every good and perfect gift. If it is not good and perfect, it is from the devil. But all too many of us are afraid of Him. The Hebrew word for this kind of fear is *yare* (Strong's, 3372). It means "to cause to be frightened, to make afraid or dread."

God the Father is love. In Matthew 22:37 Jesus said, "Thou shalt love the Lord thy God with all thy heart, and with all thy soul, and with all thy mind." We are to love God the Father, not be afraid of Him. God is the only one who loves each of us perfectly.

The Greek word *deilos*, translated fear in the New Testament, means "to dread; to be timid." By implication it means "to be faithless or fearful." Fear is equated with being faithless (Matthew 8:26, Mark 4:40, II Timothy 1:7, Revelation 21:8). Matthew 8:26 illustrates this meaning: "And He saith unto them, Why are ye fearful, O ye of little faith? Then He arose, and rebuked the winds and the sea; and there was a great calm." Mark 4:40 says, "And He said unto them, Why are ye so fearful? How is it that ye have no faith?"

Scripture records four occurrences of "little" or "no faith" concerning necessities of life (Matthew 6:30), concerning danger (Matthew 8:26), concerning working miracles (Matthew 14:31), and concerning food (Matthew 16:6-12). This kind of fear is a sin. It is a lack of faith or trust in God. If we are in fear then we are not in faith. As we have already seen, being "afraid, uneasy, or anxious, and having great fear" can cause extreme problems spiritually, physically and mentally.

Fear and faith are equal—one will always replace the other—fear is our enemy.

What are you afraid of? Here some possibilities:

Fear of losing life	Fear of a wasted life
Fear of death	Fear of the dying process
Fear of dying prematurely	Fear of disease
Fear of losing children	Fear of abandonment
Fear of foods, clothes (i.e., allergies)	Fear of the future
Fear of lack of food, clothes, etc.	Fear of man
Fear of failure	Fear of rejection
Fear of poverty	Fear of judgment
Fear of vomiting	Fear of change
Fear of the unknown	Fear of disability
Fear of pain	Fear of evil

All fears are self-fulfilling prophecies; they will come true. Satan attacks us with thoughts and fears. These fears, whether conscious or not, create a fight-flight response in our bodies and in one way or another become our reality. Fears, through automatic reflexes, set a pattern in action. We then view these as having a cause-and-effect relationship. Thus every time the same trigger occurs, the effect also occurs. As humans we have become so conditioned to these triggers and their causes and effects that we do not consciously recognize the process.

Why not choose to get rid of the bitterness, jealousy and envy, rejection and fear? God has made a way to have victory.

Note: For a complete study of these negative emotions and many others from Scripture, I suggest that you read and study my book, *Biblical Foundations of Freedom*, which describes many negative emotions and more importantly how to have victory over them. Literally thousands of people have been healed of virtually any disease as they learned to have victory over the negative emotions or thoughts that were the real causes of the disease.

God's Answer

POSITIVE EMOTIONS AND THEIR EFFECT ON HEALTH

Proverbs 4:23: "Keep thy heart with all diligence; for out of it are the issues of life."

Proverbs 14:30: "A sound heart is the life of the flesh: but envy the rottenness of the bones."

Proverbs 16:24: "Pleasant words are as an honeycomb, sweet to the soul, and health to the bones."

Proverbs 17:22: "A merry heart doeth good like a medicine: but a broken spirit drieth the bones."

Proverbs 23:7: "For as he thinketh in his heart, so is he. . ."

Many teach or imply that these verses have only a spiritual context but as we will see they apply to our physical bodies as well. Above all we must guard the heart from going astray, for out of it are the issues of life. This verse is not only about our arteries which carry the blood to all parts of the body, but also about the good and evil deeds that come from the heart (soul or center) of man (Mark 7:19-21). When one keeps the heart from evil it is an easy matter to obey the other commands of this passage (Proverbs 4:23-27).

Scripture also refers to us having something called the "reins." Have you ever considered what the reins are? The word reins comes from the Hebrew word *kilyah* (Strong's 3629) or the Greek word *nephros* (Strong's 3510). Which carry the meaning of a kidney (as an essential organ). They also figuratively mean the mind or innermost self. The term *reins* is a Hebrew idiom for the innermost thoughts and feelings.

In the ancient system of physiology, the kidneys were believed to be the seat of desire and longing, which accounts for their often being coupled with the heart (Psalms 7:9, 26:2, Jeremiah 11:20, 17:10).

The Hebrews also believed that the reins (kidneys) were the first part of the human fetus to be formed, so it may also refer to laying the foundation of a person. This is why Proverbs teaches that as we think in our hearts so will we be. It is interesting that this word carries a double meaning that connects our thoughts to our "essential organs."

We learned in the first section of this book that the endocrine system consists of many of our "essential organs," and in a broader definition, virtually every cell in our bodies. We also learned that negative emotions directly affect our nervous, endocrine and immune systems. The word *reins* is used fifteen times in Scripture. Let's look at some the verses.

Job 16:13: "His archers compass me round about, he cleaveth my reins asunder, and doth not spare; he poureth out my gall upon the ground." God wants us to serve only Him. He examines our every thought, meditation, word and deed, because He loves each of us.

Job 19:27: "Whom I shall see for myself, and mine eyes shall behold, and not another; though my reins be consumed within me."

Psalms 7:9: "Oh let the wickedness of the wicked come to an end; but establish the just: for the righteous God trieth the hearts and reins."

Psalms 16:7: "I will bless the Lord, who hath given me counsel: my reins also instruct me in the night seasons." Our thoughts are to be examined to make sure that they line up with Christ (II Corinthians 10:5). We have also learned that our bodies are barometers for what is going on in our thoughts or spirit. We have become so conditioned to our circumstances that our minds often do not recognize the fear or bitterness, but our physical bodies manifest the results of the negative emotions.

Psalms 26:2: "Examine me, O Lord, and prove me; try my reins and my heart." It is very comforting to know that God examines us because He is love; He is just and fair. It is also very comforting to give permission to God to show us any wicked way in our lives as David did in Psalms 139.

Psalms 73:21: "Thus my heart was grieved, and I was pricked in my reins." The Holy Spirit is sent to convict or prick or warn us. He warns us in our thoughts and in our bodies.

Psalms 139:13: "For thou hast possessed my reins: thou hast covered me in my mother's womb."

Proverbs 23:16: "Yea, my reins shall rejoice, when thy lips speak right things."

Isaiah 11:5: "And righteousness shall be the girdle of his loins, and faithfulness the girdle of his reins."

Jeremiah 17:10: "I the Lord search the heart, I try the reins, even to give every man according to his ways, and according to the fruit of his doings." Obedience is required under both the Old and New Covenants. Under the New Covenant Jesus says, "If you love me you will obey me" (John 14:15). The New Covenant also says in Galatians 6:7: "Be not deceived; God is not mocked: for whatsoever a man soweth, that shall he also reap."

Revelation 2:23: "...all the churches shall know that I am he which searcheth the reins and hearts: and I will give unto every one of you according to your works."

Now let's look at positive thoughts or emotions and see how they affect our health.

CARING, COMPASSION AND APPRECIATION

Heart Rate Variability: The normal or "sound" heart does not beat at a constant fixed rate. Instead, it oscillates or fluctuates. For example, a pulse rate of seventy-five beats per minute is an average of the high and low rates. It is normal for a heart rate to fluctuate from seventy to eighty and average seventy-five as in this example. But there are two heart rate variability (HRV) patterns, one that is constant and the other, erratic. In the erratic pattern there is no consistency or regular pattern. The erratic pattern is the most accurate physiological predictor of death from a heart attack (Jacobson 2000, Klieg 1987).

Research has connected our HRV pattern to how we think. Our HRV has been connected to emotional states. Individuals who have emotions that are described as caring, compassionate, or appreciative tend to have consistent or healthy HRV patterns, while those who are experiencing anger or frustration tend to have the erratic pattern, which places them at a much greater risk. Individuals who change their way of thinking from negative to positive also improve their HRV pattern and reduce their risk of heart attack or sudden cardiac death (Jacobson 2000, Tiller 1996, McCraty 1995).

GRATEFULNESS AND HOPEFULNESS

Heart Attacks or Sudden Cardiac Death: Research has also confirmed that "a merry heart doeth good like a medicine: but a broken spirit drieth the bones." Severe depression is considered a major predictor of heart disease. It is considered more dangerous than even smoking, high blood pressure or diet. One study reveals that heart patients who were recovering from a heart attack were eight times more likely to die suddenly if they were depressed than those who were grateful to be alive and hopeful for the future. Also men who were characterized as "high anxiety" (fear, worry, insecurity) were at six times the risk of sudden cardiac death than men identified as optimistic (Jacobson 2000).

PEACEFULNESS AND TRUSTING

Heart Disease: We learned earlier that "type A" behavior was listed as an anxiety and stress disorder in a pathophysiology textbook. Research has also connected two Type A behaviors with heart disease. The type A person who sets goals and does not become frustrated (peaceful, trusting) and pressured in accomplishing them is not at increased risk for heart disease. But those who become overwhelmed, pressured, or frustrated in the attempt to accomplish the goals are at a greater risk for heart disease. The other type A behavior that is associated with heart disease is unresolved conflict. When we harbor anger, resentment, or bitterness or other negative emotions towards others or ourselves we put ourselves at great risk (Jacobson 2000, McCraty 1996).

APPRECIATION AND LOVE

Infections and Immune Function: The immune system manufactures an antibody called IgA. It is found in our saliva and other body fluids. Research has shown that individuals who experienced an episode of deep appreciation or love for five minutes saw their IgA levels rise to forty percent above normal and stay elevated for more than six hours. Individuals experiencing intense anger or frustration for just five minutes were found to reduce IgA levels by fifty five percent in the first hour. The levels remained below normal six hours later after only five minutes of anger or frustration (Jacobson 2000, Research Update 1995).

LOVE FOR OTHERS

Depression, Suicidal Tendencies and Doctor Visits: The degree that we are concerned about others is also a health predictor. In a study by James Pennebaker, Ph.D., at the University of Texas at Austin, shows that the degree to which people are self- or other-focused predicts variables such as depression, suicidal tendencies and doctor visits. Those more concerned about others were healthier.

The Scriptures illustrate this in Isaiah 58:6-8: "Is not this the fast that I have chosen? To loose the bands of wickedness, to undo the heavy burdens, and to let the oppressed go free, and that ye break every yoke? Is it not to deal thy bread to the hungry, and that thou bring the poor that are cast out to thy house? When thou seest the naked, that thou cover him; and that thou hide not thyself from thine own flesh? Then shall thy light break forth as the morning, and thine health shall spring forth speedily: and thy righteousness shall go before thee; the glory of the Lord shall be thy rear guard."

LAUGHTER

Immune Function: Dr. Berk from Loma Linda School of Medicine recently studied the effects of "mirthful laughter" on the immune system. In a controlled clinical study, fifty-two healthy men viewed a humor video for one hour. Blood samples were taken ten minutes before, thirty minutes into the video and at thirty minutes and twelve hours after the video. The results showed that natural killer cell activity, plasma immuno-globulins, leukocyte markers, activated T-cells, non-activated T-cells, B-cells, interferon-gamma, and total leukocytes (white blood cells) all showed significant increase with some results lasting more than twelve hours. This is from just one hour of laughter (Berk 2001).

In another study on the effects of laughter Dr. Takahashi found that viewing a comic film for seventy-five minutes significantly elevated natural killer cell activity. Dr. Taka-hashi also presented a seventy-five-minute, non-emotional control film to the same twenty-one healthy male subjects. In this study the effect on natural killer cell activity was not significant. He also found that depression, anger and hostility suppressed natural killer cell activity (Takahashi 2001).

Dr. Hassed states "While there are inherent difficulties in structuring studies to assess the impact of humor and laughter on health, positive psychological and physiological responses to laughter have been demonstrated in a variety of settings. In particular, laughter has a role in stress hormone reduction, improving mood, enhancing creativity, pain reduction, improving immunity and reducing blood pressure (Hassed 2001).

Norman Cousins built an international business by promoting the effects of laughter. He taught how medical research has probed the effect of laughter on the human body and discovered a wide array of beneficial changes, including enhanced respiration and an increase in the number of disease-fighting immune cells (Cousins 1989).

Dr. Seaward of American University in Washington, D.C., reports that laughter has many clinical benefits, promoting beneficial physiological changes and an overall sense of well-being. Humor even has long-term effects that strengthen the effectiveness of the immune system (Seaward 1992).

Dr. Jan Ziegler reports on the physiological effect of laughing. She states that people who can laugh experience physiological changes that benefit the immune, endocrine and other systems of the body, thus demonstrating the relationship between emotions and disease (Ziegler 1995).

Have you ever noticed that you tend to get sick after becoming overwhelmed, stressed out or angry? I have learned to pay attention to my physical body because it is a better barometer of my spiritual condition that my cognitive mind. When I have caught a cold or the flu, I have learned that there is always a spiritual connection and then to be very quick to get rest and to repent for being stressed out, angry, worried or overwhelmed. Repentance brings relief, peace and the restoration of the immune system. I hope that you too are finding answers.

The issues of the heart, mind, will and emotions are critical. As we can clearly see, God knew what He was talking about when He said as we think in our hearts so will we be. Our thoughts and emotions (the issues or reins of our heart) have either a positive or negative affect on our physical hearts. Science also proves that we are to keep our hearts with all diligence, for out of it are the issues of life; that a sound heart is the life of the flesh, but envy is the rottenness of the bones; pleasant words are as an honeycomb, sweet to the soul, and health to the bones; a merry heart does good like a medicine, but a broken spirit dries the bones.

These commands from God apply to our spiritual life as well as our physical life. Remember that our bones contain all the building blocks of our immune system. The issues of our heart, our thoughts and emotions, control our immune system and therefore our health.

ISSUES OF THE SPIRIT

As important as the issues of the heart are, there is something more important. The issues of the Spirit provide the answers to the issues of the heart. Without the authority and power of God, Jesus Christ, and the Holy Spirit, we could not keep our hearts with all diligence. Without His forgiveness, there would be no help or closure to the issues of the heart.

As humans we have a body, a soul and a spirit. Our spirit enables us to communicate with Our Heavenly Father. The soul consists of our mind, will, emotions, the issues of the heart. Our bodies are the physical house for the other two. Both the spirit and soul have an effect on the body and just as systems within our body communicate, so do our spirit and soul. There is a connection between the heart and our spirit. There is also a connection between our spirit and God's Holy Spirit. Scripture also talks about evil spirits or Satan. Let's take a look at these connections.

In our study of the immune system we learned how God designed it to become trained, educated and specialized. This is also described as a maturing process.

The same is true of our "spiritual immune system." Each person is given an "innate" spiritual immune system at birth. Some have referred to this as the "eternity in our hearts." God has placed in every human a longing or empty place that only He can fill. He has also given each of us a conscience that to some degree allows us to know the difference between right and wrong, but this needs to be developed and matured. God is calling each and every person to Him, and He is also calling each of us to personal responsibility and maturity.

The first step in the maturity process is accepting Jesus as our Lord and Savior. Jesus Christ calls this being "born again." In John 3:3 Jesus said, "Verily, verily, I say unto thee, except a man be born again, he cannot see the kingdom of God." Jesus also told us that "except a man be born of water and of the Spirit, he cannot enter into the kingdom of God. That which is born of the flesh is flesh; and that which is born of the Spirit is spirit" (John 3:5-6).

I Corinthians 2:14 says, "But the natural man receiveth not the things of the Spirit of God: for they are foolishness unto him: neither can he know them, because they are spiritually discerned." In becoming "born again," our spirit becomes alive to God and our eyes begin to open to His way. Then we truly begin to discern good from evil and through the power of His name we can conquer evil in our lives.

This is where the Christian life begins. Salvation is not an end in and of itself. It is just the beginning. Often our lives become more difficult from this point on, until we learn how to fight the spiritual war—until we learn discernment (recognizing the difference between good and evil) and how to resist the devil. Sadly, most Christians do not progress past the point of a profession of faith. They do not grow or mature in Christ. They remain tied to the world and unstable in their ways (James 1:8). Their conscience becomes seared with a hot iron (I Timothy 4:2). If we are not careful, we can all become confused about right and wrong.

Scripture commands us to go on to perfection (Hebrews 6:1-2). Scripture commands us to cleanse ourselves of all iniquities if we want to be a vessel of honor in His house

(II Timothy 2:19-21). I Peter 1:16 says, "Because it is written, Be ye holy; for I am holy." This must be possible or God would not have commanded us to do it. He is a good God and would never command us to do something that was not possible. Let's look at what Paul had to say about Christian maturity.

Hebrews 5:11-14 says, "Of whom we have many things to say, and hard to be uttered, seeing ye are dull of hearing. For when for the time ye ought to be teachers, ye have need that one teach you again which be the first principles of the oracles of God; and are become such as have need of milk, and not of strong meat. For every one that useth milk is unskilful in the word of righteousness: for he is a babe. But strong meat belongeth to them that are of full age, even those who by reason of use have their senses exercised to discern both good and evil."

Just as it was two thousand years ago, believers are still immature. Most of us are still dull of hearing, needing to be taught the basic principles of Christianity. We still need "milk" and are unskillful in the Word. Those that are "full of age" have become mature by the hard work of using their senses to discern, or thoroughly distinguish good from evil and then do good.

Paul admonished us to leave behind the basic principles of the doctrine of Christ. When he says to leave the basic principles of Christ, he is not asking us to forget them or deny them. He is saying that having been fully established in them, we should then move deeper into the purposes for which God saved us in the first place.

When we begin grade school we are to learn the first principles of mathematics, science or reading. These skills are the foundation for the affairs of life and for higher education. While we are in school, they are the focus of our attention. But once we graduate, our focus turns to the concerns of adult life. Though we still use the skills we have learned, they are no longer the focus of our attention.

This is what Paul is talking about. He is saying that as we grow up in Christ, as we press on toward spiritual maturity (the high calling of God), the first principles of Christianity will be there for God to use in our lives. They will be there as a foundation to keep us grounded in truth. However, they are not to remain the central focus of our lives, for if they do, we will never grow or mature spiritually. Hebrews 5:14 defines maturity as knowing the difference between good and evil and then doing good.

What are the first principles of our faith that Paul mentioned in verse 12? Hebrews 6:1-2 tells us what they are: "Therefore leaving the principles of the doctrine of Christ, let us go on unto perfection; not laying again the foundation of repentance from dead works, and of faith toward God, Of the doctrine of baptisms, and of laying on of hands, and of resurrection of the dead, and of eternal judgment."

Paul is again encouraging us to go beyond the basic principles of Christ and move on to perfection in Christ. The word perfection means "to complete or finish." We have not completed our work or finished the course if we are still in the first principles of our faith. Would Paul teach us to go unto perfection, to complete and finish our faith, if it were not possible? Some teach that we cannot accomplish this until we die and go to heaven. This doctrine places our faith in the grave and not in the delivering power of Jesus.

Once again, the six first principles of Christianity in Hebrews 6:1-2 are:

Repentance

Faith in God through Christ
(Hebrews 6:1, Romans 3:24-25, Romans 5:1-11, I Corinthians 1:18-24, 15:1-8)

Baptisms
Baptism into Christ; Water baptism (Matthew 28:19); Spirit baptism.

Laying On of Hands when
Blessing men (Genesis 48:14)
Making offerings (Numbers 8:10)
Ordaining (Numbers 27:18, 23)
Imparting Spirit (Deuteronomy 34:9)
Blessing children (Matthew 19:15)
Healing sick (Mark 6:2, 5, 16:18, Luke 4:40, 13:13, Acts 5:12, 28:8)
Performing miracles (Acts 19:11)
Imparting gifts (I Timothy 4:14, II Timothy 1:6, Hebrews 6:2)
Imparting the Spirit of baptism (Acts 8:17-24, 9:17, 19:6)

Resurrection of the dead
(Hebrews 6:2, I Corinthians 15:4, I Thessalonians 4:13-16)

Eternal judgment
(Hebrews 6:2, Matthew 25:46, Revelation 14:9-11, 20:11-15, Isaiah 66: 22-24)
(Dake 1961).

Scripture is from God and therefore it is orderly, precise and without contradiction. I have learned to pay attention to the order in which God presents His precepts. There is always a reason for the order in which He taught or ministered. There is always a reason for what He does. These first principles are presented in this specific order for a reason. They show the order of our relationship with Him. First, we must repent; then we can believe; then baptism in water and spirit; then as His disciples, we can do His works; then resurrection and eternal life with Him.

Another way to look at maturity is from a parental standpoint. When we were little children our parents corrected our behavior. When we hit or bit another, or said bad words, they corrected the behavior. As we grew to teenagers, hopefully we left behind childish behavior and were corrected in our attitudes. And as adults we are to progress further to be responsible for our thoughts and emotions and thus how we choose to react or respond to situations in life.

Philippians 4:7-8 says, "And the peace of God, which passeth all understanding, shall keep your hearts and minds through Christ Jesus. Finally, brethren, whatsoever things are true, whatsoever things are honest, whatsoever things are just, whatsoever things are pure, whatsoever things are lovely, whatsoever things are of good report; if there be any virtue, and if there be any praise, think on these things."

Why would Scripture command us to think or meditate on only positive things; "whatsoever things are of good report"? Do you suppose that our loving and caring Heavenly Father knew how he created our bodies? Do you suppose He knew what negative thoughts or emotions would do to our health? Why do you suppose He calls these negative thoughts and emotions sin? Because He loves us and He wants to "sanctify you wholly; and I pray God your whole spirit and soul and body be preserved blameless unto the coming of our Lord Jesus Christ" (I Thessalonians 5:23).

II Corinthians 10:5-6 commands us to "Cast down imaginations [thoughts], and every high thing that exalteth itself against the knowledge of God, and bringing into captivity every thought to the obedience of Christ; and having in a readiness to revenge all disobedience, when your obedience is fulfilled."

God is commanding us to become obedient to His way of thinking because he knows what is good for us. He is also there to help us to be strong. II Corinthians 10:4 tells us that "the weapons of our warfare are not carnal, but mighty through God to the pulling down of strongholds." The strongholds are the negative thoughts and emotions (sins) that can control our lives and affect our health. Verse 5 explains that the strongholds are the imaginations or thoughts that exalt us against God.

This process of building our spiritual immune system is called sanctification. This is a process of becoming educated to the wiles of the devil so we cannot be deceived. We must become mature and know the difference between good and evil and obviously reject the evil and do the good. This is why Scripture commands us in so many places not to be just hearers of the Word but doers (James 1:22). But who or what is the devil and what are his wiles or devices?

WHAT IS SIN?

So far in this book we have clearly demonstrated, from the sciences of psychology and medicine, the effects of negative emotions (thoughts) on our physical and mental health. But science fails to understand the connection to the Spirit. Without the Spirit of God there are no answers. Without the Holy Spirit there is only eventual hopelessness. Without the Holy Spirit there is no healing or closure.

But where did these thoughts and emotions come from? Whose kingdom do they represent? Just as there is a Holy Spirit, there are also evil spirits. Ephesians 6:12

says, "For we wrestle not against flesh and blood, but against principalities, against powers, against the rulers of the darkness of this world, against spiritual wickedness in high places."

Both the Holy Spirit and evil spirits have access to each of us. The Holy Spirit comes to us in conviction asking us to deal with things in our lives so we can have a closer relationship with God. Satan and his powers and principalities come to us with condemnation and temptation. We know that evil spirits have access to us because of temptation. James 1:13 says, "Let no man say when he is tempted, I am tempted of God: for God cannot be tempted with evil, neither tempteth he any man." Temptation only comes from the devil.

God says in Hosea 4:6, "My people are destroyed for lack of knowledge..." We are also commanded not to be ignorant of the wiles of the devil. So maybe we should be asking, what are the powers and principalities of the devil that are referred to in Ephesians 6:12?

Earlier we studied what came into this world when Adam sinned. We learned that some of the most powerful negative emotions from the devil showed up in the behavior of Adam, Eve, Cain and Abel. The record in Genesis shows us that lying, shame, guilt, doubt, condemnation, jealousy, fear, unforgiveness, resentment, anger, hatred, violence and murder, etc., came into this world with the sin of one man (Romans 5:12).

Let's look at how Scripture describes these negative thoughts or emotions (sins). Remember Ephesians 6:12 says that we wrestle against powers and principalities, and spiritual wickedness in high places. Could it be that the sins that entered this world with Satan are his powers and principalities? After all, with what do we wrestle? Isn't it unbelief, doubt, rebellion, unforgiveness, resentment, anger, hatred, violence, murder, bitterness, rejection, jealousy, envy and the like? These are the sins that entered into this world with Satan through Adam, and we continue to wrestle with them today.

I have chosen to call these sins "spirits," "entities" or "beings" because the Bible uses those words to describe them. These sins are the character and manifestation of Satan and/or his spirits. Let me explain.

Numbers 5:14 says, "And the spirit of jealousy come upon him, and he became jealous of his wife." The Hebrew word used for spirit is *ruwach* (Strong's 6307). It is the same word that is used for the Spirit of God.

A lying spirit is seen in I Kings 22:23. "Now therefore, behold, the LORD hath put a lying spirit in the mouth of all these thy prophets, and the LORD hath spoken evil concerning thee."

A spirit of whoredom or idolatry is found in Hosea 4:12. "My people ask counsel at their stocks, and their staff declareth unto them: for the spirit of whoredoms hath caused them to err, and they have gone a whoring from under their God."

Isaiah 61:3 speaks of a spirit of heaviness or depression. "To appoint unto them that mourn in Zion, to give unto them beauty for ashes, the oil of joy for mourning, the garment of praise for the spirit of heaviness; that they might be called trees of right-eousness, the planting of the LORD, that He might be glorified."

Acts 16:16 speaks to a spirit of divination. "And it came to pass, as we went to prayer, a certain damsel possessed with a spirit of divination met us, which brought her masters much gain by soothsaying."

The Greek word used in the New Testament for spirit is *pneuma* (Strong's 4151). It is used both in conjunction with defining evil spirits and the Holy Spirit, just as the Old Testament used the same word for both.

In Mark 5:8, Jesus commanded an unclean spirit to come out of a man. "For He said unto him, Come out of the man, thou unclean spirit." Jesus asked this spirit its name, and the spirit's audible answer is recorded in verse 9. It claims the name, "legion, for we are many." The word "legion" was used for a Roman legion of 6,000 men. This man had thousands of demons in him that drove him to insanity. This shows graphically how demons can affect mental health.

Mark 9:25 shows Jesus casting out a deaf and dumb spirit. "When Jesus saw that the people came running together, he rebuked the foul spirit, saying unto him, Thou dumb and deaf spirit, I charge thee, come out of him, and enter no more into him." The man received the ability to speak and hear. This shows how demons can affect physical health.

In Luke 13:11-13, Jesus casts out a spirit of infirmity and heals a crooked back. "And, behold, there was a woman who had a spirit of infirmity eighteen years, and was bowed together, and could in no wise lift up herself. And when Jesus saw her, He called her to Him, and said unto her, Woman, thou art loosed from thine infirmity. And He laid His hands on her: and immediately she was made straight, and glorified God." This oppressive spirit actually affected the woman's posture and appearance.

II Timothy 1:7 says, "For God hath not given us the spirit of fear; but of power, and of love, and of a sound mind." Fear forms the basis for many mental and physical health illnesses. Fear is a sin. Fear is also another spirit that God did not give us.

There are many other Scriptural references to evil spirits negatively influencing our lives. These few examples I have provided should help you understand that Scripture repeatedly refers to various sins, diseases and infirmities as "a spirit." These evil spirits are real beings, just as is the Holy Spirit (though they are not equal in power since they are created beings and the Holy Spirit is God's Spirit). These evil spirits brought sin into this world, but they also brought mental and physical illness and death with them. If we allow them dominion in our souls, then they will manifest their natures in our character and in our bodies.

In I John 4:1-6, God instructs us, "Beloved, believe not every spirit, but try the spirits whether they are of God: because many false prophets are gone out into the world. Hereby know ye the Spirit of God: Every spirit that confesseth that Jesus Christ is come in the flesh is of God: And every spirit that confesseth not that Jesus Christ is come in the flesh is not of God: and this is that spirit of antichrist, whereof ye have heard that it should come; and even now already is it in the world. Ye are of God, little children, and have overcome them: because greater is He that is in you, than he that is in the world. They are of the world: therefore speak they of the world, and the world heareth them. We are of God: he that knoweth God heareth us; he that is not of God heareth not us. Hereby know we the spirit of truth, and the spirit of error."

God is instructing us again to acquire a "spiritual immune system" called discernment. He is instructing us to grow up and mature in Him and to test or discern all things. He is also telling us about a couple more spirits: the spirit of Truth (the Holy Spirit), and the spirit of error (Satan and his powers and principalities).

How do we know the difference between these spirits? Galatians 5:22-26 says, "The fruit of the Spirit [the Holy Spirit] is love, joy, peace, longsuffering, gentleness, goodness, faith, meekness, temperance: against such there is no law. And they that are Christ's have crucified the flesh with the affections and lusts. If we live in the Spirit, let us also walk in the Spirit. Let us not be desirous of vain glory, provoking one another, envying one another." We see that God's nature is love, joy, peace, longsuffering, grace, and mercy.

Galatians 5:19-21 tells us what the fruit or nature of the flesh is: "Now the works of the flesh are manifest, which are these; Adultery, fornication, uncleanness, lasciviousness, idolatry, witchcraft, hatred, variance, emulations, wrath, strife, seditions, heresies, envyings, murders, drunkenness, revelings, and such like: of the which I tell you before, as I have also told you in time past, that they which do such things shall not inherit the kingdom of God."

We know who we are serving by what is coming out our mouths and by what is in our thoughts. Matthew 12:34 says, "...for out of the abundance of the heart the mouth speaketh."

Whose nature do these negative emotions and behaviors line up with? Satan's nature. So in other words when we choose to sin we are in reality allowing the nature of Satan, or one of his evil spirits, to manifest through us in the same manner that we allow the Holy Spirit to manifest through us, in peace, joy, love, and forgiveness. Scripture commands us to "crucify" or destroy the flesh, the old man, the old nature, or the Adamic nature.

What Is the "Flesh" And How Do We Do This?

We need to understand that as humans we have a body, soul, and spirit. Our body is the visible flesh and all its parts. We also need to understand that the word "flesh" is used two different ways in Scripture. Many people say, "Well, that's just my old flesh.

I've got to get my flesh under control. I'm going to crucify my flesh." Do they mean they're going to kill themselves? Are they going to kill their body? Of course not.

To "crucify the flesh" has nothing to do with the physical body. It has to do with the "body of sin" (Romans 6:6). In Scripture the word flesh almost always refers to the body of sin, our old man, the old nature, the flesh, the Adamic nature or the nature of Satan. A study of the nature of Satan, the body of sin, our old man, the old nature, the flesh, or the Adamic nature reveals that they all share the same characteristics. In reality they are synonyms.

I Thessalonians 5:23 says that we are to be sanctified wholly in our spirit, soul, and body. The Bible doesn't call the body the "flesh"—it calls it the "body." The word "flesh" almost always has a spiritual meaning.

Romans 6:6 says, "Knowing this, that our old man is crucified with Him, that the body of sin might be destroyed, that henceforth we should not serve sin." We are to crucify our old man, the old nature, the flesh or the Adamic nature; thereby destroying the "body of sin," that "we should not serve sin" (Satan), so that we will not serve sin, but God. This verse equates the "old man," "the body of sin" and "sin." It teaches that we are to "crucify" or destroy the "body of sin," so that we will "not serve sin." In His death, Jesus enabled us through the power of the new nature (the Holy Spirit), to crucify and destroy the works of the devil in our lives.

"The body of sin" (Romans 6:6) is Satan and his demons, which manifest in our lives through the old nature, the flesh or the Adamic nature, which we are to destroy. The "body of Christ" is the Church, and is made up of all believers (I Corinthians 12:27).

In Romans 7:15-18, Paul says, "For that which I do I allow not: for what I would, that do I not; but what I hate, that do I. If then I do that which I would not, I consent unto the law that it is good. Now then it is no more I that do it, but sin that dwelleth in me. For I know that in me (that is, in my flesh,) dwelleth no good thing: for to will is present with me; but how to perform that which is good I find not."

Paul is examining why sometimes he does what he hates. In verse 17, he says that it was not he that sinned but the sin that "dwelleth" in him. That is a very interesting statement. He explains in verse 18 that in his flesh "dwelleth" no good thing. Paul separated himself from the flesh. He knew that the "flesh" was not really a part of "self." He accepted responsibility for his sins but taught that we are to crucify the flesh or old nature.

Mankind was created (chosen) before the foundations of the world, perfect (Ephesians 1:4). We were created in the image of God (Genesis 1:26), and we were created with free will (the ability to choose). When Adam chose to obey Satan and thus sin, his spirit and that of all mankind died to God. This is why we must become "born again" to be saved (John 3:3). While I do not believe we were created with an old nature, all of mankind is born with the old nature or flesh as a result of Adam's sin.

Paul also said in Romans 7:23-25, "But I see another law in my members, warring against the law of my mind, and bringing me into captivity to the law of sin which is in my members. O wretched man that I am! Who shall deliver me from the body of this death? I thank God through Jesus Christ our Lord. So then with the mind I myself serve the law of God; but with the flesh the law of sin."

Jesus is our deliver from the body of death. He is our deliver from sin and disease. He came to heal the brokenhearted and set the captives free (Isaiah 61:1-3, Luke 4:18-19).

Christian maturity is the process of destroying the old nature, the flesh, the old man, the law of sin, or the Adamic nature that was added to us, by Satan, when Adam sinned. To achieve Christian maturity is to become Christlike, it is to become holy as God is holy, it is to purge ourselves of all iniquity, it is to become vessels of honor fit for His service. This life is just a training ground, to prepare ourselves to be His kings and priests for all eternity.

With these thoughts in mind I want to suggest a radical but essential idea. I suggest that sin is more than just an action or a thought or falling short or missing the mark. As sovereigns of our own free will, when we choose to sin we open the door for Satan's demons to manifest their nature through us. Wow! That is a scary thought! Consider this carefully.

Remember, Satan is a created being and the only authority that he has over us is that which we allow. If you know Jesus as Lord and Savior, then He has given you all authority and power over the devil and his devices. Through the name of Jesus all things are possible. Nothing is impossible, even victory over sin, disease and Satan! Through Christ there is true closure and victory. Through Christ broken hearts are healed. This is why the New Covenant is better than the Old Covenant. Through the indwelling of the Holy Spirit we can have victory over the devil and sin.

Matthew 19:26: "But Jesus beheld them, and said unto them, With men this is impossible; but with God all things are possible."

Mark 9:23: "Jesus said unto him, If thou canst believe, all things are possible to him that believeth."

Mark 10:27: "And Jesus looking upon them saith, With men it is impossible, but not with God: for with God all things are possible."

Mark 14:36: "And he said, Abba, Father, all things are possible unto thee."

We also need to remember that we are the temple of Lord. I Corinthians 3:16 says, "Know ye not that ye are the temple of God, and that the Spirit of God dwelleth in you?" We become the temple of the Lord when we become born again and then His Spirit dwells in us. It is His Spirit that gives us the power and authority to destroy or crucify the old nature or the nature of Satan that is still in us. This is a process called sanctification.

As believers, God owns our spirit, but this process of maturity is called sanctification and is fought in our soul. Our soul consists of our intellect, mind, emotions, memory, thoughts and will. It is in this area of our existence that we fight against Satan. It is in this part of us that Satan tempts, entices, and sometimes controls believers and non-believers. As we cleanse ourselves of all sin and iniquity, we gain victory, and destroy the works of the devil. We accomplish this one sin, one thought, one emotion, and one iniquity at a time. This is why II Corinthians 10:5 teaches us to cast down imaginations [thoughts and emotions], and every high thing that exalteth itself against the knowledge of God, and bringing into captivity every thought to the obedience of Christ."

Some Christians are snared by a theological trap that claims, "I'm born again, I'm spirit-filled, Jesus paid the price, it is finished, and I'm immune to the devil." "All my past, present and future sins are automatically forgiven." If so, why are they oppressed, depressed, filled with diseases and have all types of evil operating in their lives? Why do they constantly repeat the same old lies, even when they know the truth?

Let's wake up, acknowledge and learn about our enemy, and then defeat him. We have the power and ability to do this because the provision has been made, and the debt has been paid. Under the New Covenant we have the Holy Spirit living in us. But the work of Jesus on the cross and His resurrection must be appropriated in our lives each day. We must forgive others or God does not forgive us (Matthew 6:14-15). If we confess our sins He will cleanse us (I John 1:9). What happens if we do not forgive others or do not confess our sins? We must become doers of His word and not hearers only (Romans 2:13, James 1:23-25).

Being "born-again" doesn't make us immune to evil. It means we have the power to overcome evil. Jesus died for sin as the ultimate sacrifice and rose again to give us the power to defeat Satan (I John 2:14, 4:4). This is why the New Covenant is better than the Old. We now can have the power to overcome the works of the devil.

The blood of Jesus is the ultimate atonement for the forgiveness of sins. The Old Testament animal sacrifices provided a covering for sins, but not forgiveness. Jesus' blood provides total forgiveness of sins, if we forgive others and ask God to forgive us. His resurrected life gives us access to the victorious power of the Holy Spirit.

While the Cross brought forgiveness, the power of Christian faith comes from the indwelling of the Holy Spirit. In this way we have all three members of the Godhead— Father, Son and Holy Spirit—living in and through us.

Jesus said, "If you have seen Me, you have seen the Father" (John 14:9). This should be true in our lives. We should be manifesting the nature of God as Jesus did, so that people see God's nature in our actions, hear Him in our speech, and understand Him in our attitudes. This can happen only through the power of the Holy Spirit acting in and through us. The Holy Spirit has been sent to convict us of our sins and then help us to defeat the lies of the devil in our lives.

Remember there was no sin, death, disease, sorrow or suffering before Adam and Eve sinned, and according to Revelation there will be no suffering, death, tears, or sorrow in the new heavens and the new earth (Revelation 21:4).

For an in-depth discussion of these topics please read *Biblical Foundations of Freedom* and *The Continuing Works of Christ.*

DOES GOD ALLOW EVIL IN THIS WORLD?

The New Testament equates God to love and names Him as light, the rewarder of those who diligently seek Him, the giver of every good and perfect gift, and the beginning and the end. The Old Testament names Him the Creator, Redeemer, Shepherd, Savior, Provider and many other positive names. His names also describe His nature. If His nature consists of these attributes, how can there be evil in the world?

"God allowed this cancer (or other negative event) to happen" is a timeworn cliché. Insurance companies label large storms as "acts of God." Philosophers and theologians ask if God "allowed" Hitler to kill millions of Jews during World War II. Did God "allow" all the male babies under age two in Bethlehem to be murdered by Herod, in his vain effort to kill the baby Jesus?

While ministering to people, we find many that go through life angry and bitter at God. They blame Him for a family tragedy or personal loss. Why do so many people see God as arbitrary and capricious, as someone that walks around carrying a big stick ready to punish them? Why are so many people afraid of God?

I have heard pastors and other Christians confidently say that God in His sovereignty allows evil, but He uses it for our good as an opportunity for Him to demonstrate His grace and mercy. This verbal salve is supposed to make it all better, make it okay that God allowed evil to happen.

Are any these statements accurate?

What does the word "allow" mean? Does it mean that if we choose to allow something to happen, that to some degree we approve or condone that action? Of course it does. If we choose to allow our children to do something, aren't we then responsible to some degree for the consequences of that action?

If God allows evil to happen, does that imply that to some degree He approves or condones it? Would it make Him responsible for that evil action? To be responsible for evil requires the commission of a sin. Does God ever sin? Of course not! Something is wrong with our human reasoning when we allege that God allows evil to happen.

Isaiah 45:7 says that The LORD created evil. What does this mean? The Hebrew word for "create" is *baw-raw* (HSN-1254) and it means "to bring about; bring into existence." The Hebrew word for "evil" is *rah* (HSN-7451). It is never translated "sin." It is translated in the following ways: "evil" (Isaiah 45:7, Genesis 2:9, 17, 3:5, 22); "calamity" (Psalms 141:5); "adversity" (I Samuel 10:19, Psalms 94:13, Ecclesiastes 7:14); "grievous" (Proverbs 15:10); "sorrow" (Genesis 44:29); "trouble" (Psalms 27:5, 41:1, 107:26); "distress" (Nehemiah. 2:17); "bad" (Genesis 24:50, 31:24, Leviticus

27:10-14); "affliction" (II Chronicles. 20:9, Zechariah 1:15); "misery" (Ecclesiastes 8:6); "sore" (Deuteronomy 6:22); "noisome" (Ezekiel 14:15, 21); "hurt" (Genesis 26:29); and "wretchedness" (Numbers 11:15).

God created the law of sowing and reaping, and those who sow sin will, for certain, reap evil. God decreed that misery, wretchedness, sorrow, trouble and distress will result from sin (Galatians 6:7-8). The Hebrew word *rah* (HSN-7451) is translated "evil" 442 times, and it is never with the idea that God created sin. People sow their own sin and reap their own evil. The responsibility for both is theirs. God gave the law and it provided penalties for breaking the law. In light of this, we all should examine what we have been taught, or what we believe. Who is really responsible for evil?

Scripture is replete with references to the two kingdoms all mankind inhabits. Satan is called the "god of this world" and the "prince and power of the air" (II Corinthians 4:4, Ephesians 2:2). He heads an earthly kingdom.

Jesus sits at the right hand of God in the third heaven, but His spirit lives within us. We are the temple of the Lord. His is a heavenly kingdom from which He rules the universe.

Satan's goal is to destroy us. He employs clever lies and principalities with their demons to persuade us to participate in evil and sin. God comes to us through the Holy Spirit and His Word, and wants us to embrace the truth and be set free from Satan's power.

In God's manifold wisdom, He created all of us with a free will. Our free will allows us to choose how to live. We have the option to follow God and His precepts, or Satan, the god of this world. These are the only two choices.

The ability to choose is valuable to each of us, but in order to choose there must be choices. Though God created good and evil, evil is not a sin until it results in an action.

Our free will is also very important to God. He wants each of us to freely choose Him as He has already chosen us. This reveals the heart of God. God is Love.

Have you ever been able to make someone love you? No! Has anyone ever tried to make you love him or her? Love requires an act of our free will. Love is an action and a choice. God wants each of us to choose a love relationship with Him, where we remain faithful to Him. It is the only kind of relationship that has any meaning to it. It is an intimate fellowship that only God can have with each of us.

The word fellowship found in Ephesians 3:9 means "a partnership or joint effort." This type of fellowship can only happen if both parties voluntarily agree. God wants us to choose to love Him as He has already chosen to love us! "And to make all men see what is the fellowship of the mystery, which from the beginning of the world hath been hid in God, who created all things by Jesus Christ; To the intent that now unto the principalities and powers in heavenly places might be known by the church the manifold wisdom of God" (Ephesians 3:9-10).

Does this understanding of choosing to love God cast a different light on our relationship with Him? Does this cast a different light on our responsibility to properly exercise our free will?

Everything bad that has ever happened to us on earth was planned in hell and executed by one of Satan's demons. These bad consequences happen because of one or more of the following three aspects.

First, because this is a fallen and cursed world, things will go wrong—bad things will happen. There are natural disasters, diseases, and other calamities that result from the curse. But these are still the result of sin and Satan. This was a perfect world before Satan's temptation of Adam and Eve led them to sin, and it will be again when God provides the new heavens and the new earth. The blind man in John 9 is an example of this type of calamity. But remember that Jesus healed him.

Second, exercising our free will, people choose to follow Satan and thus commit evil acts. These evil acts hurt innocent people. This is what Hitler, Herod and many others have done throughout history. In our choices to follow Satan and not God, each of us has also hurt innocent people.

Third, we suffer the consequences of our own sins. These consequences are something "evil" that enters our lives. As a result of our sins, God turns us over to "our own devices" (Proverbs 1:27-30). We will reap what we sow, in this God will not be mocked (Galatians 6:7). Our choice to entertain negative emotions has a corresponding result in our physical body.

God never allows evil. Mankind allows evil by making wrong choices. If we choose to practice evil then we alone are responsible for the consequences. We cannot blame God for evil.

II Corinthians 10:6 says, "And having in a readiness to revenge all disobedience, when your obedience is fulfilled." Are you ready to "revenge all disobedience"? When you revenge (stop) disobedience, then your "obedience is fulfilled."

We cannot blame God when we choose to disobey Him. Romans 5:12 says, "By one man [Adam] sin entered into this world [mankind]." Sin did not enter this world by God. The verse goes on to say "all have sinned." Thus, all of us are just as guilty of sin as was Adam. However, we cannot blame him for our problems since we have the same choice, whether or not to follow God or Satan, that he did.

Romans 5:18-19 says, "Therefore as by the offense of one [Adam] judgment came upon all men to condemnation; even so by the righteousness of one [Jesus] the free gift came upon all men unto justification of life. For as by one man's disobedience many were made sinners, so by the obedience of one [Jesus] shall many be made righteous."

God the Father loves us so much that He gave His only begotten Son that we might have life! By our disobedience we deserve death, but His love grants us life if we choose to accept it.

Sowing sin reaps evil. The decision of what to sow—God's good or Satan's evil—

is each person's. God never allows evil. Allowing evil violates His Holy nature. We alone must bear the responsibility for sin and evil.

One of Satan's greatest tactics is to blame God for his evil deeds.

In Genesis 3, we see how Satan falsely blamed God for "withholding something good" from mankind. If we have been blaming God for some event or attitude in our lives, now is the time to recognize who is really responsible. Our enemy is not God. Our enemy is not ourselves. Paul said in Romans 7:17, "Now then it is no more I that do it, but sin that dwelleth in me." Let's recognize Satan as our true enemy, and stop blaming God and ourselves.

Discernment comes from learning to know the difference between good and evil, and then making the choice to agree with God by doing good. This is the mark of a mature Christian. Let's use godly discernment to destroy the lies of Satan that give him a foothold in our lives!

The bottom line is that God is Love. All of His acts, even those we don't understand, are motivated by His love.

Hebrew Idiom of Permission

God's Word is clear as to the nature of the true God—He is always good. In direct contrast to God's loving nature is the devil, our adversary, the thief who wants to do nothing but steal and kill and destroy (John 10:10). The devil is always bad. In order to live in God's power, we must maintain a clear mental picture of the goodness of our loving heavenly Father and the badness of the devil. God never imparts evil to mankind. People who think that God makes them sick, injures them, or kills them are attributing darkness or evil to God, and that is wrong because God is light and in Him is no darkness at all (I John 1:5).

Of course there are many apparent contradictions in the Bible that stem from the erroneous idea of God's hurting or killing someone. Most can be reconciled with the proper understanding of the figure of speech, or idiom. An idiom is a colloquialism, a peculiar manner of speaking, or an expression with a meaning that cannot be understood from the words alone. An idiom can also be described as a usage of words in a culture that has a meaning different from a strict dictionary definition. In *Figures of Speech Used in the Bible*, E.W. Bullinger explained that the Hebrew language has an idiom of permission, which is a unique usage of words where active verbs are sometimes used "to express, not the doing of the thing, but the permission of the thing which the agent is said to do."

For example, when Exodus 10:20 says "the Lord hardened Pharaoh's heart" it means, "the Lord permitted Pharaoh's heart to be hardened." When II Samuel 6:7 says, "God smote him [Uzzah]," it more accurately means, "God permitted him to be smitten." When Genesis 19:24 records that "the Lord rained upon Sodom and upon Gomorrah brimstone and fire," it must be understood as "the Lord permitted brimstone and fire to rain upon Sodom and Gomorrah." The same is true in the story of Job and the calamities that fell upon him in chapters one and two.

We must realize the only sense in which God permitted any of these things to happen, is found in the fact that He gave men and angels free will. God gave Pharaoh the chance to resist Him and harden his own heart (Exodus 4:21, 9:12, 10:1, 20, 27, 11:10, 14:8, Romans 9:18). Each time was also a chance to repent and obey, but he refused. In the same way the gospel saves or damns, softens or hardens, all who hear it today (Romans 2:4-11, II Corinthians 2:15-16). As the sun hardens clay but softens wax, so it is with truth. The results reveal the nature of the materials. God did not personally cause any of these situations; mankind did, in our choices or free will.

Renewing of the Mind

So far we have taught many things about experience, emotions and disease. But the next few words are the most important words in this entire book.

Jesus has the ability to renew our minds, to purge our conscious of experiences such as traumas and fears, and heal our broken minds and bodies. He can restore our neural pathways, activate the proper genes, heal the genetics and restore us in body, soul and spirit. But He has requirements that we must meet.

Several times in scripture God commands someone to get off their duff and go to work. In Job 38:3, God command Job to "Gird up now thy loins like a man; for I will demand of thee, and answer thou me." God had had enough of Job's self-pity and self-righteousness and demanded that Job act like a man and take responsibility for his actions.

In I Peter 1:13 we are also commanded us to "gird up the loins of your mind, be sober, and hope to the end for the grace that is to be brought unto you at the revelation of Jesus Christ." This means to brace up, to be strong and face the challenges and experiences of this life because we can win and have victory in Jesus. We are commanded to be sober, which means to live righteously, and hope to the end for the grace and salvation that are for us in Christ.

I Peter 1:14 tells us how we are to be righteous: "As obedient children, not fashioning yourselves according to the former lusts in your ignorance." Do not pattern after your former life of sin (Ephesians 2:1-3). You are new creatures and you must live new lives (II Corinthians 5:17-18).

I Peter 1:15-16 further explains how were are to live this life: "But as he which hath called you is holy, so be ye holy in all manner of conversation; Because it is written, Be ye holy; for I am holy." God expects us to be holy as He is in this life. We can do this because of the power of the Holy Spirit and the blood of Jesus.

Hebrews 9:11-14 says: "But Christ being come an high priest of good things to come, by a greater and more perfect tabernacle, not made with hands, that is to say, not of this building; Neither by the blood of goats and calves, but by his own blood he entered in once into the holy place, having obtained eternal redemption for us. For if the blood of bulls and of goats, and the ashes of an heifer sprinkling the unclean, sanctifieth to the purifying of the flesh: How much more shall the blood of Christ, who through the eternal Spirit offered himself without spot to God, purge your conscience from dead works to serve the living God?"

Christ is our High Priest under the new and better covenant. "How much more shall the blood of Christ, who through the eternal Spirit offered himself without spot to God, purge your conscience from dead works to serve the living God?" The blood of Jesus is there to purge our conscience or minds from all the sins and experiences that have damaged it. But there are requirements that we must meet.

Romans 12:1-2 says: "I beseech you therefore, brethren, by the mercies of God, that ye present your bodies a living sacrifice, holy, acceptable unto God, which is your reasonable service. And be not conformed to this world: but be ye transformed by the renewing of your mind, that ye may prove what is that, good, and acceptable, and perfect, will of God."

He is there to renew our minds if we will let Him. But again there are requirements that we must meet. The real purpose for all believers in this life is to meet those requirements—to become holy as He is holy. How do we do this?

II Timothy 2:19-21 says: "Nevertheless the foundation of God standeth sure, having this seal, The Lord knoweth them that are his. And, Let every one that nameth the name of Christ depart from iniquity. But in a great house there are not only vessels of gold and of silver, but also of wood and of earth; and some to honour, and some to dishonour. If a man therefore purge himself from these, he shall be a vessel unto honour, sanctified, and meet for the master's use, and prepared unto every good work."

Our true calling in this life is to become a vessel of honor fit and prepared for every good work, not only in this life but in all eternity. We become vessels of honor by purging ourselves through the blood of Jesus of iniquities, all dead works, all sins. We are required to forgive those that have hurt us or God will not forgive us (Matthew 6:14-15). We are required to confess our sins so that He can cleanse us of all unrighteousness (I John 1:9). If we confess He is faithful to forgive us. We are required to seek first the kingdom and God and His righteousness (Matthew 6:33).

Obedience is required if we want His blessing.

As we repent and forgive, He cleanses us. He removes all the anger, bitterness, guilt, regret and sorrow. He provides closure; He resolves all the issues and traumatic experiences from life. He takes all the pain away. As this happens spiritually there are direct physical responses in our bodies. As our minds are renewed and purged, our bodies are also renewed.

A Study of Specific Diseases

So far we have looked at negative and positive emotions and how they can affect our immune system. We have also seen God's connection to our health. He has told us in many ways that obedience is required if we want to experience His blessings. He has required obedience because He loves us. He knows our bodies and how they are destroyed with sin. He wants each of us to experience this life abundantly. That is why He has warned us so many times to be careful what we sow because that is what we will reap. Now I want to change direction in this study to take a look at many specific diseases and the specific thoughts and negative emotions that we believe to be their cause.

In our research we have learned that our bodies are excellent barometers of the spiritual aspect of our lives. We have learned to trust physical reactions to tell us what is really going on in our thoughts, emotions and then in our relationship with the Lord. Most of us have become so conditioned to anxiety, stress, fears, and other negative emotions (sins) that we do not cognitively recognize them in our lives. Our discernment has become so confused and clouded by the things of this world, we do not understand or even perceive our own thoughts and emotions. And beyond this, many do not even recognize or know what sin is.

An example of this is found in a recent study by the Department of Psychiatry at Emory School of Medicine (Heim). His study revealed that women with a history of childhood abuse showed an elevation of interleukin 6 (a hormone that stimulates inflammation), an increased prevalence of chronic pelvic pain, and increased numbers of multiple other physical complaints.

The November 2002 issue of *Focus on the Family* magazine features an article about Dr. Larimore that confirms this clinical study. The opening paragraph relays an interview Dr. Larimore had with a caller named Sue, who was suffering from chronic pelvic pain. "He tells her that prior trauma, such as (sexual) abuse from childhood, can manifest itself in chronic pelvic pain and inflammation." We have also learned that the location of unexplained pain is often a clue to the root cause of the pain. In Sue's case it was bitterness toward the perpetrator. Forgiveness heals the broken heart and the broken body.

When I had environmental illness, one of the symptoms I experienced was muscle cramps, as a result of exposure to synthetic fabrics. I remember sitting at my desk absorbed in my work, and suddenly realizing that my foot was cramping. I had no knowledge of exposure to a fabric or any knowledge of a fear of a fabric. I did not cognitively recognize any fear. I did not know or understand that I was in fear. But my body told me otherwise.

As I learned to trust the physical reactions to reveal to me what my unconscious thoughts were, I gained victory. I learned to repent for the fear of the fabric simply because my foot was cramping, and then to command the fear and cramping to go, in Jesus' name. When I did this, the cramping immediately stopped. Many others have experienced the same results (see the allergy profile for more information).

Negative thoughts and experiences, and their conditioning effects, have a tremendous effect on our physical and mental health. We need to learn to pay attention to our physical symptoms because our bodies have more discernment than our minds do.

DISEASE CATEGORIES

As part of this discussion, I want to briefly discuss the various categories that most diseases fit into. A basic understanding of these categories will help us in our study of specific diseases. We have already discussed anxiety and fear disorders. Now, I want to discuss four additional categories of diseases: hypersensitive reactions, inherited or generational dysfunction, inflammatory responses, and psychosomatic diseases. Let's look at each of these individually.

Hypersensitive Reactions (HSR)

The inappropriate responses of our bodies to allergens, autoimmunity and alloimmunity can be collectively classified as hypersensitivity. Hypersensitivity is an altered immune reaction to an antigen (McCance 1998). It is important to note that allergies, autoimmunity, and alloimmunity are referred to as inappropriate immune responses. In other words, these only happen when our immune system is not functioning properly.

Diseases caused by hypersensitivity are characterized by immune functions that create inflammation, and result in the destruction of healthy tissue. Also, hypersensitivity reactions can be immediate or delayed. Reactions that occur within minutes are termed immediate hypersensitivity reactions. Delayed hypersensitivity reactions may take several hours to appear and are at maximum severity days after exposure to the antigen. The reaction is caused or activated by cytokines, which are controlled by our thoughts and emotions (Berk 2001, Dentino 1999, Lutgendorf 1999, Maes 1995, 1999, 1998). The most rapid, immediate and/or severe reaction is anaphylaxis. The symptoms include itching, vomiting, abdominal cramps, diarrhea, localized swelling and breathing difficulties. In more severe cases the symptoms might include blood vessel collapse, closure of the throat from swelling, low blood pressure and shock (McCance 1998).

It is also very interesting to note that allergies, autoimmunity, and alloimmunity are differentiated by the source of the antigen that is causing the immune response. Allergies are an immune response to something in our environment. Autoimmunity or autoimmune diseases are an immune response against our own body. Alloimmunity is an immune response against other people. Medically this happens when our bodies form antibodies to blood transfusions, skin grafts or an unborn baby during pregnancy (Rh incompatibility) (McCance 1998).

These three physical responses also have a fascinating spiritual component. God created the environment. In food or environmental allergies there is a fear of what we believe to be the allergen. But in reality, it is something that God has made, thus this really expresses a fear or distrust of God. In autoimmune disease, the immune system is attacking its own body. We have learned that this response happens as a result of a broken relationship with oneself (self-hatred). Alloimmune disease is a reaction to others which results from or causes a broken relationship with other people. Let's look at Scripture and see how this ties in.

Matthew 22:35-40 says, "Then one of them, which was a lawyer, asked him a question, tempting him, and saying, Master, which is the great commandment in the law? Jesus said unto him, Thou shalt love the Lord thy God with all thy heart, and with all thy soul, and with all thy mind. This is the first and great commandment. And the second is like unto it, Thou shalt love thy neighbour as thyself. On these two commandments hang all the law and the prophets."

A lawyer in this passage asked Jesus a trick question. "Master, which is the great commandment in the law?" The Jews had over six hundred man-made laws and he was positive that he would cause an offense through his question. But Jesus understood his intent and surprised everyone with His answer. Jesus said that we are to love God the Father with all our heart, soul and mind, and that we are to love our neighbors as ourselves. This means that we must love ourselves or we cannot love our neighbor.

These two commands are so important that Jesus said all the law and the prophets hang on them. These two commandments are the sum of all divine revelations and responsibility. We are commanded to love our neighbor, as we love ourselves. If we hate ourselves, are we then to also hate our neighbor? Of course not! We have learned that if we do not love and respect ourselves, we cannot love others or God. In ministry we explore our relationships with others, with ourselves and with God the Father. In these broken relationships we find the cause of most of our problems and diseases in life. If the Bible is not working for you, you will find the answer in the healing of these relationships.

Our ministry process leads people to discover how their relationships with God, self and others have been broken. If there is any emotional pain such as anger, unforgiveness, resentment, hatred, shame, guilt or regret in a memory, then there is bitterness in that memory. As we have already seen these negative emotions have many different negative effects on our immune system. This negative effect can include any of these three types of hypersensitive reactions.

If we are blaming God, others, or ourselves for our problems, we are always wrong. God the Father is the giver of every good and perfect gift (James 1:17). Therefore, if it is not good and perfect, it is not from God. If we are blaming God for any calamity in this life, we are wrong. If we are blaming others, then we are in bitterness. We cannot control what others do, but we can control how we choose to respond. There will not be a negative immune response if we respond according to God's Word. If we blame ourselves, we have fallen into self-bitterness. We are to do as Paul taught in Romans 7:17. We are to separate others and ourselves from the action (sin) and forgive. This means that we are to take full responsibility for our sins in a Biblical way. Scripture never teaches us to blame ourselves in anyway. The only proper scriptural response to our sins or the sins of others is to repent or to forgive. We are never to place blame on anyone. To choose not to forgive is the same as judging.

The Lord's Prayer (Matthew 6:12) teaches to ask Our Father to forgive us in the same manner that we forgive others. Do you really want to ask God to do this? If you do not understand this, Jesus made it very plain in Matthew 6:14-15: "For if ye forgive men their trespasses, your heavenly Father will also forgive you: but if ye forgive not men their trespasses, neither will your Father forgive your trespasses."

I John 1:9 says, "If we confess our sins, he is faithful and just to forgive us our sins, and to cleanse us from all unrighteousness." Remember this verse begins with an "if." If we confess, He will forgive. What happens if we do not confess? Forgiveness and repentance are not options; God requires them if we want to be forgiven. As we learn to forgive and repent, thus letting Jesus heal our broken hearts and our broken relationships, the inappropriate immune response stops and our bodies heal.

Please read and study *Biblical Foundations of Freedom* and *Continuing Works of Christ* for further discussion on these topics.

Now I want to look at each of these hypersensitive reactions individually.

ALLERGIES

When our immune system is functioning properly, it builds immunity to antigens. In other words a properly functioning immune system creates specialized T-cells and B-cells that form antibodies, which attack and kill antigens (invaders). But a malfunctioning immune system creates an immune response to things in our environment that should not be harmful to us, things that God has made. This improper immune response to something in our environment is called an allergy.

This reaction occurs because of two sets of negative emotions: bitterness and fear. First, negative emotions such as unforgiveness, resentment, anger, shame, guilt, regret, sorrow, and the other negative emotions associated with bitterness, are immunosuppressants. They can also cause the immune system to act improperly and become hypersensitive. As a result, antibodies are created to various foods or the air that we breathe, creating swelling, itching, stomachaches, or far more serious reactions.

The second negative emotion is fear. We develop a fear toward what we have learned to associate the reaction in our bodies with. In the HSR or the allergy reaction, we become trained or conditioned in a Pavlovian manner (see classical conditioning and placebo) to react to what we have come to believe are allergens to us. The fear of the supposed allergen trains or conditions the immune system to respond in a HSR, even when we do not cognitively recognize the allergen or even the fear.

The answer is also twofold. First, we must recognize and repent for the bitterness, self-bitterness, jealousy and envy, and rejection (i.e., all the negative emotions). We must let Jesus heal our broken hearts in every way. This stops the alarm or flight-fight response, thus allowing our nervous and endocrine (hormonal) systems to settle down. Both of these systems affect the immune system and its response. In this process our immune system returns to normal. Positive emotions greatly enhance the immune system.

Second, we must get rid of every fear. Fear powerfully affects our nervous, endocrine and immune systems. This kind of fear is really a sin. In this fear we are really saying "God, I do not trust you." This kind of fear is the opposite of faith. If you are in fear, you cannot be in faith. If you are in faith, you will not be in fear. For a full discussion of these subjects, read and study *Biblical Foundations of Freedom*.

AUTOIMMUNITY

Autoimmunity is a misguided or inappropriate immune response against the body's own organs or cells. In this abnormal response, the immune system builds antibodies to, and attacks, its own body. Autoimmunity is really an allergy to one's own body. Something has fooled the immune system into attacking the body as if it were bacteria, virus or other invader. Antibodies then can be developed for any organ or cell in the body. In this reaction, there is almost always inflammation. Inflammation can be the evidence of an abnormal immune response (Singh 1994, 1997).

Vijendra K. Singh, Ph.D., a Research Associate Professor at Utah State University, has over twenty years of experience in neurobiology and immunology research. Recently Dr. Singh's research has focused on central nervous system disorders, particularly infantile autism and Alzheimer's disease, with a special focus on autoimmunity in autism. Dr. Singh has authored more than a hundred scientific publications and made numerous presentations at conferences worldwide. He is considered a pioneer in his field and an international authority on autoimmunity and autism. He serves on the scientific board of the Autism Autoimmunity Project, New Jersey.

Antibodies are measured by what are called titers. An antibody titer is the level of a given antibody, that is, how much of that antibody is present. For example an anti-neuronal antibody is an antibody that specifically acts against nerve cells or neurons, and/or neurological processes. This is what caused my nerve endings to die, in what was diagnosed as peripheral neuropathy. Antibodies can be developed to brain cells, nerve cells, organs, blood vessels, blood, or any other part of the body (Singh 1994, 1997).

Additionally, Dr. Singh's research links autoimmunity to all nervous system diseases. Included in his list are conditions such as autism, obsessive-compulsive disorder (OCD), Multiple Sclerosis (MS), Alzheimer's, schizophrenia and major depression. The main component in nervous system disease is really autoimmunity. Dr. Singh goes on to say that he is convinced that the immune response is important, not just for the nervous system, but for basically any disease in the body (Singh 1994, 1997).

Dr. Singh also refers to the works of Dr. Susan Swedo's group regarding OCD. They were actually administering an immune therapy known as plasmapheresis when they observed an association between group-A streptococcus infection and OCD. While providing therapy to address the infection, it was found that the patient's OCD symptoms were reduced by plasmapheresis (plasma). It was also learned that there was a decrease in antineuronal antibody titers in response to therapy. So with plasmapheresis they were able to reduce the antibody titers as well as see behavioral benefits to the patients, thus demonstrating the autoimmune connection (Singh 1997).

We have previously studied many negative emotions such as depression or anxiety. These negative emotions can directly affect the cells of the immune system and either up or down regulate the secretion of proinflammatory cytokines (IL-6), that cause inflammation. Inflammation has been linked to several conditions or diseases including cardiovascular disease, osteoporosis, arthritis, type-2 diabetes, certain cancers (including multiple myeloma, non-Hodgkin's lymphoma and chronic lymphocytic leukemia), Alzheimer's disease, and periodontal disease (Cohen 2000, Ershler 2000, Kendall 2002).

Once again, it is important to note that Dr. Singh's research shows that inflammation is nothing but an abnormal immune response (Singh 1994, 1997). Other research shows that the body is responding to what is going on in the brain, and not to what is going on in the environment. This same study demonstrated how negative self-appraisal —blaming oneself for negative events—is linked to poorer health outcomes (Taylor).

A pathophysiology medical textbook lists the following disorders as autoimmune disorders:

Endocrine System: hyperthyroidism (Grave's Disease), autoimmune thyroiditis, primary myxedema, insulin-dependent diabetes, Addison's disease, premature gonadal failure (ovary), orchitis (testes), female infertility, male infertility, idiopathic hypoparathyroidism, partial pituitary deficiency.

Skin: pemphigus vulgaris, bullous pemphigoid, dermatitis herpetiformis, vitiligo.

Neuromuscular Tissue: polymyositis, multiple sclerosis, myasthenia gravis, polyneuritis, rheumatic fever, cardiomyopathy, postvaccinal or postinfectious encephalitis.

Gastrointestinal System: celiac disease, ulcerative colitis, Crohn's disease, pernicious anemia, atrophic gastritis, primary biliary sclerosis, chronic active hepatitis.

Eye: Sjogren's syndrome, uveitis.

Connective Tissues: ankylosing spondylitis, rheumatoid arthritis, systemic lupus erythematosus (SLE), mixed connective tissue disease, polyarteritis nodosa, scleroderma, Felty syndrome, antiphospholipid antibody syndrome.

Renal System (kidney): immune complex glomerulonephritis, Goodpasture's Syndrome.

Hematologic System (blood): idiopathic neutropenia, idiopathic lymphopenia, autoimmune hemolytic anemia, autoimmune thrombocytopenic purpura.

Respiratory System: Goodpasture's syndrome. (McCance 1998)

The answer is to search out and repent for any way that you have put or are putting yourself down. When God looked at His creation in Genesis, chapter one, He called it "very good." If you are saying anything about, or doing anything to, yourself that is less than "very good" you are cursing yourself. Additionally, you are cursing God since He created you in His image.

If you add this list of autoimmune diseases to those listed as anxiety and stress disorders from the same medical textbook that we listed earlier, we have covered the great majority of all diseases.

ALLOIMMUNE

Alloimmune diseases occur when the immune system of one person produces an immune response against the tissues of another person. This happens with immune reactions against blood transfusions, skin grafts, and organ transplants. It is also a major factor in miscarriages where an immune reaction occurs against the unborn baby (Rh incompatibility, spontaneous abortions) (McCance 1998). We have found that a husband or wife can be allergic to their spouse.

Again the answer is to search out and repent for all the bitterness and fear in our lives. We need to carefully examine our feelings and emotions toward God, others and ourselves.

Inflammatory Response

Inflammatory responses are being associated with more and more diseases. As we have just read they are associated with all reactions in allergies, autoimmune and alloimmune diseases.

A November 6, 2002, Associated Press article reported two new studies from the *Journal of the American Medical Association (JAMA)* that add to the rapidly growing body of evidence that inflammation in the bloodstream can be a powerful predictor of heart disease. These findings could help explain why people with no known risk factors such as high cholesterol or high blood pressure can still have heart attacks.

One JAMA study found that levels of an enzyme, myeloperoxidase (MPO), were elevated in people who had had heart attacks, heart bypass surgery and narrowed coronary arteries. The other study linked IL-6 to an increased risk of death in heart patients. Both substances are associated with inflammation.

In recent years, doctors have come to suspect that inflammation, whether triggered by an infection or some other condition, can damage the walls of heart arteries, making them more prone to the fatty buildups that can lead to heart attacks.

MPO Levels

One of the two studies found that patients with the highest levels of MPO, which is normally found in infection-fighting white blood cells, had a twenty-fold greater risk of heart disease than those with the lowest levels. Inflammation is an indicator of infections. High levels were even found in people with no significant heart disease and with no risk factors such as high cholesterol and high blood pressure.

Cleveland Clinic researchers said that may help explain why heart attacks frequently occur in people previously thought to be healthy. "What is most exciting, is that this marker appears to be significantly better at predicting risk for atherosclerosis, or hardening of the arteries, than blood tests now used," which include cholesterol tests, said Dr. Stanley Hazen, who coordinated the research. He noted that about fifty percent of heart attack patients have normal cholesterol levels.

Interleukin 6 Tied to Death Risk

The second JAMA study involved more than 3,000 Scandinavian patients and found that high levels of IL-6 increased the risk of death in patients hospitalized with chest pain and other heart attack symptoms. IL-6 has been previously linked in other studies with inflammation and heart disease (Cohen 2000, Ershler 2000, Kendall 2002).

Patients whose blood tests showed high IL-6 levels faced a more than threefold risk of dying within 6-12 months of initial hospitalization, compared with patients with low levels. The findings suggest that testing for IL-6 could help determine which patients would benefit most from such treatments, said researchers Eva Lindmark and colleagues from Uppsala University Hospital in Sweden (Associated Press Nov. 6, 2002).

C-reactive Protein

The November 2002 edition of *The New England Journal of Medicine*, reported another study comparing C-reactive protein and low-density cholesterol (LDL, "the bad cholesterol") in predicting first cardiovascular events. C-reactive protein and LDL cholesterol were measured in 27,939 apparently healthy American women, who were then monitored for eight years for the occurrence of myocardial infarction (heart attack), stroke, coronary revascularization (bypass surgery), or death from cardiovascular causes.

The study revealed that seventy-seven percent of all events occurred among women with LDL cholesterol levels below 160 mg, and forty-six percent occurred among those with LDL cholesterol levels below 130 mg. The conclusion is that the C-reactive protein level is a stronger predictor of cardiovascular events than the LDL cholesterol level (Ridker 2002).

The point is that inflammation is a marker for a dysfunction in the immune system that is usually categorized as an autoimmune response. As Dr. Singh teaches, "inflammation is nothing but an abnormal immune response" (Singh 1994, 1997).

We have also seen in other studies that negative emotions such as depression or anxiety can directly affect the cells of the immune system and either up, or down, regulate the secretion of proinflammatory cytokines (interleukin 6) which causes inflammation (Kendall 2002).

Generational or Inherited Dysfunction and Disease

When we hear the words "genetic" or "generational" we usually react in fear and in one way or another proclaim that there is nothing we can do. We believe that we have been victimized by a cruel quirk of nature. Often "generational" or "genetic" becomes an escape from personal responsibility. But, as we learned in the study of the brain, the genes are affected by experience. In other words the way we react to an experience affects which genes are activated and how our nervous system develops. Both positive and negative thoughts and emotions affect gene development and activation (Siegel 1999).

We also studied earlier how cytokines act by binding to specific receptors at the cell membrane, setting off a cascade that leads to the enhancement or inhibition of a number of cytokine-related genes in the nucleus of the affected cells (Berk 2001). In Dr. Berk's work we see genes affected by cytokines (proteins) that other studies show are affected by thoughts and emotions (Kendall 2002). I believe that as time goes on, a greater volume of research will confirm this spiritual/emotional connection.

In a very practical way our negative ways of thinking and reacting (sins), as well as our positive thoughts and coping mechanisms, are passed on to our children. We can see in the pathologies of life and in Scripture how our children mimic our behavior.

Numbers 14:18: "The Lord is longsuffering, and of great mercy, forgiving iniquity and transgression, and by no means clearing the guilty, visiting the iniquity of the fathers upon the children unto the third and fourth generation."

Exodus 20:5: "Thou shalt not bow down thyself to them, nor serve them: for I the Lord thy God am a jealous God, visiting the iniquity of the fathers upon the children unto the third and fourth generation of them that hate me."

What do these verses mean? I have heard some teach that these are just "Old Testament curses" that have no application for today. First, God's Word is never a curse. The only curse comes from how we misuse or misapply His Word.

Unrighteousness brings with it a consequence. It is God's will that all serve Him.

When He says that He is a "jealous God," He is saying that He is zealous for each and every person that He created. It is His will that none perish. It is His will that every human experiences His love and mercy. But in the sovereignty of our free will, many say "no" to Him.

It also needs to be stated that this is not an issue of salvation. Ezekiel 18 and many other passages teach that we will all stand alone before God and answer for our own sin at the day of judgment. But there is an application for today.

As parents, we pass on our way of thinking, our way of dealing with the challenges of life, and our behaviors to our children and our children's children. If mom was extremely fearful, her children will also be fearful. If dad is angry and bitter, his children will approach life with the same attitude. We see all the behaviors, attitudes and pathologies of this life passed on to our offspring.

If a person has been sexually, emotionally or physically abused, he will probably abuse others and/or himself. He has been conditioned and learned "that is how it is done." If dad was a liar, then the son and daughter will probably be a liar also. We see this in the story of Abraham.

Abraham was afraid that the king would kill him and take his wife Sarai. So he lied to Pharaoh and told him that Sarai was his sister. Later Abraham traveled to the land of the Philistines where Abimelech was king. He told the exact same lie again. Then forty years later, Abraham's son Isaac, and his wife Rebekah, traveled into the land of the Philistines, where Abimelech was still king. Isaac told the exact same lie that his father told forty years earlier.

Isaac had two sons, Esau and Jacob. Rebekah, who had already lied, along with her husband Isaac, got into a discussion with Jacob over the birthright and together they deceived Isaac and lied to him. Now we have another generation of liars, Abraham, Isaac and Jacob. It doesn't stop there.

Jacob had twelve sons. Ten of the sons were jealous of Joseph. They killed an animal, kidnapped Joseph, dipped his coat of many colors in the blood, took it back to their father and said that an animal had just killed Joseph (Genesis 37). They lied to Jacob. If it had not been for the intercession of Judah to sell Joseph into slavery, Joseph would have been killed. Now we have four generations of liars. Not only that, Jacob's wife Rachel lied to her father, Laban, over the issue of idols (Genesis 31:19). Now we've got men and women lying.

If you look into your own life, I believe that you can find examples of similar behaviors or attitudes that have passed down through your generations. As we have already learned, negative emotions and behavior have severe consequences in our mental and physical health. This is the practical application of these verses.

There are also several verses that demonstrate repentance for the sins of the fathers: Nehemiah 9:1-2: "Now in the twenty and fourth day of this month the children of

Israel were assembled with fasting, and with sackclothes, and earth upon them. And the seed of Israel separated themselves from all strangers, and stood and confessed their sins, and the iniquities of their fathers." Daniel 9 and Leviticus 26:40-45 are other examples.

Passages from Mark 9, Luke 9 and Matthew 17 relate the story of a father with a sick son. In each of these accounts, Jesus rebukes a "faithless" and/or "perverse generation." As you read these accounts, you will also notice that Jesus did not (and I believe could not) heal the boy until after the father repented of his unbelief and asked Jesus to help his unbelief.

Mark 9:17-27 says, "And one of the multitude answered and said, Master, I have brought unto thee my son, which hath a dumb spirit; And wheresoever he taketh him, he teareth him: and he foameth, and gnasheth with his teeth, and pineth away: and I spake to thy disciples that they should cast him out; and they could not. He [Jesus] answereth him, and saith, O faithless generation, how long shall I be with you? How long shall I suffer you? Bring him unto me. And they brought him unto him: and when he saw him, straightway the spirit tare him; and he fell on the ground, and wallowed foaming. And he asked his father, How long is it ago since this came unto him? And he said, Of a child. And ofttimes it hath cast him into the fire, and into the waters, to destroy him: but if thou canst do any thing, have compassion on us, and help us. Jesus said unto him, If thou canst believe, all things are possible to him that believeth. And straightway the father of the child cried out, and said with tears, Lord, I believe; help thou mine unbelief. When Jesus saw that the people came running together, he rebuked the foul spirit, saying unto him, Thou dumb and deaf spirit, I charge thee, come out of him, and enter no more into him. And the spirit cried, and rent him sore, and came out of him: and he was as one dead; insomuch that many said, He is dead. But Jesus took him by the hand, and lifted him up; and he arose."

In Mark 9:21, Jesus asked the father how long the boy had been sick, and the father said since childhood or infancy. In verse 22 the father says, "but if thou canst do any thing, have compassion on us, and help us." This was the desperate cry of a father for his son: "Help, if you can." He did not believe that Jesus really could or would heal his son. In verse 23, Jesus looked at that father and he said, "If you can believe...?" In others words, "It's not a matter, of if I can, it's a matter if you can believe." But the father was so discouraged and so disappointed and so beat up by the spirit of unbelief and the spirit that made his son deaf, dumb and mute, he wasn't able to believe God. He wasn't able to believe the promise of God.

In verse 24, the father of the "child cried out, and said with tears, Lord, I believe; help thou mine unbelief." Then Jesus cast out the dumb and deaf spirit and the boy was healed. He cast out the spirit and the boy was healed after the father repented for his unbelief. It was the father's unbelief that prevented the disciples from casting the demon out. Unbelief also prevented Jesus from doing the works of the Father in healing this boy.

The dumb and deaf spirit blinded the spiritual eyes of the father, seeking to prevent him from believing. But it was not just the father's sin. It was in the generations. Sometimes we really want to believe that God can and will heal, but the healing does not happen. There is a generational sin of unbelief that must be repented of and broken.

The passages continue to say "this kind comes out by prayer and fasting." It is usually taught that "this kind" refers to the demon. I believe that Jesus is referring to the sin of unbelief that comes out by prayer and fasting.

I firmly believe that "all things are possible" with God. But as you study Scripture, you will see that only one thing prevented Jesus from doing His work. Only unbelief stopped Jesus from doing mighty miracles (Mark 6: 4-6).

We believe that it is appropriate to confess iniquities of the past generations as well as those in our lives. We find that it is very important to recognize the iniquities and unbelief (sins) in our families and our lives and then repent. In doing this, we break the cycle and establish a new generation in righteousness. We have led hundreds of people in this type of prayer and have seen them set free of many bondages. This is how the Blood of Jesus renews our minds (Hebrews (9:14).

There are also verses that teach that His righteousness is forever.

Isaiah 51:7-8: "Hearken unto me, ye that know righteousness, the people in whose heart is my law; fear ye not the reproach of men, neither be ye afraid of their revilings. For the moth shall eat them up like a garment and the worm shall eat them like wool: but my righteousness shall be for ever, and my salvation from generation to generation."

Let's make this true in our lives and families.

Psychosomatic Disease

This term is often misunderstood. Many believe that a psychosomatic disease is "all in your head." Nothing could be further from the truth. *Taber's Medical Dictionary* defines psychosomatic disease as:

> Pertaining to the relationship of the mind and body; to disorders that have a physiological component but are thought to originate in the emotional state of the patient. When used so, the impression is created that the mind and body are separate entities and that a disease may be purely somatic in its effect or entirely emotional. This partitioning of the human being is not possible; thus no disease is limited to only the mind or the body. A complex interaction is always present even though in specific instances a disease might on superficial examination appear to involve only the body or the mind (Taber's 1997).

The Merck Manual has this to say about psychosomatic medicine:

> The fact that psychological stress can precipitate or alter the course of even major organic diseases has long been apparent but very difficult for physicians

to accept and comprehend. Emotions obviously can affect the autonomic nervous system and, secondarily, cardiac rate, sweating, or bowel peristalsis. But can a reaction affecting the mind (brain) alter immune responses? The answer is becoming clear. Psychoimmunology is now an established area of scientific research, and both animal and human studies demonstrated the interrelationship (Merck 1996).

Indeed it is difficult to find a disease that is not psychosomatic. Many in medical science teach that as many as eighty percent of all diseases are psychosomatic. I personally believe that the percentage is much higher. As you look back at the anxiety and fear disorders, the hypersensitivity reactions, the infectious disorders, cancers, autoimmune disease, and even the inherited disorders, it very easy to correlate negative emotions with all these various diseases or disorders.

Our mind-body connection is far more extensive than most want to believe. But the answer to our questions is found in "the things of the Spirit."

SPECIFIC DISEASE PROFILES
Warning: Quick Fixes Usually Don't Work

Often people are looking for a quick fix, and they usually do not work. We strongly encourage you to work through all areas of your life that do not line up with God's Word. If you go to only the "spiritual root" listed for a specific disease and disregard other issues in your life, you probably will not have the result you are looking for.

It is God's will for us to cleanse ourselves of all iniquities (II Timothy 2:20-21). He is a God of relationship. Sin separates Christians from Him in our daily walk. We should choose to seek His face and not His hand; we should choose relationship over healing. If we are willing to put relationship first, the blessing will follow. But it may not be the "blessing" that we are looking for. Let me explain what I mean.

Several months ago a lady named Carol called wanting help. Carol had a very severe case of adult onset diabetes. She was in her early sixties, almost blind, her kidneys have failed and she can hardly walk because of neuropathies in her feet. The doctors told her that she had less than six months to live.

I visited with her and asked if she could and would separate her healing from her relationship with the Lord. In other words, I asked her if she would commit to loving and serving God, even if she were not healed. I was asking her not to make her relationship with God subject to, or contingent upon, her physical healing in any way. She said that she could.

I began to lead Carol through our ministry process of identifying the broken relationships in her life, with her husband, father and mother, brothers and sister, God and herself. We then spent several sessions forgiving those who had hurt her and asking God to forgive her for her sins, and also learning to forgive herself.

At the beginning of every follow-up session, we always re-check our work to make sure we are being effective. We check our work by reviewing the memories that we have previously prayed through, to see if there is any emotional pain left in them. If there are emotional pains, such as unforgiveness, resentment, or anger at another person, then there is still bitterness in that memory. If there are emotional pains, such as shame, guilt, regret or sorrow in a memory of something we have done, then there is still self-bitter-ness. If the bitterness has returned, there is either another facet or deeper level of the bitterness, or the person has taken it back. We consider forgiveness to be completed when there is no longer any emotional pain in the memories. We have also learned that we need to be careful to work through each and every memory. Each memory that has pain is a root of bitterness.

As I am writing this in January 2003, it has been a year since I first met Carol and she has not been physically healed. She is still on dialysis, her eyes still do not work well and she still has trouble walking. But she is still alive, and most importantly, Carol is at peace and loving her life. God is using her to help and minister to others. Her family relationships have been healed and she has become a vessel of honor, fit for His service (II Timothy 2:19-21).

Carol is now looking at this life as a training ground for all of eternity. She is looking through eternal eyes and realizing that the few years in this life are for the purpose of preparing ourselves for all eternity. Would she like to be healed physically? Of course, but more importantly, she has been healed spiritually and is ready to meet God when her time comes. She has peace. What else is more important?

Even though God heals about seventy percent of those who come to us for physical healing, we do not have all the answers. Please join us in prayer for the other thirty percent. Sometimes people do not want to cleanse themselves of all iniquities and sometimes we do not know why the healing does not take place. But if people apply the Word of God to their lives, there is always a spiritual healing. The broken heart is always healed.

Warning: How Not to Minister

In our compassion sometimes we want to tell others why they are sick. Do not tell someone they have a sin because they have a disease. If you do this, you will only cause an offense. You cannot minister to anyone without his or her permission. Remember, we have all sinned. God brings sinners to Himself through His love. Love your brother. Do not judge him. In the manner that you judge others is the standard that you have set for yourself and that is the manner by which God will judge you (Matthew 6:9-15). Also remember, that when we learn we have a sin, we "shout Hallelujah!" because we have learned the answer to a challenge in our life. We cannot deal with a sin if we do not recognize it as a sin. Recognition is the first step to victory. If we choose to deal with the sin, we can become closer to Our Father (James 4:8).

Medical Disclaimer: I am not a medical doctor, nor do I intend for anyone to use this work as a diagnostic tool, or in any other way, to practice medicine. We do not, nor will we ever, advise anyone to stop medications or stop seeing their doctor. We strongly advise you to consult your medical doctor on all medical decisions.

The format that we have chosen for the profiles is to first describe the disease, and second, to provide the spiritual and emotional strongholds that we have found to be most common in the specific disease. To learn how to have victory over the strongholds, please read and study *Biblical Foundations of Freedom*.

Acne

An inflammatory disease of the pilosebaceous gland, characterized by papules, pus-filled cysts, blackheads, inflamed nodules and pustules. Hormonal changes at puberty are what most doctors claim to be the major cause. We believe that the guilt and anxiety coming from conflict and peer pressure cause the body to produce too much histamine, which causes the outbreaks.

Spiritual/Emotional Strongholds: Anxiety, fear, insecurity, depression, and low self-esteem.

Repent and renounce these strongholds, including unbelief, and break agreement with them. Take responsibility for them in your life and break their power over you.

References:

Layton, Alison M. *Scientific evidence supports link between acne and depression.* Journal of Cutaneous Medicine and Surgery.

Acne. Merck Manual 16th Edition, p. 2429.

Addictions or Addictive Personality

This is defined as the involvement, for a variety of reasons, in one of several forms of repetitive behavior such as gambling, dangerous or reckless activities, or eating disorders. The term is best used to indicate dependence on narcotics, drugs, alcohol, tobacco or even food (Taber's 1997). We can also become addicted to TV and other things that are not harmful physically.

The addictive personality is running and hiding from the pain of negative events of the past. The addicted person or the addictive personality is a person who is self-medicating to cover the hurts and pain of life. They do not, or believe that they cannot, face the situations, and then they cover them with something. Our mouths are a contact point of security. As little children we put our thumbs in our mouths to satisfy ourselves. As we become older we learn to put cigarettes, drugs, alcohol or food into our mouths to satiate ourselves. We learn to put something in the mouth to cover the pain and insecurities.

Spiritual/Emotional Strongholds: Anxiety, fear, insecurity, depression, low self-esteem, and unforgiveness.

Instead of self-medicating, learn to forgive those who have hurt you and ask God to forgive you for your judgments. Only Jesus can heal the broken heart.

Addison's Disease

A progressive autoimmune disease of the adrenal cortex. It causes the adrenal glands to atrophy, thus resulting in hyposecretion of cortisol and aldosterone. There is also an increased excretion of sodium and a decreased excretion of potassium causing dehydration and low blood pressure. Hypoglycemia, hyperpigmentation, weakness and fatigue are early signs of the disease. Adrenal "crisis" can result in serious consequences, such as renal (kidneys) shutdown and vascular collapse.

Spiritual/Emotional Strongholds: Self-hatred and guilt.

Repent and renounce these strongholds, including unbelief, and break agreement with them. Take responsibility for them in your generations, forgiving those who have hurt you.

References:

Marguiles, Paul. *Addison's Disease: The Facts You Need To Know.* Cornell University Medical College.

Acquired Immune Deficiency Syndrome (AIDS)

AIDS is caused by the HIV virus, which severely weakens the immune system. The virus is most often transmitted through blood or semen during sexual intercourse and by the use of needles. It can be transmitted by dental caries, if there is infection and someone has an opening that leads directly into the blood stream. It can also be transmitted through breast milk, spinal cord fluid and amniotic fluid. The virus infects the t-helper cells (the most important cells in the immune system), rendering parts of the immune system ineffective. This results in opportunistic lung and eye infections, skin cancer, neurological dysfunction, and a variety of other syndromes. It is debilitating and fatal. The virus has an amazing ability to mutate, giving it the ability to hide and evade capture.

Medical and physiological studies involve ways of preventing the disease, through various means of protection or behavior modification (Kelly 2002). Most cases can be prevented by obedience to Scripture.

Spiritual/Emotional Strongholds: Anxiety, fear, fornication/uncleanness, rebellion, and addictions.

Repent and ask God for forgiveness. Make sure that you have forgiven yourself. Make sure that there is no shame or guilt in you from your past sins.

References:

Recer, P. Gallant, J. and Margolick, J. Researchers: *HIV Hides in Cells*, John Hopkins University.

Ho, D. Diamond A., AIDS Research Center, N.Y., Centers for Disease Control, Division of HIV/AIDS Prevention.

Alzheimer's Disease

A progressive deterioration of brain cells causing dementia. Dementia means to "remove or reduce the mind." Recently researchers have found antibrain antibodies, thus labeling it an autoimmune disorder. The proteins, tau and beta amyloids, are responsible for causing plaque and neurofibrillary tangles in the brain.

Associated symptoms may include depression, emotional outbursts, insomnia, incontinence, delusions, weight loss and gait disorder. It affects ten percent of people in the U.S. over 65 and fifty percent over 85. There is a higher incidence among African-Americans.

Recent studies are linking negative emotions such as depression or anxiety to the oversecretion of a pro-inflammatory cytokine (inteleukin-6), which causes inflammation. These same studies are linking inflammation with Alzheimer's disease (Cohen 2000, Ershler 2000, Singh 1994, 1997).

Additionally, Alzheimer's and other dementia patients may also display worsening anger, as they lose the ability to control their emotions. The anger has always been there, but as they lose control it manifests. Scientists call this "emotional incontinence." This supports the connection to negative emotions that have been buried and over time create the inflammation that causes the damage to the brain.

Spiritual/Emotional Strongholds: Self-hatred, guilt, loss of identity, depression, and anxiety.

References:

Singh, V. *Selected Work on Alzheimer's Disease*, Utah State University, Biotechnology Center.

Flicker, L. *Alzheimer's The Tangled Brain*, University of Western Australia.

Amyotrophic Lateral Sclerosis (ALS or Lou Gehrig's Disease)

Amyotrophic Lateral Sclerosis is a progressive motor neuron disease, resulting in paralysis and frequently death. Only five percent of cases are inherited with an autosomal dominant inheritance. There is research showing excess glutamate (a brain chemical) in the nerve synapse resulting in cell death. One theory is that in vulnerable persons strenuous exercise causes neurotoxins to be released, damaging anterior horn cells. There is also an autoimmune component involved. The symptoms vary, depending on the part of the nervous system that is affected; usually the anterior horn cells and bulbar motor nuclei are affected. Muscle weakness and wasting, muscle twitching, spasticity, muscle shaking, difficulty with speech and swallowing are common symptoms. It is diagnosed usually in middle age and is more common in men than women.

Approximately fifty percent of those diagnosed with ALS die within three years of the first symptoms, while ten percent may live ten years or more. On the rare occasion a person may live as long as twenty-five years (Merck 1997).

Dr. V.K. Singh teaches that the main component in nervous system disease is really autoimmunity. If you examine central nervous system diseases closely, you will find that for almost each condition there is a suspicion of autoimmune process involvement (Singh 1994, 1997).

Spiritual/Emotional Strongholds: Fear, anxiety, self-hatred, self-rejection, and occultism.

Repent and renounce these strongholds, including unbelief in your generations, taking responsibility for them and breaking their power over you. Take authority over them casting them out in Jesus name.

References:

Amyotrophic Lateral Sclerosis: Lou Gehrig's disease. American Family Physician March, 15, 1999.

Amyloidosis

Amyloidosis is a bone marrow disorder. Abnormal proteins (amyloids) arise out of the bone marrow and accumulate in specific organs, which can lead to organ failure. Amyloid build-up occurs as a result of plasma cell dyscrasia (blood cell disease). It is often found in the presence of multiple tumors arising from the bone marrow. The organs most affected are the kidney, heart, liver and peripheral nervous system. Onset is usually after the age of 40.

Spiritual/Emotional Strongholds: Broken heart, rejection, bitterness, and self-rejection.

Repent and renounce any bitterness for those who have rejected you. Take responsibility for any generational rejection and fear, resulting in you rejecting yourself and/or others.

References:

Nyirady, Judith. *Amyloidosis, Primary Systemic.* Dermatology, UMDNJ-New Jersey Medical School.

Ankylosing Spondylitis

A chronic, progressive, autoimmune disorder characterized by arthritis, pain and inflammation. It usually affects the joints and ligaments of the spine and hip, resulting in fusion of the joints and bones. Young white males are affected three times more than women.

Spiritual/Emotional Strongholds: Inherited rejection, self-hatred, guilt, and pain.

Repent and renounce any of these generational strongholds, including unbelief, and break agreement with them. Take responsibility for these strongholds in your generations. Forgive those who have hurt you. Break the power of these strongholds in your life and cast them out.

References:

Matsen, F. Leopold, S. and Gardner, G. *Ankylosing Spondylitis*. University of Washington Sports Medicine.

Ankylosing Spondylitis. American Autoimmune Related Diseases Association, Washington D.C.

Aplastic Anemia

Aplastic anemia is bone marrow failure, leading to a decrease in blood cells supplying oxygen and nutrients to the body's tissues and organs. The bone marrow becomes unable to produce red and white blood cells and platelets, due to reduced bone marrow mass. The body becomes susceptible to bleeding, organ failure and infection. There is an autoimmune component involved. Early symptoms are fatigue, bruising, shortness of breath, pallor and bleeding gums.

Spiritual/Emotional Strongholds: Broken heart, rejection/abandonment (usually by the father), self-rejection, and guilt.

Repent and renounce these strongholds in your generations, forgiving those who have hurt you. Take responsibility for your bitterness and rejection of others and walk in the freedom and acceptance that God has made available in Christ.

References:

About This Cancer. The Sidney Kimmel Comprehensive Cancer Center, John Hopkins.

LeWine H., *Aplastic Anemia*. InteliHealth, Harvard Medical School.

Arnold-Chiari Malformation

A group of defects in the back of the brain stem, causing herniation of the cerebellum into the spinal cord. These herniations, cause headaches/pressure in the neck, blurred/double vision, muscle spasms, decreased sensation in arms, hands, legs and feet, difficulty walking, foot drop, loss of balance, dizziness, frozen shoulder, loss of sense of smell and taste.

Dr. Singh teaches that the main component in nervous system disease is really auto-immunity. If you examine central nervous system diseases closely, you will find that for almost each condition there is a suspicion of autoimmune process involvement (Singh 1994, 1997).

Spiritual/Emotional Strongholds: Self-hatred, anger, rebellion, fear, and occultism.

Repent and renounce any of these strongholds in your generations, taking responsibility for them and breaking agreement with them. Forgive those who have hurt you, separating them from their sins.

References:

Fact Sheet: What is Arnold-Chiari? World Arnold-Chiari Malformation Association. Duke University for Human Genetics.

Bejjani G., *Neurosurgery Focus*, Vol. 11, 1, July 2001.

NINDS Chiari Malformation Page. National Institute of Neurological Disorders and Stroke.

Arthritis

The two most common forms of arthritis are osteoarthritis and rheumatoid arthritis. Osteoarthritis, or degenerative joint disease, is the most prevalent non-inflammatory joint disease. It is the degeneration and loss of cartilage in the joints. Rheumatoid arthritis is an inflammatory, systemic, autoimmune joint disease that causes chronic inflammation of connective tissues, primarily in the joints.

Arthritis is among the leading causes of pain and disability. It is estimated that 37 million persons have arthritis (Center for Disease Control 1990). Fifty percent of the people in their 70s and 80s suffer from osteoarthritis, and one percent of the general population suffers from rheumatoid arthritis (Kendall 2002).

Research shows that negative emotions such as depression or anxiety can directly affect the cells of the immune system and either up or down regulate the secretion of proinflammatory cytokines. Proinflammatory cytokines create inflammation, pain, loss of function) in many parts of the body. Inflammation has recently been linked to several conditions or diseases, including arthritis (Cohen 2000, Ershler 2000, Kendall 2002). When asked about the cause of disease flares, persons having rheumatoid arthritis most often list stress as the primary cause (Affleck 1987).

Spiritual/Emotional Strongholds: Self-hatred, anger, anxiety, and fear.

Repent and renounce these strongholds, including unbelief, and break agreement with them.

Asperger's Syndrome

A neurological disorder that is classified as an autistic spectrum disorder. Asperger's syndrome is characterized by severe social withdrawal, few facial expressions, dyslexia, repetitive behaviors, clumsiness, sensitivity to sounds, and a preoccupation with a particular subject or interest. Individuals with Asperger's lack common sense and lack the ability for abstract thinking. Unlike with autism, language and cognition are not affected.

Dr. Singh teaches that the main component in nervous system disease is really autoimmunity. If you examine central nervous system diseases closely, you will find that for almost each condition there is a suspicion of autoimmune process involvement (Singh 1994, 1997). (See Autism)

Spiritual/Emotional Strongholds: Inherited deaf and dumb spirit, matriarchal control, depression, self-rejection, and occultism.

Repent and renounce these strongholds, including unbelief, and break agreement with them. Parents, take responsibility for these in your generations and break their power off of your children. Take authority for them and cast them out of your children.

References:

Edelson S. *Asperger's Syndrome*. Center for the Study of Autism, Salem, Oregon.

Asthma

Asthma is a chronic respiratory disease characterized by reversible airway obstruction, which is usually accompanied by inflammation of tissues of the airways and/or constriction airway smooth muscles (Busse 1988). Symptoms include wheezing, cough, difficulty in breathing, and chest tightness. Anxiety, fear, sadness, and suggestion can affect asthma. It is also associated with an elevated prevalence of anxiety and depressive disorders (Kendall 2002).

The National Heart, Lung, and Blood Institute defines asthma as an immune system process (NHLBI 1997). As we have already demonstrated in many other studies, negative emotions create the immune process that results in inflammation (Cohen 2000). Patients with asthma, especially children, appear particularly likely to suffer from psychological problems, particularly anxiety disorders (Bussing 1996, Vila 1999, Wambolt 1998). With the number of children born or conceived out of wedlock and the prevalence of divorce, it is no wonder children experience anxiety and fear, and that asthma is one of the fastest growing diseases in children. Asthma is usually accompanied by colic, allergies and weak immune systems, which allow repeated ear and bronchial infections (see colic profile).

Asthma and other chronic respiratory diseases are three times more common in those with panic disorder than among the general population (Spinhoven 1991, Zandbergen 1991). In other words, asthma is really caused by anxieties and fears that cause inflammation and the rigidity of the airway passages. Psychology suggests biofeedback training, Yoga and hypnosis as possible treatments (Kendall 2002). We suggest forgiveness, repentance, and deliverance as the true cure for the anxiety and fears.

We have also observed the tendency for asthma sufferers to breathe in a very shallow manner. In their fear of an airborne allergen or cold, they consciously or unconsciously reduce the rate and depth of breathing. This can result in migraine headaches. This is why migraines at times are treated with oxygen.

Spiritual/Emotional Strongholds: In children: Inherited abandonment, rejection and fear. These issues can start while the child is still in the womb if the child was born or conceived out of wedlock, if the child was not wanted in any way, or if there was arguing and strife during the pregnancy. In Adults: the issues could have begun in the womb or later in life. The anxiety, worry, and fear of antigens, such as cold, exercise, airborne allergens, or foods can cause the onset of asthma.

Repent and renounce these strongholds, including unbelief, and break agreement with them. Parents, take responsibility for these strongholds in your life, on both sides of the family, and break their power off of your children. Reassure your children that they are loved and wanted and give them your blessing.

References:

Roumelotis P. *The Asthma Corner: What Causes Asthma?* The Children's Wellness Center, Montreal, Canada.

Asthma: A Concern for Minority Populations. National Institute of Allergy and Infectious Diseases.

Astrocytoma

A brain tumor arising from brain cells called astrocytes. Astrocytoma is the most common type of brain tumor found in children. "Low grade" is slow-growing and less serious. "High grade" is fast growing and aggressive. Grades 3 and 4 are considered malignant (cancerous). Most often the thalamus and hypothalamus are affected.

Spiritual/Emotional Strongholds: Inherited bitterness/unforgiveness, self-bitterness, and occultism.

Parents, take responsibility for, and repent and renounce, these strongholds in your generations. Forgive those who have hurt you and break agreement with bitterness. Then break the power of these strongholds over your children.

Reference:

Kelly P. *Astrocytomas.* New York Univ. Med. Center, NY.

Attention Deficit Disorder (ADD)/Attention Deficit Hyperactivity Disorder (ADHD)

A developmental disorder, exhibiting inappropriate inattention, difficulty getting organized, mood swings, impulsivity, low stress tolerance, speech and hearing disorders and self-destructive behavior. It affects five percent of school age children, and is seen ten times more frequently in boys. It is diagnosed in boys more often partially because our schools do not want to deal with active boys. Instead they choose to medicate them.

In this disorder we usually find very intelligent children that are often bored and confused. The boredom may be from school experiences that do not challenge them and then they stop doing the work and get behind and then give up. The confusion often comes from situations or experiences in the home where usually dad is absent physically, emotionally, or spiritually, and mom becomes the source of income and/or support. There may not be the normal attachment to both parents.

We also often see children who are not disciplined or trained. They are not disciplined to have specific times to do their homework, bedtimes or meal times. There is a lack of structure that brings security into their lives. Other situations or experiences that bring insecurity and confusion such as inconsistent parental relationships, fighting, arguments, violence, and divorce also pay a large role in the development of a child's ability to think and express themselves. Emotional, sexual, physical, verbal abuse or other traumas also can be part of the equation. Unresolved loss leads to disorganized infant response patterns (Siegel 1999).

Psychologist call this disorganized/disoriented attachment. The child's relationship with their parent or caregiver may become disorganized and disorientated in any way that the child does not feel secure. Children with disorganized/disoriented attachment have been found to have the most difficulty later in life with emotional, social, and cognitive impairments (Siegel 1999).

Parents who have unresolved attachment (relationship) issues tend to have infants that also have disorganized/disoriented attachment or relationships (Main and Hesse 1990). In other words, the way we relate to others and ourselves is learned from our parents, and it can be learned even before we are born.

Spiritual/Emotional Strongholds: Inherited confusion, anger, rejection, fear, abandonment, matriarchal control, rebellion, self-rejection and low self-esteem.

Parents, repent and renounce any of these strongholds in your life and generations (on both sides of the family). Take responsibility for them and break agreement with them. Take authority over these strongholds in your children and break their power. Bless your children.

References:

What is Attention Deficit Disorder? The Greater Rochester Attention Deficit Disorder Association.

Autism

Autism is a developmental disorder that is characterized by impaired development in communication, behavior, and social interactions. It affects males four times more than females. Serotonin dysfunction and immune abnormalities play a role in autism.

Vijendra Singh, Ph.D., a research professor in the Biotechnology Center at Utah State University, has over 20 years of experience in neurobiology and immunology research. He serves on the scientific board of the Autism Autoimmunity Project, New Jersey, and is considered a pioneer in his field and an international authority on autoimmunity and autism. His focus is on the interaction between the immune and nervous systems.

Dr. Singh teaches that the main component in all nervous system disease is really autoimmunity. He has said, "If you examine central nervous system diseases closely, you will find that for almost each and every condition, there is a suspicion of auto-immune process involvement. In some diseases, such as MS, there is a large body of research to support this, and in others it has not been as clearly established as it needs to be (i.e., Alzheimer's and autism) but I think this will happen in the future" (Singh 1994, 1997).

Spiritual/Emotional Strongholds: Inherited deaf and dumb spirit (coming out of matriarchal control), rebellion, and self-rejection.

Parents, repent and renounce these sins in your generations and life (on both sides of the family), taking responsibility for them and breaking agreement with them. Take authority over these strongholds in your children.

References:

Dagg, Paul. *Excerpt from Pervasive Developmental Disorder: Autism.* eMedicine.

Singh, Vijendra. *Autism, Autoimmunity and Immunotherapy.* Dept. of Biology and Biotechnology Center, Utah State University.

Bacterial Meningitis

An inflammation of the meninges (covering of the brain and spinal cord), due to bacterial infections. Predisposing factors include weakened immune system, respiratory and ear infections, and head trauma. Bacterial meningitis often occurs in children under the age of 5. Common symptoms are fever, headache, stiff neck, irritability and seizures. If left untreated, brain damage, hearing loss and death may occur. Inflammation indicates an improper immune response (Singh 1994, 1997).

Spiritual/Emotional Strongholds: Inherited anxiety, fear, rejection, and abandonment issues that are weakening the immune system.

Parents, repent and renounce any of these strongholds and take responsibility for them. (See colic, allergy or asthma profile.)

References:

Kumar, Ashir. *Bacterial Meningitis.* Michigan State University College of Medicine and EW Sparrow Hospital.

Behcet's Syndrome

A rare, chronic, relapsing autoimmune disorder resulting in over-inflammation of the blood vessels. Symptoms include mouth ulcers, arthritis, eye inflammation, skin lesions, genital ulcers, loss of balance and hearing loss, personality changes, brain inflammation, Irritable Bowel Syndrome (IBS) and nervous system disorders.

Spiritual/Emotional Strongholds: Self-hatred, guilt, fear and loss of identity.

Repent and renounce any of these strongholds, including unbelief, in your generations. Take responsibility for them and break agreement with them.

Bell's Palsy

A sudden form of facial paralysis affecting the seventh cranial nerve. It usually improves in six weeks' time. In addition to one-sided facial paralysis, other symptoms include headache, eye pain and drooping, drooling and hypersensitivity to sounds. It is often caused by a viral infection.

Dr. Singh teaches that the main component in nervous system disease is really autoimmunity. If you examine central nervous system diseases closely, you will find that for almost each condition there is a suspicion of autoimmune process involvement (Singh 1994, 1997).

Spiritual/Emotional Strongholds: Anxiety, worry, fear, self-hatred, and occultism.

Repent and renounce these strongholds in your life and in your generations. Take responsibility for them and break agreement with them.

References:

Swanson, Jerry. *What is Bell's Palsy?* Mayo Clinic Foundation for Education and Research, MayoClinic.com

Benign Prostatic Hyperplasia (Enlarged Prostate)

BPH is a common prostate disorder among men over 60. As men grow older their prostate gland grows larger, obstructing their urinary flow. It is believed to be caused by a hormonal imbalance and by overstimulation. As some men age their testosterone levels decrease and their DHT and estrogen levels increase causing the cells in the prostate to grow.

Spiritual/Emotional Strongholds: Self-bitterness, fornication, performance, anxiety, and worry.

Repent and renounce any of these strongholds in your life and in your generations. Take responsibility for these strongholds and break agreement with them.

References:

Wehle, Michael. Lisson Scott, *Benign Prostatic Hypertrophy: Which Nonoperative Strategies Are Best?* The Physician and Sportsmedicine, Vol. 30, No. 4, April 2002.

Berger's Disease (IgA Neuropathy)

An autoimmune kidney disorder where there is inflammation of the glomeruli (which filter blood to form urine). There is an abnormal rise in the production of IgA, which affects adversely the nervous system and glomeruli, resulting in blood in the urine, and neuropathy. When the kidneys are no longer able to filter properly, the body becomes toxic, which can lead to chronic renal failure. High blood pressure, back pain and bloody urine are often the first symptoms reported.

Spiritual/Emotional Strongholds: Self-hatred, guilt, and unforgiveness.

Repent and renounce these strongholds in your generations, taking responsibility for them and breaking agreement with them. Forgive those who have hurt you and separate them from their sins.

References:

Levy, M. *Idiopathic recurrent macroscopic hematuria and mesangial IgA deposits in children.* Clin. Nephrol. 1973, 1: 63.

Michelk, D. *Idiopathic mesangial IgA glomerulonephritis in childhood: Review of the literature.* Eur. J. Ped. 13: 134, 1980.

Hogy, R. *IgA nephropathy: Natural history and prognostic indices.* Contrib. Nephrol. 40: 214, 1984.

Levy, M. *Berger's disease in children: Natural history and outcome.* Medicine 64: 157, 1985.

Friedman, A. *IgA nephropathy*. Contemp. Peds. Nov. 1987, p.53.

Bipolar Mood Disorder (Manic-Depression)

An alternating of full-blown manic (frenzy) and depressive episodes. An increase of norepinephrine and a decrease in serotonin in the brain have been observed. Onset usually begins in the teen years.

We find that serotonin shortages are caused by negative emotions, especially those directed at ourselves.

Spiritual/Emotional Strongholds: Depression, anger, anxiety, and lack of discernment.

We must learn to understand that not all thoughts are to be obeyed. II Corinthians 10:5 teaches us to take every thought captive and examine it, to see if it lines up with God's word. I believe that all humans hear voices (thoughts and impressions that vary in intensity). Our goal as Christians is to separate God's voice from Satan's. We do this by testing what we are being told to do, by the Word of God. We must learn to think and test all things before we act. In my opinion, this disorder is closely related to obsessive compulsive disorder.

Repent and renounce any of these strongholds and break agreement with them. Take responsibility for them in your generations.

References:

Young, L.T. Warsh, J.J. Kish, S.J. Shannak, K. and Hornykeiwicz, O. *Reduced brain 5-HT and elevated NE turnover and metabolites in bipolar affective disorder*. Department of Psychiatry, Institute of Medical Science, University of Toronto, Canada.

Shear, Kathleen. *Anxiety and Bipolar Disorder*. University of Pittsburgh, Anxiety Disorders Clinic.

Merck Manual, *Mood Disorders*. 16th Edition pp. 1592-4.

Bursitis

Inflammation of the bursa (tiny fluid-filled sacs that surround and protect joints) either due to injury (or repetitive motion), infection, or inflammatory disorders (i.e., gout, rheumatoid arthritis, scleroderma). When the synovial cells (joint cells) become inflamed they grow in thickness. Symptoms may include swelling, pain upon motion and decreased range of motion.

Recent studies are linking negative emotions such as depression or anxiety to the oversecretion of a pro-inflammatory cytokine (inteluekin-6), which causes inflammation. These same studies are linking inflammation with rheumatoid arthritis and other inflammatory disorders (Cohen 2000, Ershler 2000).

Spiritual/Emotional Strongholds: Anxiety, fear, worry, self-bitterness, or injury.

Repent and renounce these strongholds in your life, breaking agreement with them and breaking their power.

References:

Talbot-Stern, Janet. *Bursitis*. Departments of Emergency Medicine and Surgery, University of Sydney, Royal Prince Alfred Hospital.

Paoloni, Richard. Department of Emergency Medicine, Royal Prince Alfred and Concord Hospitals.

Cancers

Bernie Siegel, M.D., in his book *Love, Medicine and Miracles*, reports from several studies that we have already cited, proving the direct connection between the nervous, endocrine, and the immune system. Dr. Siegel states:

> The immune system, then, is controlled by the brain, either indirectly through hormones in the blood stream, or directly through the nerves and neurochemicals (neurotransmitters). One of the most widely accepted explanations of cancer, the "surveillance" theory, states that cancer cells are developing in our bodies all the time, but are normally destroyed by the white blood cells, before they can develop into dangerous tumors. Cancer appears when the immune system becomes suppressed and can no longer deal with this routine threat. It follows that whatever upsets the brain's control of the immune system, will foster malignancy.
>
> This disruption occurs primarily by means of the chronic stress syndrome, first described by Hans Selye in 1936. The mixture of hormones released by the adrenal glands as part of the fight-or-flight response, suppresses the immune system. This was all right, in dealing with the occasional threats our ancestors faced from wild beasts. However, when the tension and anxiety of modern life keeps the stress response "on" continually, the hormones lower our resistance to disease, even withering away the lymph nodes. Moreover, there is now experimental evidence that "passive emotions," such as grief, feelings of failure, and suppression of anger, produce over-secretion of these same hormones, which suppress the immune system (Siegel 1998).

As we studied earlier, this "experimental evidence," is no longer experimental. The association of stress with cancer has led investigators to identify the personality or behavioral profile of the typical individual who is at an increased risk for cancer. Now referred to as "type C," such an individual is characterized by denial and suppression of emotions (especially anger), "pathological niceness," avoidance of conflicts, exaggerated social desirability, harmonizing behavior, over-compliance, over-patience, high rationality, and a rigid control of emotional expression.

This pattern, usually concealed behind a facade of pleasantness, appears to be effective as long as environmental and psychological homeostasis is maintained, but collapses in the course of time, under the impact of accumulated strains and stressors, especially those evoking feelings of depression and reactions of helplessness and hopelessness. As a prominent feature of this particular coping style, excessive denial, avoidance, suppression and repression of emotions and one's own basic needs, appears to weaken the organism's natural resistance to carcinogenic influences (Baltrusch 1991).

These and other findings have led researchers to recommend that, "more attention should be paid to the manipulation of the psyche, in the prevention and management of cancer" (Miller 1977).

Additionally, there are many other clinical studies that link psychological interventions to cancer outcomes or survival. One study reported that twenty-nine percent of the control group died after six years, while only nine percent of subjects of the experiment died (Fawzt 1990, 1993). Richardson also reported higher survival rates for intervention patients (Richardson 1990). Other studies that treated cancer patients with poor prognoses with psychological intervention resulted in significant increase in survival time (Spiegel 1983, 1989, 2001).

The only true "psychological intervention," is found in the forgiveness through Jesus Christ. Only Jesus can bring closure to the hurt and pain of this life. Only Jesus can heal the broken heart and thus heal the negative emotions and experiences. It is only through the forgiveness of Jesus Christ that we can be set free. If our immune system is not functioning properly, many different diseases can have their way in our bodies including cancer.

Now let's look an individual cancers and the specific negative emotions that suppress the immune system.

BLADDER CANCER

Bladder cancer is three times higher in men than in women. It is the fourth leading cancer in American men. Smoking, chronic bladder infections, and exposure to chemicals all contribute to bladder cancer. Blood in the urine is the most common symptom.

Spiritual/Emotional Strongholds: Fear, anxiety, addictions, and unforgiveness.

Repent and renounce any of these strongholds, including unbelief. Take responsibility for these in your generations and break their power.

References:

Parker, S.L. et al. *Cancer Statistics*, 1996. A Cancer Journal for Clinicians: 46:(1)5-27, 1996.

Cohen, S.M. and Johansson. *Epidemiology and etiology of bladder cancer.* Urologic Clinics of North America 19(3):421-428, 1992.

Badalament, R.A. et al. 1987. *The sensitivity of flow cytometry compared with conventional cytology in the detection of superficial bladder carcinoma.* Cancer, 59(12):2078-2085.

Wheeles, L.L. et al. 1993. *Consensus review of the clinical utility of DNA cytometry in bladder cancer.* Cytometry, 14:478-481.

Sarosdy, M. et al. 1995. *Result of a multicenter trial using the BTA test to monitor for and diagnose recurrent bladder cancer.* J Urol, 153(4):75A.

BONE CANCER (OSTEOSARCOMA)

Osteosarcoma is the most common type of bone cancer in children. Very weak immune systems are the major factor in this disease.

Spiritual/Emotional Strongholds: Inherited broken heart, bitterness, abandonment, and fear.

Parents, repent and renounce these strongholds, including unbelief, and break agreement with them in your generations (both sides of the family).

References:

Cancer Facts Bone Cancer: Questions and Answers. 1/20/1999 National Cancer Institute.

Neoplasms of Bones and Joints, Merck Manual 16th Edition. pp. 1350-1.

BREAST CANCER

It is defined as the growth of abnormal cells in the breast. When breast cancer is in the ducts, it is in the earliest stages. When it invades the breast tissue and has spread to other organs, it is stage IV, or the worst stage. Family history, never bearing a child or having a first child after 30, late menopause, and benign breast disease are some risk factors of this disease. We have often observed broken relations with other female members in the family. Recent studies show an increased risk due to Hormone Replacement therapy (Women's Health Initiative 2002) and mammograms.

Spiritual/Emotional Strongholds: Bitterness (unforgiveness often involving female family members), anxiety, and fear.

Repent and renounce any of these strongholds, including unbelief, and break agreement with them. Take responsibility for these strongholds in your generations and break their power over you.

References:

Wahrman Miryam, *The Breast Cancer Genes*. Jewish Virtual Library, A Division of the American-Israeli Cooperative Enterprise.

Richardson Andrea, *Breast Cancer: Causes and Risk Factors*. Dept. of Pathology, Brigham and Women's Hospital.

Mammograms: Samuel Epstein, M.D., Chairman of the Cancer Prevention Coalition and Professor Emeritus of Environment and Occupational Medicine, University of Illinois School of Public Health, Chicago, warns that screening mammography poses significant and cumulative risks of breast cancer for premenopausal women. The routine practice of taking four films of each breast annually results in approximately

1 rad (radiation absorbed dose) exposure, which is about 1,000 times greater than that from a chest x-ray. The premenopausal breast is highly sensitive to radiation; each 1 rad exposure increases breast cancer risk by about one percent, with cumulative ten percent increased risk for each breast over a decade's screening. These risks are even greater for younger women subject to "baseline screening."

Dr. Epstein further warns that:

(1) Radiation risks are some four-fold greater, for the one to two percent of women who are silent carriers of the ataxia-telangiectasia (A-T) gene; by some estimates this accounts for up to twenty percent of all breast cancers.

(2) Mammography is ineffective, because missed cancers are common in premenopausal women due to dense breasts, and also in postmenopausal women on estrogen replacement therapy.

(3) Mistakenly diagnosed cancers are common. The cumulative risks of false positives can reach as high as one hundred percent over a decade's screening.

Dr. Epstein teaches that monthly breast self-examination, following brief training, coupled with annual clinical breast examination by a trained health care professional, is at least as effective as mammography in detecting early tumors, and is also safe.

Research by John Gofman, M.D., Ph.D., shows that past exposure to ionizing radiation, primarily medical x-rays, is responsible for about seventy-five percent of the breast-cancers in the United States. For more information you can read his book, *Preventing Breast Cancer,* on line at http://www.ratical.com/radiation/CNR/PBC /indexT.html.

BURKITT'S LYMPHOMA

Burkitt's Lymphoma is a cancer of the B-cells, most common in boys age 7-11. It is thought to be caused by the Epstein-Barr virus. Bone marrow, lymph nodes, kidneys, and often the bowel are affected.

Spiritual/Emotional Issues: Inherited rejection (usually by the father), bitterness, fear of rejection, and abandonment.

Parents, repent and renounce any of these strongholds, including unbelief, in your life and generations. Take authority over them in your children, breaking their power and cast them out.

References:

Burkitt's Lymphoma. Vanderbilt Medical Center.

Quinn, J. 1983. *Burkitt's Lymphoma.* In Altman, A. and Schwartz, A. ed. *Malignant Diseases of Infancy.* Childhood and Adolescence. W.B. Saunders, p. 268.

Ziegler, J. 1982. *Burkitt's Lymphoma.* Cancer J. Clinicians 32 (3): 144.

Jenkins, R. 1984. *The treatment of localized non-Hodgkin's lymphoma in children.* J. Clin. Onco. 2 (2): 88.

Ziegler, J. 1977. *Epstein-Barr virus and human malignancy.* Ann. Int. Med. 86:323.

CHRONIC MYELOID LEUKEMIA (CML)

CML is a slowly progressive cancer, causing an overgrowth of white blood cells. Symptoms may include anemia, fatigue, weight loss, and abdominal pain. It affects women more often than men and occurs mostly in adults from the ages of 40-70.

Studies show that negative emotions such as depression or anxiety can directly affect the cells of the immune system and either up or down regulation of the secretion of proinflammatory cytokines, which create inflammation (swelling, pain, loss of function) in many parts of the body. Inflammation has recently been linked to several conditions or diseases including multiple myeloma, non-Hodgkin's lymphoma, chronic lymphocytic leukemia, Alzheimer's disease, and periodontal disease (Cohen 2000, Ershler 2000, Kendall 2002).

Spiritual/Emotional Strongholds: Rejection (usually by a father), broken heart, bitterness, self- rejection, depression, and anxiety.

Repent and renounce any of these strongholds, including unbelief, and break agreement with them. Forgive those who have hurt you and separate them from their sins. Take responsibility for your responses. Take authority over them and break their power over you. Walk in love with yourself and your fellow man.

References:

Leukemia. Mayo Clinic Education and Research.

What is Leukemia? The University of Texas, MD Anderson Cancer Center.

Leukemias – U.S. Racial/Ethnic Cancer Patterns. National Cancer Institute. cancer.gov.

CERVICAL CANCER

Growth of cancer cells in the cervix, most commonly caused by the human papilloma virus (HPV), during sexual contact. Cervical cancer is the fifth most common cancer in the world and the second major cause of cancer-related death in women, preceded only by breast cancer (Larsen 1988). Smoking, low socioeconomic status, many sexual partners, young age at first intercourse, and high parity (many pregnancies) are some other risk factors (Friedman 1996).

Spiritual/Emotional Strongholds: Fornication, adultery, lack of self-esteem, infirmity and bitterness.

Repent and renounce these strongholds, including unbelief, in your life and your generations. Take responsibility and break agreement with them. Forgive those who have not loved you properly and separate them from their sins.

References:

Cervical Cancer. National Cancer Institute.

COLON CANCER

Growth of abnormal cells in the colon. It is ranked second among cancer deaths in the U.S. Five percent of all colon cancers are caused by genetic abnormalities, and occur before the age of 40. Colon cancer is usually seen in older populations and is more common in women. Native Alaskans have the highest incidence followed by African-Americans, Japanese, and Samoans. However, the mortality rates are growing among whites.

Genes can be affected by negative thoughts and emotions. As we have studied earlier, cytokines act by binding to specific receptors at the cell membrane, setting off a cascade that leads to the enhancement or inhibition of a number of cytokine-related genes in the nucleus of the affected cells (Berk 2001). In Dr. Berk's work we see genes affected by cytokines that other studies show are affected by thoughts and emotions (Kendall 2002, Siegel 1999).

Spiritual/Emotional Strongholds: Bitterness, anger, slander, accusation, and fear.

Repent and renounce any of these strongholds, including unbelief, in your life or your generations. Take responsibility for any of these and forgive those who have hurt you. Take authority over these and break their power over you.

Reference:

2001 Statistics, American Cancer Society.

HODGKIN'S DISEASE

This cancer begins in lymphatic tissue, which includes the lymph nodes, spleen, bone marrow, thymus, and related lymph vessels that are part of the body's immune system. The cancer cells found in Hodgkin's are called Reed-Sternberg cells of B-cell lineage. The Epstein-Barr virus may be a contributing factor to this disorder.

Interleukin-13, a cytokine produced by the immune system, is overproduced by Hodgkin's cancerous cells. The incidence of Hodgkin's disease is higher in white affluent males than females and more often seen in the 17-25 and 70-85 age groups.

Spiritual/Emotional Strongholds: Rejection (often by a father), broken heart, bitterness, performance and drivenness.

Repent and renounce all of these strongholds, including unbelief, and break agreement with them. Forgive all those who have hurt you and separate them from their sins. Take responsibility for your wrong responses.

References:

What is Hodgkin's Disease? American Cancer Society.

Adult Hodgkin's Disease. Lymphoma Information Network.

Sternberg Cell Genome Expression Supports a B-Cell Lineage. Journal of The Society of Hematology (July 15, 1999) Georgetown University Medical Center, Washington D.C., Human Genome Sciences, Inc. Rockville MD, the National Cancer Institute, National Institute of Health, Bethesda Maryland, and The University of Milano-Bicocca, Milan, Italy.

LEUKEMIA

A cancer of the bone marrow and blood. There are four categories: myelogenous or lymphatic, each of which can be acute or chronic. The most common type is acute myelogenous leukemia (AML). The incidence is higher in Caucasian males. Chronic myelogenous leukemia (CML) and chronic lymphatic leukemia (CLL) are slow growing and increase dramatically over the age of 40. Symptoms of leukemia are easy bruising and bleeding, anemia, infections, night sweats and fatigue.

Negative emotions such as depression or anxiety cause the release of proinflammatory cytokines, which cause inflammation. Inflammation has been linked to chronic lymphocytic leukemia (Cohen 2000, Ershler and Keller 2000, Kendall 2002).

Spiritual/Emotional Strongholds: Rejection (usually by a father), broken heart, bitterness, self-bitterness, and self-rejection.

Repent and renounce any of these strongholds, including unbelief. Take responsibility for these strongholds in your generations. Forgive those who have hurt you.

References:

Leukemia. The Leukemia and Lymphoma Society.

Berenson, Jim. *Leukemia Causes. Oncology Channel*. West Los Angeles VA Medical Center, 11301 Wilshire Blvd., Los Angeles, Ca. 90073.

LIVER CANCER

The uncontrolled growth of abnormal cells in the liver. Chronic hepatitis B and C infections, alcoholism, and drug addiction are all associated with liver cancer. Symptoms may include weakness, nausea, upper abdominal pain, fever, weight loss, dark colored urine, loss of appetite, and yellow color of the skin and eyes, pale or clay colored stools.

Spiritual/Emotional Strongholds: Bitterness, infirmity, and addictions.

Repent and renounce any of these strongholds, including unbelief, and break agreement with them. Take responsibility for your actions and forgive those who have hurt you.

References:

Liver Cancer. Columbia Weill Cornell Cancer Centers, 2001.

LUNG CANCER

The uncontrolled growth of abnormal cells in one or both lungs. More than eighty percent of all lung cancer is related to smoking and other carcinogens (radon gas and asbestos). There are several types, depending on the area of the lung they are growing in. Symptoms include fatigue, cough, blood in sputum, wheezing and persistent chest, shoulder and back pain.

Spiritual/Emotional Strongholds: Bitterness, addictions, anxiety, and fear.

Repent and renounce any of these strongholds, including unbelief, and break agreement with them. Forgive all those who have hurt you and separate them from their sins. Take responsibility for them and break their power over you.

References:

What is lung cancer? American Cancer Society.

MULTIPLE MYELOMA

Cancer of the plasma cells (part of the immune system) of the blood known as myeloma cells. These myeloma cells tend to collect in the bone marrow forming tumors. When these cells collect in multiple bones it is called multiple myeloma. Some causes may be radiation exposure, viruses, genetic mutations and a weakened immune system. Symptoms include bone pain, bruising, weakness, fatigue, weight loss, and frequent infections. It is more common in the elderly.

Recent research connects negative emotions such as depression and anxiety to the secretion of pro-inflammatory cytokines that cause inflammation. Inflammation has been linked to a spectrum of conditions, including multiple myeloma (Ershler and Keller 2000, Kendall 2002).

Spiritual/Emotional Strongholds: Broken heart (coming out of rejection), bitterness, self-rejection, fear, anxiety and depression.

Repent and renounce any of these strongholds in your life and generations. Take responsibility for these strongholds and break their power over you and your children.

References:

About Myeloma. Multiple Myeloma Research Foundation

NON-HODGKINS LYMPHOMA

A group of cancers of the lymphatic system. It is the fifth most common type of cancer in the U.S. The exact cause is unknown, although chemicals causing genetic mutations are suspected in some cases. Symptoms include painless swelling in the lymph nodes of the neck, underarm, or groin, fevers, fatigue, weight loss, itchy skin and nausea. Individuals with autoimmune diseases and weakened immune systems are at higher risk. It occurs in all ages but more commonly in pre-adolescence and after 55. Whites are affected more than African-Americans. Vietnamese men have the second highest rate.

Recent research connects negative emotions such as depression and anxiety to the secretion of proinflammatory cytokines that cause inflammation. Inflammation has been linked to a spectrum of conditions, including non-Hodgkin's lymphoma (Ershler and Keller 2000, Kendall 2002).

Spiritual/Emotional Strongholds: Self-bitterness, rejection (often by a father), anxiety, bitterness, self-rejection, guilt, fear of rejection, and depression.

Repent and renounce any of these strongholds, including unbelief. Forgive those who have hurt you and separate them from their sin.

References:

Non-Hodgkins Lymphoma Risks. Oncology Channel. Stanley J. Swierzewski, Founder.

OVARIAN CANCER

Cancer cells growing in the ovaries, the woman's sexual glands, responsible for secreting progesterone and estrogen. It occurs most often in post-menopausal women in their 50s. Women at risk are those who have family members with a history of ovarian cancer, obesity, those who take estrogen, childless women, and women who enter menopause later than usual.

Spiritual/Emotional Strongholds: Bitterness (due to absence of positive fathering), self-rejection (of her sexuality), and self-hatred.

Repent and renounce these strongholds, including unbelief, and break agreement with them. Forgive those who have hurt you and separate them from their sins. Take responsibility for these sins in your generations and break their power over you (also see the PMS and menopause profiles).

References:

Increased Risk of Ovarian Cancer is Linked to Estrogen Replacement Therapy. National Cancer Institute.

Berenson, Jim. *Ovarian Cancer*. Oncology Cancer West Los Angeles VA Medical Center. 11301 Wilshire Blvd. Los Angeles, Ca.

PANCREATIC CANCER

The growth of malignant cells in the pancreas. It is the fourth leading cause of cancer deaths in the U.S. Smokers are at risk for this disease twice as much as non-smokers. Also, diabetics are more prone to this disease. This disease is more common in males in the 60-80 age group and is increasing among African-Americans.

Spiritual/Emotional Strongholds: Bitterness, self-bitterness, addictions, fear, and anxiety.

Repent and renounce any of these strongholds, including unbelief, and break agreement with them. Take responsibility for these sins in your generations and break their power over you.

References:

Confronting Pancreatic Cancer. The Lorenzen Cancer Foundation Pathogenesis, diagnosis and treatment. Edited by Reber. Humana Press; Totowa, New Jersey, 1998.

Pancreatic Disease; Second Edition. Edited by Johnson and Imrie. Springer-Verlag; Great Britain, 1999.

Feig, Berger, Furman, Lippincott, Williams, and Wilkins. *The M.D. Anderson Surgical Oncology Handbook*, Second Edition. Philadelphia, Pennsylvania, 1999.

PROSTATE CANCER

It is the most common form of cancer among men in the U.S. Eighty percent of prostate cancer patients are over 65 years of age and there is a higher incidence in African-American men. Symptoms may include painful urination, interruption of urine flow, blood in the urine, low back pain and painful ejaculation, and erectile dysfunction.

In a recent article, science (the drug company) is bragging about a great discovery in prostrate cancer prevention. The article stated that if a thousand 63-year-old men started taking the drug Finasteride, only forty-five would get prostate cancer within the next seven years, compared with sixty who would be expected to develop the cancer without the drug. This one of only two drugs that have ever been discovered that "prevents" cancer.

But other experts warn that while the drug appeared to reduce the overall number of cancers, men on the drug may be at greater risk for more aggressive tumors. (Anchorage Daily News, Remedy for baldness also may help prevent prostate cancer. June 25, 2003) The drug is also marketed to reduce hair loss under the name, Propecia.

What is not mentioned, is the actual number deaths. Did the drug actually prevent people from dying? Remember this the best that medicine has to offer.

Spiritual/Emotional Strongholds: Bitterness/unforgiveness (often toward males in the family), fornication, and fear.

Repent and renounce any of these strongholds, including unbelief, if applicable, and break agreement with them. Take responsibility for these and forgive those who have hurt you and separate them from their sins.

References:

Gilbert, Tom. *More Sex, More Cancer?* New York State Office of Mental Health, NYC Region.

SKIN CANCER

Ultraviolet radiation from the sun is the main cause of skin cancer. Artificial sources of UV radiation, such as sun lamps and tanning booths, can also cause skin cancer. Melanoma is the most deadly form of skin cancer and it is the fifth most common cancer in men. Basal cell cancer is the most common form of skin cancer and least dangerous if detected early. Squamous cell cancer is the second most common form of skin cancer and if not treated early can spread to the lymph nodes. Fair skinned people are at the highest risk. Australia and South America have the highest incidence of skin cancer.

Spiritual/Emotional Strongholds: Bitterness and self-neglect (not taking proper care of one's temple).

Repent and renounce any of these strongholds, including unbelief, and break agreement with them. Take responsibility for these in your life and break their power.

References:

What you need to know about skin cancer. National Cancer Institute.

Uterine Cancer

The most common cancer among women during the postmenopausal years. It begins in the lining of the endometrium and develops over a period of years. Exposure to increased levels of estrogen, diabetes, obesity, having never been pregnant, estrogen replacement therapy (HRT), irregular ovulation, and many years of menstruation all play a role in uterine cancer. Symptoms include heavy bleeding, pelvic pain, weight loss, pain during intercourse and painful urination. (also see the PMS and menopause profiles)

Spiritual/Emotional Strongholds: Bitterness, self-bitterness and fear.

Repent and renounce any of these strongholds, including unbelief, and break agreement with them. Forgive those who have hurt you and separate them from their sin. Take responsibility for these strongholds in your generations and break their power over you.

References:

Uterine Cancer. University of Michigan Health System 1500 E. Medical Center Dr. Ann Arbor, MI 48109.

Uterine Cancer. InteliHealth, Harvard Medical School's Consumer Health Information.

Waldenstrom's Macroglobulinemia

A rare blood cancer affecting the plasma cells resulting in thick blood. IgM antibodies are produced in large amounts, invading the bone marrow, lymph nodes and spleen. There is excess protein found in the blood, which interferes with normal immunity. Some people have no symptoms and others may have these symptoms: bleeding easily, enlarged spleen and lymph nodes, visual problems, confusion, fatigue, headache, dizziness, loss of coordination and weight loss. It usually occurs in people over the age of 65.

Spiritual/Emotional Strongholds: Self-bitterness, broken heart, bitterness, confusion, and fear.

Repent and renounce any of these strongholds, including unbelief, and break agreement with them. Take responsibility for these strongholds in your generations and break their power over you.

References:

Waldenstrom's Macroglobuinemia. Cancer Facts. National Cancer Institute.

Candidiasis

An infection, caused by a fungus (typically candida albicans), causing either localized infection or more severe overwhelming illness. Infants, the elderly, individuals on antibiotics or with compromised immune systems are more susceptible to this illness. Some manifestations of this infection are fatigue, pain, allergies, thrush, vaginitis, bronchitis, sinusitis, esophagitis, rashes, athlete's foot, systemic candidiasis (in the blood stream), affecting major organs and affecting mood and cognition.

Candidiasis is usually found along with severe allergies, malabsorption and other anxiety and stress disorders. Candidiasis usually disappears when the other diseases are addressed.

Spiritual/Emotional Strongholds: Broken heart, anxiety, worry, infirmity, bitterness.

Repent and renounce any of these strongholds, including unbelief, and break agreement with them. Forgive those who have hurt you and separate them from their sins.

References:

Henderson Sean O., *Candidiasis*. Dept. of Emergency Medicine, University of Southern California School of Medicine. January 2, 2002.

Carpal Tunnel Syndrome

Inflammation of the tendons in the wrist which is sometimes due to repetitive movement, sprains or to metabolic conditions such as rheumatoid arthritis, pregnancy, diabetes, menopause, hypothyroidism, and vitamin B-6 deficiency. The inflammation causes swelling and compression on the median nerve that causes the symptoms of CTS. Symptoms may include sharp pains in the wrist, cramping, tingling and numbness in the hand and fingers and insomnia due to flare-ups at night.

Other studies also show that negative emotions such as depression or anxiety can directly affect the cells of the immune system and either up or down regulation of the secretion of proinflammatory cytokines. Proinflammatory cytokines create inflammation (swelling) in many parts of the body. (Cohen 2000, Ershler 2000, Kendall 2002). Inflammation is also evidence of an autoimmune response (Singh 1994, 1997).

Spiritual/Emotional Strongholds: Anxiety, fear, drivenness, self-hatred, depression.

Repent and renounce any of these strongholds, including unbelief, and break agreement with them. Take responsibility for these in your generations and break their power over you.

References:

Carpal Tunnel Syndrome. JAMA Vol. 288 No. 10 Sept.11, 2002. American Society for Surgery of the Hand, Harvard Medical School's Consumer Health Information.

Celiac Disease

This is a inflammatory response of the small intestine caused by the ingestion of the protein gluten found in wheat and rye. The inflammation decreases the surface area of the intestine available for nutrient and fluid absorption. It usually occurs around two years of age but can occur at any age. Symptoms may include diarrhea, weakness, iron deficient anemia, fatigue and rashes.

Dr. Alessandro Ventura, of the Universita di Trieste, Italy, and colleagues say in the August issue of the Journal of Pediatrics that patients with celiac disease often have high levels of diabetes, and thyroid-related autoantibodies that disappear when the patients are placed on a gluten-free diet.

This is an autoimmune disease, where the body has created an allergy to gluten and then creates antibodies to specific organs. Allergies are immune responses that may also be related to or cause an autoimmune response (Singh 1994).

Spiritual/Emotional Strongholds: Inherited fear, anxiety, self-hatred, and guilt.

Repent and renounce these strongholds, including unbelief, in your generations and break agreement with them.

References:

Organ-Specific Autoantibodies Linked to Dietary Gluten in Celiac Disease Patients. J Pediatr. 2000: 137:263-265.

Chronic Fatigue

An unexplained persistent chronic fatigue lasting for six months or more. CFIDS is usually accompanied by low blood sugar and an autoimmune disease (thyroiditis). Other symptoms include impairment in short term memory and concentration, muscle and joint pain, headaches, yeast infections, hypotension, asthma, gastritis, nonrefreshing sleep, sore throat, tender lymph nodes and postexertional fatigue lasting more than twenty-four hours. It occurs in women twice as often as men. Chronic fatigue patients also show increases in the cytokine, interleukin-6 (Costello 1998). Interleukin-6 is a proinflammatory hormone that creates inflammation in the body. This explains the muscle and joint pain. The over secretion of IL-6 is caused by anxiety and depression (Cohen 2000).

In this disease we often see a drivenness to make others happy, or a drivenness to gain approval from others, especially overachieving parents. The person simply wears out from trying to gain approval by keeping others happy.

Spiritual/Emotional Strongholds: Self-hatred, anxiety, drivenness, performance, low self-esteem, guilt, and depression.

Repent and renounce any of these strongholds and forgive those who have hurt you. Take responsibility for your responses. Take authority over them and break their power over you.

References:

Definition of Chronic Fatigue Syndrome. Center for Disease Control.

Chronic Pain Syndromes

In recent years, many volumes of research have focused on the contributions of psychological factors in understanding pain (Kendall 2002). Dr. Mark B. Weisber of the Minnesota Head and Neck Pain Clinic says, "We have no question that pain is both physical and psychological in every patient. Patients' emotions may be setting off autonomic nervous system responses that aggravate physical symptoms."

It is also interesting to note many studies, in which physical factors, including severity of an injury or the physical demands of the job, do not appear to contribute as much to pain becoming chronic as do psychological factors. In fact, the best predictors of the transition from an acute injury to a chronic disability are psychiatric factors (Gatchel 1999, Kendall 2002). Psychological factors are predictors of long-term disability for pain syndromes as well as pain severity (Boothby 1999; Johansson 2000). In another study psychosocial variables accounted for fifty-nine percent of the variance in disability associated with chronic pain (Burton 1995). Depression and other negative emotions have a great effect on pain (Staats 1999, Weiss 1989). Negative emotions can and do cause real pain. Psychological factors do predict long-term disability.

Our anxieties and fears greatly affect our sensitivity to feelings and sensations in our body and the perception of pain. These same anxieties and fears are an impediment to recovery from chronic pain. In chronic pain, pain-related anxiety and fear may actually accentuate the pain (Crombez 1999). Chronic pain patients with elevated pain-related anxiety tend to anticipate higher levels of pain than those with low anxiety and fear. The fear or anticipation of pain often results in poor health outcomes (McCracken 1993). For more information read the profile on headaches.

CHRONIC BACK PAIN

Back pain is usually due to emotional stress, anxiety, fear, worry, anger, frustration, etc. These emotions cause the contraction of the muscles and a decrease in blood flow to the skeletal muscles and nerves in the back. In a study designed to evaluate psychological treatments in the prevention of chronic low back pain in patients with sciatica, the best predictor of disability was the refusal of treatment (Hasenbring 1999). It has been proven in many studies that cognitive-behavioral treatments are effective in treating chronic back pain (Kendall 2002). The only effective "treatment" is found in forgiveness and repentance. It is only through these principles of God's word that anxiety, anger, fear and other strongholds can be broken.

Spiritual/Emotional Strongholds: Anxiety, worry, fears, anger, drivenness, and bitterness.

Repent and renounce any of these strongholds, including unbelief, and break agreement with them. Forgive those who have hurt you and separate them from their sins. Take responsibility for these strongholds in your generations and break their power over you.

CHRONIC PELVIC PAIN

A recent study by the Department of Psychiatry at Emory School of Medicine revealed that women with a history of childhood abuse showed an elevation of Interleukin-6 (a cytokine which stimulates inflammation), an increased prevalence of chronic pelvic pain, and increased numbers of multiple physical complaints (Heim).

The November 2002 issue of the *Focus on the Family* magazine features an article about Dr. Larimore. The opening paragraph relays an interview he had with a caller named Sue, who was suffering from chronic pelvic pain. "He tells her that prior trauma, such as abuse from childhood, can manifest itself in chronic pelvic pain and inflammation."

Spiritual and emotional strongholds: Anger, bitterness (at the perpetrator), shame, guilt, regret, sorrow (directed at self), and depression.

Forgive the one who abused you. Repent if you did not tell anyone about the abuse. Forgive yourself for not telling, and taking the perpetrator's sin into you. Command the bitterness and shame to go. Command the trauma from the abuse to go and ask the Holy Spirit to cleanse your mind from all the sights, sounds, feelings and smells associated with the abuse.

PAIN (PSYCHOGENIC)

Chronic physical pain without any organic cause.

Spiritual/Emotional Strongholds: Hatred, unforgiveness, depression, unhealthy introspection, oppression, and self-pity.

Repent and renounce any of these strongholds, including unbelief, and break agreement with them. Take responsibility for these in your generations and break their power over you (see the fibromyalgia profile).

References:

Psychogenic Pain Syndromes. The Merck Manual of Diagnosis and Therapy Ch. 167.

Colic

Abdominal pains in infants that make them very uncomfortable, causing crying and even screaming. It usually occurs between the ages of two weeks and five months and more often in boys.

Colic usually precipitates allergies, asthma, and weak immune systems that result in frequent bronchial and ear infections. Usually we find that somehow the child has perceived that he was not wanted. If child was conceived out of wedlock, born out of wedlock, was the wrong gender, the parents were not ready to be pregnant, or there was fighting and stress during the pregnancy the unborn baby has abandonment, rejection, and fear issues in his life. It is these issues that predispose to colic, allergies, asthma, and weak immune systems in children.

We usually do not minister directly to the children. We teach the parents what to do and ask them to minister to their own children. Things that the parents have done cause this disorder and when they repent the child is healed. It is important to identify the circumstances or door points for the rejection.

There are four steps to this ministry. First, repent to the child for their sin (i.e., not wanting them, born or conceived out of wedlock, etc.), and ask the child for forgiveness. This should be accomplished with love and words carefully chosen not to introduce more pain or rejection into the child. Second, cast out the spirits of fear, rejection, abandonment, and trauma that came to the child in these circumstances. Third, give the child a father's, and a mother's blessing, if possible. Fourth, in the name of Jesus command the colic, allergies, asthma, etc. to go. When the parents have done this, the child has always been healed, even a two-month-old baby.

Spiritual/Emotional Strongholds: Fear of abandonment, rejection, fear, trauma and insecurity.

Reference:

The PDR Family Guide, Encyclopedia of Medical Care (1997).

Chronic Obstructive Pulmonary Disease (COPD)

Any chronic respiratory disease such as emphysema and bronchitis and asthma that are characterized by obstruction to air flow. These diseases cause irreversible lung damage by weakening and breaking the air sacs within the lungs. Smoking is the number one cause of COPD.

Spiritual/Emotional Strongholds: Self-hatred, anxiety, fear, lack of trust in God, and addictions.

Repent and renounce any of these strongholds, including unbelief, in your life and generations. Take responsibility and break agreement with them. Take authority over them and break their power.

References:

Breathlessness in America: New Survey Reveals Impact of Chronic Obstructive Pulmonary Disease. American Lung Association.

Costochondritis

Costochondritis is an inflammatory process of the costosternal joints (sternum) that causes chest pain and tenderness. Minor repetitive trauma, inflammatory diseases and anxiety all are contributors to this disease. It is more common in women than in men.

Spiritual/Emotional Strongholds: Anxiety, fear, insecurity, and depression.

Repent and renounce any of these strongholds, including unbelief, and break agreement with them. Take responsibility over them and break their power over them.

References:

Flowers, Lynn. *Costochondritis*, eMedicine, Eastern Virginia Medical School, Portsmouth Naval Medical Center.

CREST Syndrome

CREST is an acronym, for five features of this syndrome: calcinosis, Raynaud's syndrome, esophageal dysmotility, sclerodactyly, and telangiectasia. It is a less serious form of scleroderma (a chronic autoimmune disease of the connective tissue) which is confined to the skin of the fingers and face. Calcium deposits in the skin cause hardness, limited motion and pain. There are spasms of the blood vessels supplying blood to the fingers, and dilated vessels in the face. The esophagus is affected as well with less motility. There is a higher incidence of CREST syndrome among women then men.

Spiritual/Emotional Strongholds: Self-hatred, hardness of heart, guilt, and fear.

Repent and renounce any of these strongholds. Break agreement with any of these strongholds in your life, including unbelief. Take responsibility for them and break their power over you.

References:

CREST Syndrome. November 2, 2001

Crohn's Disease

Inflammation of the lining of the digestive tract, usually affecting the lower portion of the small intestine. It is an autoimmune disease where the immune system is attacking the digestive tract. It affects men and women equally. The major symptoms include diarrhea, weight loss and pain.

Spiritual/Emotional Strongholds: Rejection, self-rejection, self-hatred, codependency, false burden bearing, and guilt.

Repent and renounce any of these strongholds, including unbelief, and break agreement with them. Take responsibility for them in your generations and break their power over you.

References:

Crohn's Disease, National Institute of Health. NIH Publication No. 00-3410 April 2000.

Cushing's Disease

A rare hormonal disorder, caused by prolonged exposure of the body's tissues to high levels of cortisol. Excess cortisol is secreted, because of continued anxiety and fear (Jacobson 2000).

Symptoms include upper body obesity, round face, fatigue, weak muscles, high blood pressure, high blood sugar, irritability, thin fragile skin, anxiety and depression. People taking steroids for asthma and other inflammatory diseases may suffer from this syndrome. Alcoholics, people suffering with panic disorders and depression, and those malnourished all are at risk for this disease. It usually affects individual from the ages of 20-50.

Spiritual/Emotional Strongholds: Fear, anxiety, victimization, self-hatred, guilt, and depression.

Repent and renounce these strongholds, including unbelief, and break agreement with them. Take responsibility over them and break their power.

References:

Cushing's Syndrome, National Institute of Health, Publication No. 02-3007.

Cystitis

Bladder inflammation. There are two major types: bacterial or idiopathic (no known cause). In idiopathic cystitis there is usually the congregating of white blood cells around the bladder due to an autoimmune response.

Spiritual/Emotional Strongholds: Fear, anxiety, self-hatred, infirmity, and uncleanness.

Repent and renounce any of these strongholds, including unbelief, and break agreement with them. Take responsibility for them in your generations.

Cysts

Benign harmless growths, that may grow anywhere in the body. Some grow due to hormones and others are due to bacteria, parasites, or unknown causes.

Spiritual/Emotional Strongholds: Anxiety, fear and self-bitterness.

Repent and renounce any of these strongholds and break agreement with them. Take responsibility for them in your generations.

References:

Bunch, Bryan, 1999. *The Family Encyclopedia of Disease: A Complete and Concise Guide to Illness and Symptoms*. Scientific Publishing Inc., Published by W.H. Freeman and Company, New York.

Deep Vein Thrombosis (DVT)

DVT is a blood clot, in the blood vessels commonly of the calf or thigh, interfering with the blood flow in the vein. It can cause life-threatening complications if the clot breaks away and travels to the lungs. Some risk factors include, sitting for long lengths of time, obesity, cancer, stroke, varicose veins, pregnancy, recent surgery, and chronic swelling of the legs or feet.

Spiritual/Emotional Strongholds: Anger and rage.

Repent and renounce these strongholds, including unbelief, taking responsibility for them in your generations and breaking agreement with them.

References:

Deep Vein Thrombosis. MD Travel Health. From the New England Journal of Medicine.

Degenerative Disc Disease

The aging process, occupational stress, trauma, addictions and dehydration affecting the discs (shock absorbers) in the vertebrae of the spine. This occurs by micro-trauma and tearing of the disc and facet joints, resulting in degeneration. Symptoms may include back, hip pain and leg pain. Metabolic diseases and depression are also contributors to this disease.

Spiritual/Emotional Strongholds: Anxiety, fear, addiction, and depression.

Repent and renounce any of these strongholds and break agreement for them. Take responsibility for them and break their power.

References:

Lumbar Degenerative Disc Disease, eMedicine.

Dementia

A decline in cognitive and intellectual function. Memory is often the first cognitive function to become affected. It occurs when brain cells die, due to various metabolic, vascular and neurological diseases. Chronic stress releases cortisol, which destroys memory cells. Vascular disease, depression, and neurological diseases can cause dementia. Alzheimer's is the most common cause. Antibrain antibodies have been discovered in Alzheimer's patients (Singh 1997).

Recent studies are linking negative emotions such as depression or anxiety to the over secretion of a pro-inflammatory cytokine (IL-6), which causes inflammation. These same studies are linking inflammation with Alzheimer's disease (Cohen 2000; Ershler 2000).

Spiritual/Emotional Strongholds: Anxiety, fear, and self-bitterness.

Repent and renounce any of these strongholds, including unbelief, and break agreement with them. Take responsibility for them in your generations and break their power.

References:

Dementia and Memory Loss. Mayo Foundation for Education and Research. December 18, 2000.

Sapolosky, Robert and McGaugh, James. *The Human Brain How Stress Affects Memory*. The Center of Neurobiology of Learning and Memory at the University of Calif.

Depression (Unipolar)

Major depression occurs when people experience "episodes" of severe depression, that can last for months. Depressed people feel a sense of worthlessness, hopelessness and helplessness, and experience social withdrawal, loss of motivation, sleep disorders, weight loss or gain, and often suicidal feelings. In each of these feelings or emotions, the person has believed the lies of the devil. Each of these thoughts or emotions would be considered sins in Christian terms.

Clinically, depression is defined as a shortage of serotonin, a neurotransmitter. Drugs called serotonin re-uptake inhibitors are often prescribed for treatment. These drugs attempt to make serotonin last longer in the nerve synapse, but they cannot create or cause the body to produce more serotonin. The shortage of serotonin and the resulting depression are caused by negative emotions. Negative thoughts and emotions, especially self-hatred and guilt, cause the restriction or reduction of serotonin production. Psychology also refers to depression as a negative emotion (Cohen 2000, Ershler 2000, Kendall 2002).

Spiritual/Emotional Strongholds: Self-Bitterness, self-condemnation, guilt, anxiety, hopelessness, anger, rage, and hostility.

Repent and renounce any of these strongholds, including unbelief, and break agreement with them. Take responsibility for them and break their power over you.

References:

Depression Unipolar Disorder. The Merck Manual of Diagnosis and Therapy. Section 15. Psychiatric Disorders Chapter 189. Mood Disorders.

Dermatitis

Inflammation of the skin that is not contagious. There are several types: contact dermatitis, neurodermatitis, seborrheic dermatitis, stasis dermatitis and atopic dermatitis.

Medications usually contain an antihistamine. Anxiety and fear are the cause of most skin disorders (McCantz 1998, Jacobson 2000). Anxiety causes the body to produce too much histamine, which can cause outbreatks.

Spiritual/Emotional Strongholds: Fear, anxiety and insecurity.

Repent and renounce these strongholds, including unbelief, and break agreement with them.

References:

Dermatitis. Mayo Foundation for Education and Research. May 02, 2002

Diabetes

Type 1 (insulin dependent) is an autoimmune disorder of the pancreas. It is characterized by impaired insulin production by autoaggressive T-cells and high blood sugar and ketoacidosis results. Type 1 diabetes usually develops before the age of 18.

Type 2 is usually called "adult onset" and results from insulin resistance. This is a condition in which the body fails to properly use insulin combined with insulin deficiency. It is also an autoimmune disorder of the pancreas. Oversecretion of cortisol blocks insulin and excess cortisol is produced from anxiety and fears, which produce a fight-flight response (Jacobson 2000).

According to Greg Nichols, Ph.D., a senior researcher with Portland, Oregon, based Kaiser Permanente Center for Health Research, depression is two times more prevalent in people with diabetes than in people without diabetes. Nichols' most recent study found that not only do depression and diabetes often go hand in hand, but also that depression may have a significant role in causing diabetes. Further studies at Washington University in St. Louis have found that patients with depression exhibit less stable blood glucose control than patients without depression (Nichols 2003).

Most research in behavioral medicine is about the management of this disease.

Psychobehavioral intervention can have a positive impact on physical and emotional well being for people living with diabetes (Kendall 2002). But very little research involves the prevention or cure. The answer is again found in the negative emotions that cause the autoimmune response and the resulting inflammation.

Negative emotions such as depression or anxiety can directly affect the cells of the immune system and either up or down regulate the secretion of the proinflammatory cytokine, Interleukin-6 (Cohen 2000). Interleukin-6 also signals the liver to make C-reactive protein (Jacobson 2001). C-reactive protein (CRP) is considered by many researchers to be the most sensitive measurement of inflammation.

University of Texas scientists have discovered that the level of CRP in the blood is closely related to severity of diabetes. CRP levels were thirty-three percent higher in patients with mild diabetes and approximately twice as high in patients with major diabetes, compared to people without diabetes. In this study the patients were given a 1200 IU daily supplement of vitamin E to reduce the inflammation. After three months the CRP levels dropped dramatically. In those with mild diabetes the level returned to normal, and those with major diabetes, the level reduced to that of those with mild diabetes (Devaraj 2000).

Other research also demonstrates that inflammation is linked to several conditions or diseases including cardiovascular disease, osteoporosis, arthritis, type 2 diabetes, certain cancers (including multiple myeloma, non-Hodgkin's lymphoma, chronic lymphocytic leukemia), Alzheimer's disease, and periodontal disease (Cohen 2000, Ershler 2000, Kendall 2002).

Spiritual/Emotional Strongholds: Rejection (usually by a father), self-rejection, self-hatred, guilt, anxiety, fear, and depression.

Repent and renounce any of these strongholds and break agreement with them. Take responsibility for them in your generations.

References:

Diabetes, Arthritis and Other Autoimmune Diseases. Institute for Cancer, Aging and Antioxidant Research.

Endocrinology and Type 1 Diabetes — Insulin Dependent Diabetes (IDD). The Endocrine Society and The Hormone Society Bethesda, Maryland.

HLA-DQ and Type I Diabetes. Center for Disease Control.

Dissociative Disorder (DID) or Multiple Personality Disorder (MPD)

This disorder is charatarized by abrupt shifts in states of mind. In severe cases the person may even claim to be or switch into a different person or personality. The person usually develops different personalities or parts or fragments of themselves as a protection from trauma or horror that has been a part of their life. They disassociate into personalities that usually coincide with certain ages in their life. They create these personalities because the real life experiences were too horrible for them to cope with.

Disorganizedly attached children and their parents with unresolved trauma or grief each have the potential to activate incoherent, conflictual, or unstable mental models. Abrupt shifts in states of mind can occur within these individuals, leading to a disorganized form of behavior externally and to the experience of a dissociation in consciousness internally Unresolved traumatic experience or unresolved grief can be revealed through this disorganization (Siegel 1999). According to Dr. Siegel the problem or answer is found in the unresolved traumatic experiences. This confirms our experience.

In my experience the real person shares the memories and feelings of the other personalities or fragmented parts of themselves. Some teach that each of these fragmented parts must be integrated, and then each personality individually led to accept Jesus as their savior. I do not agree with this. I believe that scripture teaches that we are each individually and wonderfully made. God created only one of each of us, not many individuals within each of us. Therefore I believe that these personalities are not from God and are not good. In the long term they bring disaster and prevent the person from receiving God's peace and joy that only comes through forgiving the abusers. In forgiveness, the shame and guilt are also healed.

We have had good success by leading the person in forgiving each person that abused him. In doing this the traumatic experiences are resolved. We work through each and every memory of each personality, beginning with the youngest. I do not allow the alters to speak, but we work through the bitterness and traumas they've experienced. These memories are healed as the bitterness, pain, fear, shame, guilt, and trauma are removed by the blood of Jesus from their lives, the need for the false protection supposedly provided by the alter or dissociation, is thus satisfied.

As this process progresses, the person begins to realize that the personality or alter was actually holding them in bondage to the shame and guilt of what was done to them and/or what they did. The fact that they were forced does not remove the guilt and shame. Almost every sexually abused person in some way blames him or herself or carries shame and guilt for what was done to him or her. Once this is realized, the healing progresses very rapidly. Asking for forgiveness, and forgiving oneself, is extremely important. This is how the shame and guilt are removed.

All people disassociate in some way in their lives. A daydream is a mild form of disassociating. It is an escape from reality. Scripture does not teach us to escape or run from life. Scripture teaches us to deal with life in the power of Jesus.

Usually these personalities were formed as children. I agree that they did not know or have the ability to deal with the situation at the time, but usually we are not ministering to a child, but to an adult who can make adult decisions. The fact remains that the acts they were forced to participate in were sin. All sin must be forgiven and cleansed. This process removes all the shame, guilt, anger, and hatred and the person finds a place of peace knowing that he is forgiven, cleansed, clean, and righteous before the LORD. He is free! He can walk with his head up.

Diffuse Idiopathic Skeletal Hyperostosis (DISH)

DISH is also known as Forestier's disease and anklylosing hyperostosis. It is a form of degenerative arthritis (autoimmune). There is calcification along the sides of the vertebrae of the spine. Calcifying of tendons is also involved, sometimes resulting in tendonitis and bone spurs. Diabetes has been implicated in this disease. The most common symptom is stiffness in the back.

Spiritual/Emotional Strongholds: Self-bitterness, self-hatred, guilt, and fear.

Repent and renounce these strongholds, including unbelief, and break agreement with them. Take authority over them, breaking their power, and cast them out.

References:

Diffuse Idiopathic Skeletal Hyperostosis. eMedicine

Diverticulitis

Diverticulitis is the inflammation of an abnormal pouch (the diverticulum) in the colon. When the muscle of the colon wall becomes weakened, a hernia can form in the gut. Often the diverticulum is the result of constipation (straining). When these pouches become infected, abdominal pain, fever, and diarrhea or constipation are common symptoms. In severe cases, fistulas or bowel obstructions may develop.

Spiritual/Emotional Strongholds: Anxiety, fear, and anger.

Repent and renounce any of these strongholds in your life, including unbelief, taking responsibility for them. Take authority over them breaking their power and cast them out. Walk in the freedom made available to you in Christ Jesus.

References:

Nichols, Trent and Thomsa, Paul. *Diverticulosis Definitions of Diverticulosis and Diverticulitis.* The Center for Nutrition and Digestive Disorders, Hanover, PA

Dyslexia

This is a learning disability that affects reading. Many people think dyslexia is seeing letters or words backwards and that it is a visual problem. However this is untrue; it is a language-processing problem. Dyslexics do not use the same neural networks in the brain as normal readers. It is a breakdown in "phoneme awareness," or making connections between the sounds of the words and the symbols. They often have diffi-culty with sounding out words, reading comprehension, memory, spelling, learning names of letters, and accuracy in reading. The question is, what has caused their brains to be wired differently?

In this disorder we usually find very intelligent children that are often bored and confused. The confusion often comes from situations or experiences in the home where dad is absent physically, emotionally or spiritually, and mom becomes the source of income and/or support. There may not be the normal attachment to both parents.

We also often see children who are not disciplined or trained. They are not disciplined to have specific times to do their homework, bedtimes or meal times. There is a lack of structure that brings security into their lives. Other situations or experiences that bring insecurity and confusion such as inconsistent parental relationships, fighting, arguments, violence, and divorce also play a large role in the development of a child's ability to think and express themselves. Emotional, sexual, physical, verbal abuse or other traumas also can be part of the equation. Unresolved loss leads to disorganized infant response patterns (Siegel 1999).

Psychologists call this disorganized/disoriented attachment. The child's relationship with their parent or caregiver may become disorganized and disorientated in any way that the child does not feel secure. Children with disorganized/disoriented attachment have been found to have the most difficulty later in life with emotional, social, and cognitive impairments (Siegel 1999).

Parents who have unresolved attachment (relationship) issues tend to have infants that also have disorganized/disoriented attachment or relationships (Main and Hesse 1990). In other words the way we relate to others and ourselves is learned from our parents, and it can be learned even before we are born.

Spiritual/Emotional Strongholds: Inherited fear, insecurity, rebellion, rejection, and abandonment.

Repent and renounce any of these issues (divorce, abandonment, passive father and dominant mother) in your life and generations, and break agreement with them. Take responsibility for them and break their power.

References:

Thorne Glenda, *What is Dyslexia?* Vice President of services and clinical psychologist at the Center for Development and Learning.

Rao, Caroline. *Differences in Dyslexic and Normal Brains.* June 20th issue of Lancet (351:1849-52).

Dysmenorrhea (Menstrual Cramps; also see PMS)

Primary dysmenorrhea is painful menstrual cramping without any pathology present. It is often due to an increase in prostaglandins. GI symptoms usually accompany this disorder. It affects forty percent of all menstruating women.

My studies show that PMS symptoms are related to shame or guilt associated with being a female. Somehow the woman has learned to resent being a female or at least the monthly cycle. She has developed a fear and resentment about how God made the female body to function. This can come from several sources: She has been taught that she will have pain and that she just has to put up with it; often there has been abuse that would not have happened if she were not a girl; the parents got a girl when they wanted a boy and the girl works to gain acceptance; an overbearing mother; observed preferential treatment of males; and the shame from early development. These are some of the examples of resentment of being a female that we have observed.

Spiritual/Emotional Strongholds: Self-hatred, bitterness, victimization, pain, fear, anxiety, and self-neglect (overweight, lack of exercise, poor nutrition etc.).

Repent and renounce these strongholds, including unbelief, and break agreement with them. Take responsibility for them and break their power.

References:

Dysmenorrhea. eMedicine.

Ear Infections (Chronic)

Repeated infections of the middle ear causing pain and swelling, which may lead to hearing loss. This is part of group of diseases including asthma, allergies, colic and bronchial infections that are part of what we call the abandonment profile. The abandonment and rejection usually begins in the womb in one or more of the following ways: conception/birth out of wedlock, wanting the opposite sex, arguing and fighting during pregnancy, adoption, parents not wanting a baby, etc. (See colic and allergy profiles.)

Spiritual/Emotional Strongholds: Inherited fear of abandonment, rejection, fear, insecurity, and infirmity.

Parents, repent and renounce these strongholds, including unbelief, and break agreement with them. Take authority over these strongholds, breaking their power over your child. Make sure that your words promote security in your child.

Eating Disorders

There has been extensive research into the causes of these disorders. The research explores media pressure, peer pressure, family factors such as entanglements and criticism, low self-esteem, and body dissatisfaction. A core feature in eating disorders is an obsession with slimness. Therefore it is not surprising that the media is often blamed for the increasing incidence of eating disorders on the grounds that media promotes images of the ideal slim physiques. Peer pressure plays a role because young girls learn certain attitudes and behaviors from their peers, both by way example and by teasing (Levine 1994).

Families also play a large role by praising slenderness and the self-control in achieving "slimness" (Branch 1980). Sometimes this is done as a manipulating tool; this may not cause the disorder, it helps to perpetuate it. Case reports and studies in families with eating disorders find the families to be enmeshed, intrusive, hostile, and negative toward the person with the disorder (Shoebridge 2000). Eating disorder patients, generally describe a critical family environment, with coercive parental control (Haworth-Hoepper 2000). Patients who perceive a lack of family communication, parental caring, and parental expectations as well as those who report sexual or physical abuse, are at increased risk for developing eating disorders (Haudek 1999, Neumark-Sztainer 2000). Eating disorders may also represent a way of coping with problems of identity and personal control (Polivy 2002).

Women who have suffered sexual abuse, have a family history of alcoholism and mood disorders have a higher incidence of eating disorders (Polivy 2002). These negative situations and emotions are usually internalized and result in some form of self-hatred, which is the primary emotional or spiritual cause of this disorder.

Anorexia and bulimia are the predominant eating disorders; let's look at the disorders individually.

ANOREXIA NERVOSA (AN)

Young females starve themselves, sometimes to death. Previous to the 1960s, anorexia was very rare, but today it is much more prevalent in Western societies.

BULIMIA NERVOSA (BN)

An eating disorder of epidemic proportions where one loses control over eating and engages in "binging and purging" (overeating followed by self-induced vomiting). The use of laxatives, diuretics and excessive exercise are common following a binge. The highest risk groups are college-age women, although this disorder can begin later in life. Complications of this eating disorder are gastric rupture, loss of tooth enamel, esophagitis and esophageal cancer.

AN and BN, are part of the obsessive compulsive spectrum disorder. Recent research is also referring to OCD as an autoimmune disease. When treated with immune enhancing drugs, the OCD effect diminishes or even completely subsides for a time (Singh 1997).

Spiritual/Emotional Strongholds: Self-hatred, low self-esteem, depression, denial, anger, addictions, and insecurity.

Repent and renounce any of these strongholds and break agreement with them. Take responsibility for them in your generations and break their power over you.

References:

Bulimia nervosa, Merck Manual. 16th Edition pp. 2280-1.

McAlpine, Donald. *Eating Disorders at Midlife*. Mayo Clinic, Rochester, NY.

OBESITY

There is a continuing debate whether to classify this as an eating disorder or as an addiction. Regardless of the name, the profile does not change. Obesity is the result of an imbalance in the intake of calories and the expenditure of energy, resulting in an increase of fat cells in the body. In other words, the person eats too much, substituting food for love. Mood disorders, anxiety and fears, thyroid imbalance, low serotonin levels, addictive personalities and some medications can all contribute to this disorder. When refined carbohydrates flood the brain with the neurotransmitters serotonin, nor-epinephrine and dopamine, they create a temporary sense of well being, but addictive cravings develop.

As in all addictions the person is self-medicating to cover the hurts and pain of life, instead of forgiving and repenting to heal the broken heart. Only Jesus can heal the broken heart and then only if we are obedient.

It is estimated each year that 90,000 deaths are tied to obesity. A *New England Journal of Medicine* study reveals that excess wieght is a factor is many deaths caused by cancer. The research says that as many as fourteen percent of cancer deaths in men, and twenty percent of cancer deaths in women, may be caused by excessive weight (*Anchorage Daily News* 4-24-03).

Spiritual/Emotional Strongholds: Anxiety, fear, abandonment, emptiness, rage (coming out of abuse, often sexual), depression, self-bitterness, and low self-esteem.

Repent and renounce any of these strongholds and break agreement with them. Take responsibility for these strongholds on both sides of your family tree. Take authority over them, breaking their power over you.

References:

Sheppard, Kay. 1998. *The Biochemistry of Food Addiction.* Northwestern Lutheran Sept. 1998.

Baacke, Linda. 1998. *A cycle of addiction.* Northwestern Lutheran Sept. 1998.

Eclampsia

A serious complication of pregnancy that typically occurs after the twentieth week of gestation. Symptoms include high blood pressure, seizures, intracranial bleeding, coma, headache, abdominal pain, confusion, generalized swelling, protein in the urine, anemia, liver damage, and fetal growth retardation. Eclampsia is most common in women younger than 20 years of age. Women with hypertension, diabetes, connective tissue or vascular disease are at higher risk for eclampsia.

Spiritual/Emotional Strongholds: Fear of abandonment, anger, and self-hatred.

Repent and renounce any of these strongholds in your life, including unbelief, and break agreement with them. Take responsibility for these strongholds and breaking their power and cast them out.

References:

Brooks, Michael. *Pregnancy, Eclampsia.* Department of Emergency Medicine, Bethesda North Medical Center.

Endocarditis (Non-Bacterial)

Non-bacterial endocarditis occurs when white blood cells congregate around the heart muscle, causing inflammation.

Spiritual/Emotional Strongholds: Self-hatred and guilt.

Repent and renounce strongholds, including unbelief, and break agreement with them. Take authority over them and break their power. Forgive yourself and others and walk in the freedom God made available to you in Christ

Endometriosis

A gynecological disorder where there is the presence of endometrial tissue found growing outside of the women's uterus into the pelvic cavity. Infertility, pain, bowel and bladder problems are some of the problems it can cause. There is no known cause; some theories are immunologic disorders, retrograde menstruation and hormonal imbalance.

The profile that we have seen includes guilt and shame coming from sexual abuse or promiscuity and/or a dislike of being a female as in the PMS profile.

Spiritual/Emotional Strongholds: Self-hatred, guilt, victimization, and insecurity.

Repent and renounce any of these strongholds, including unbelief, in your life. Forgive those who have victimized you and separate them from their sins. Take responsibility and break their power over you.

References:

Center for Endometriosis Treatment and Research Etiology. Sloane Hospital for Women Dept. of Obstetrics and Gynecology

Environmental Illness (EI)

A chronic disease, involving immune memory distortion, resulting in autoimmune diseases. EI sufferers become ill after eating, breathing, or absorbing small amounts of normally safe chemicals. It is an extreme form of allergies (see hypersensitivity reactions). The immune system "overreacts," as the sufferer overreacts by fearing their environment. Some symptoms include: fatigue, confusion, nausea, dizziness, difficulty breathing, loss of sleep, frequent colds, sinus infections, bronchitis, asthma, rashes, hives, personality changes, headaches, sensitivity to touch, memory loss, brain fog, joint pain, swollen limbs, food allergies and poor digestion. The reactions may be immediate or delayed, and mild or severe. In severe cases, people become allergic to all foods, magnetic fields, all fabrics—literally everything.

We have worked with many cases of this disease. Usually they are sensitive people who have had their hearts broken through abusive situations. As they learn to forgive others and themselves, and learn to deal with the fears, they completely recover (see the allergy profile).

Spiritual/Emotional Strongholds: Fear, anxiety, broken heart, unhealthy introspection, self-hatred, and self-pity.

Repent and renounce any of these strongholds, including unbelief, and break their power over you. Come out of agreement with the lie that your environment is making you sick. Forgive those who have hurt you and separate them from their sins.

References:

Brenneman, Lew. *What is Environmental Illness (EI)?* Immunology Medical Associates. brenn@sfo.com

Epilepsy (Idiopathic)

A condition where seizures occur regularly. Seizures are a disruption of normal brain electrical activity. Idiopathic is a term used when the seizure disorder has no identifiable cause. This type usually begins between the ages of 5-20, but can occur at any age. There are usually no other abnormalities present. There is often a family history of seizures.

Spiritual Strongholds: Deaf and dumb spirit, guilt, and occultism.

Repent and renounce any of these strongholds, including unbelief, and break agreement with them. Take responsibility for them in your generations and break their power over you and your children.

References:

Epilepsy and GABA Brain Briefings. Society for Neuroscience Aug. 1996.

Epilepsy Overview and Treatment. UCLA Pediatric Neuropsychiatry

Erectile Dysfunction (ED),

ED or impotence may be due to many physical and psychological causes. Hormonal and neurological imbalances, hypertension, diabetes, stress, depression, alcoholism and drugs are a few of the disorders or causative factors involved.

Spiritual/Emotional Strongholds: Fear, anxiety, self-hatred, depression, guilt, and anger.

Repent and renounce any of these strongholds, including unbelief, and break agreement with them. Forgive yourself and others and take responsibility for your responses. Take authority over these strongholds, breaking their power, and cast them out.

References:

Erectile Dysfunction Causes. Urology Channel Physician Board

Essential Tremor

A neurological disorder of unknown cause involving hand tremors, which is often inherited. Nervousness and medications that increase adrenaline levels increase the tremor. The condition is slowly progressive and worsens over time.

Fear and anxiety (Jacobson 2000) usually cause excessive adrenaline. Dr. Singh's research, also points to an autoimmune component in all neurological disorders (Singh 1994, 1997).

Spiritual/Emotional Strongholds: Fear, anxiety, self-hatred, and occultism.

Repent and renounce any of these strongholds, including unbelief, and break agreement with them. Take authority over them breaking their power and cast them out.

Reference:

Hain, Timothy. *Essential Tremor*. Northwestern University Medical School, Chicago, IL.

Coping with Essential Tremor. What is Essential Tremor? International Tremor Foundation.

Fear (see Phobic or Anxiety and Stress Disorders)

Fibrocystic Breast Syndrome

A disorder of the breast, where benign lumps filled with fluid develop. They often become tender and swell just before a period begins. Women who have irregular periods, who never have had children, or who have a history of breast cancer are at higher risk for this syndrome.

Spiritual/Emotional Strongholds: Self-bitterness and resentment (towards females in the family).

Repent and renounce any of these strongholds and break agreement with them. Take responsibility for these in your generations and break their power over you.

References:

Comforth Trace, *Understanding Breast Changes*. Women's Health.

Fibromyalgia Syndrome

A non-inflammatory disorder characterized by widespread pain, fatigue, depression, headaches and non-restorative sleep. Immune system changes have been found along with low serotonin levels. Eighty percent of all people with fibromyalgia are women. Many women with this illness have grown up in abusive homes and the disease is often triggered by a stressful event (i.e., divorce, death of a loved one, marital problems, loss of a job, burn out). This disease is usually centered on the feelings of not being nurtured, protected or taken care of.

Spiritual/Emotional Strongholds: Anxiety, fear, trauma, self-hatred, depression, and drivenness.

Repent and renounce any of these strongholds and break agreement with them. Forgive those who have hurt you. Repent for looking to a person for your security instead of to God which is a form of idolatry.

References:

Fibromyalgia, Merck Manual 16th Edition. Chapter 114 p. 1369-70.

Flesh Eating Bacteria (Necrotizing Fasciitis)

Necrotizing fasciitis is a progressive, chronic inflammatory infection of the subcutaneous tissue. A bacteria known as group-A strep pyogenes attacks the soft tissue and fascia (sheath covering the muscle), becoming gangrenous (dead). This bacterium is able to hide itself from the immune system, allowing it to spread rapidly. Symptoms include blisters, pain, fever, rapid heart rate, low blood pressure and altered level of consciousness. It is often found after trauma or surgical wounds in individuals with compromised immune systems. Mortality rate is twenty to twenty-five percent.

Spiritual/Emotional Strongholds: Anxiety, fear, insecurity, infirmity, and occultism. Search out any negative emotion.

Repent and renounce any of these strongholds, including unbelief, and break agreement with them. Take responsibility for any of these curses in your generations on both sides of the family tree.

References:

Maynor, Michael. *Necrotizing Fascitis*, (eMedicine) Louisiana State University School of Medicine.

Frigidity (female loss of sexual drive)

Frigidity is often the result of hormonal imbalance, stress, sexual abuse, alcohol abuse, side effects of medications, depression, and poor relationships. Medical textbooks list this as an anxiety and stress disorder (McCance 1998, Jacobson 2000).

Spiritual/Emotional Strongholds: Anxiety, fear, depression, victimization, guilt, and depression.

Repent and renounce any of these issues. Take responsibility for them in your life and generations, and break agreement with them.

References:

Female Sexual Arousal Disorder. American Psychiatric Association. *Diagnostic and statistical manual of mental disorders*, fourth edition. Washington, DC: American Psychiatric Association, 1994.

National Institutes of Health, National Institute of Mental Health, NIH Publication No. 95-3879 (1995.)

Fungal Infections (Chronic)

Fungi cause a wide variety of diseases in humans. In healthy bodies we have an innate immunity to them, but with a compromised immune system they are serious infections. Individuals with diabetes, cancer, AIDS, Hodgkin's disease, TB, emphysema, leukemia, burns, or on steroids are at higher risk. A few fungal diseases are: candidiasis or yeast infections, ringworm, aspergillosis (causing a serious pulmonary pneumonia in compromised patients), mycotic keratitis causing eye infections of the cornea, blastomycosis, which causes lesions on the skin and lungs, and many others.

Spiritual/Emotional Strongholds: Fear, anxiety, bitterness, and infirmity.

Repent and renounce any of these issues in your life and generations. Take responsibility for them and break agreement with them.

References:

Gardner, Amanda. *Fungal Infections a New Health Threat People with weakened immune systems particularly vulnerable.* Health Scout News Reporter Nov 7-2002 University of Maryland Medicine.

Systemic Fungal Infections, Merck Manual 16th Edition. Ch. 11 p. 169

Gallbladder Disease

Two common gallbladder diseases are cholelithiasis, or gallstones, and cholecystitis, or inflammation of the gallbladder. These diseases take years to develop and when symptoms begin, biliary colic (gallbladder pain), nausea, and vomiting are common symptoms. Gallstones are made up of cholesterol. Factors that elevate cholesterol in bile are obesity, estrogen, aging, and rapid weight loss. Women are more affected than men.

Spiritual/Emotional Issues: Bitterness, self-bitterness, and fear.

Repent and renounce any of these issues that may be in your life or generations. Take responsibility for them and break agreement with them.

References:

Soper, Nathaniel J. *Gall Bladder Disease.* Washington University School of Medicine, St. Louis, Missouri.

Digestive Disease Center, Mayo Clinic, Rochester, Minnesota.

Gastritis

Inflammation of the gastric mucosa. Infection, alcohol, bile, anxiety, and fears that increase the pepsin and acid secretion are some contributors. Inflammation is an immune response indicating an autoimmune component (Singh 1994, 1997).

Spiritual/Emotional Strongholds: Fear, anxiety, self-hatred, lack of trust in God, addictions, and insecurity.

Repent and renounce any of these strongholds and break agreement with them. Take responsibility for them and cast them out.

References:

Gastritis, Merck Manual 16th Edition. Ch. 51 p. 764.

Gingivitis

A gum disease, where there is chronic inflammation due to bacteria, resulting in bone loss and eventually, loss of teeth. Smoking dramatically increases the risk for this disease. Individuals with diabetes are also at greater risk for gingivitis. Inflammation is a marker for an autoimmune response (Singh 1994, 1997).

Spiritual/Emotional Issues: Anxiety, fear and self-hatred.

Repent and renounce any of these issues and break agreement with them. Take responsibility for them and break their power over you.

References:

Periodontal diseases: pathogenesis and microbial factors. American Academy of Periodontology. 1: 926-32.

Johnson, G.K. et al., 1994. T*he effect of smoking on the response to periodontal therapy*. J Clin Periodontol 21: 91-7.

Glomerulonephritis

A serious kidney disease, where there is inflammation of the kidneys' filters (glomeruli). These filters become inflamed and scarred and unable to filter waste and excess water from the blood. Dialysis and eventually a kidney transplant may be needed. Infection and hypersensitive vasculitis, are two main causes. Symptoms include protein in the urine, fatigue, high blood pressure and swelling. Males are affected twice as often as females.

The inflammation indicates an autoimmune response (Singh 1994, 1997).

Spiritual/Emotional Roots: Fear, anxiety, insecurity, and self-anger.

Repent and renounce any of these issues if applicable and break agreement with them. Take responsibility for them in your life and generations.

References:

Kazzi, Amin Antoine. *Glomerulonephritis*, Division of Emergency Medicine, University of California at Irvine Medical Center

Gout

A chronic painful arthritic disease of the joints, usually affecting the great toe and hands. It is an autoimmune disorder whereby uric acid builds up in the blood stream, forming uric acid crystals in the joint. Then antibodies attack the joint, causing more inflammation. Obesity, alcohol, rich-food intake, and diabetes all contribute to this disease. Research has shown that the negative emotions of depression and anxiety cause the release of proinflammatory cytokines that cause inflammation and arthritis (Kendall 2000).

Spiritual/Emotional Issues: Self-bitterness, guilt, and addictions (alcohol and food).

Repent and renounce any of these issues and break agreement with them. Take responsibility for them in your life and generations.

References:

Gout, National Institute of Arthritis and Musculoskeletal and Skin Diseases NIAMS/National Institutes of Health (NIH). 1 AMS Circle, Bethesda, MD 20892-3675. NIH Publication No. 02-5027. Publication Date: April 2002

Grave's Disease (Hyperthyroid Disease)

An autoimmune hyperthyroid disorder. The immune system attacks the thyroid making the thyroid produce too much thyroid hormone. The symptoms include increased appetite and heart rate, tremors, nervousness, inflammation and swelling of the eyes, and high blood pressure. It targets women seven times more than men (McCance 1998).

Spiritual/Emotional Strongholds: Anxiety, fear, self-hatred, and guilt.

Repent and renounce these strongholds, including unbelief, and break agreement with them. Take responsibility for them in your life and generations. Take authority over them, break their power over you, and cast them out.

Guillain-Barre Syndrome

An inflammatory disorder of the peripheral nerves often preceded by a viral infection such as herpes. There is a rapid onset of weakness, paralysis of the legs, arms, diaphragm (breathing muscle), and face. Autonomic nervous system dysfunction occurs in more severe cases. Most people recover from GB, but some may have long-term disabilities, and five percent die from respiratory failure. The inflammation indicates an autoimmune response (Singh 1994, 1997).

Spiritual/Emotional Strongholds: Anxiety, fear, self-hatred, insecurity, and occultism.

Repent and renounce any of these strongholds, including unbelief, and break agreement with them. Take responsibility for them in your life and generations, breaking their power over you.

References:

Guillain-Barre Syndrome (GBS), Merck Manual 16th Edition. Ch. 131 p.1521.

Hair Loss

Hair loss can be caused by many different reasons. Stress, major surgery, medications, hair dye, and menopause are some causes of hair loss. If your thyroid gland is overactive or underactive, your hair may fall out. Hair loss may occur if male or female hormones known as androgens and estrogens are out of balance.

Spiritual/Emotional Strongholds: Fear, anxiety, trauma and self-hatred.

Repent and renounce any of these strongholds, including unbelief, and break agreement with them. Take responsibility for these in your generations and break their power over you.

References:

Hair Loss and its Causes, American Academy of Family Physicians (AAFP).

Tobler, Randy. *What can a woman do to stop hair loss?* Well Journal.

Hashimoto's Disease (Hypothyroidism)

A thyroid disorder where the thyroid produces too little thyroid hormone. Symptoms are fatigue, coarse dry hair, hair loss, rough dry skin, constipation, low body temperature, depression, irritability, leg cramps, memory loss, loss of sex drive, and abnormal periods. Often it is due to antibodies attacking the thyroid (Hashimoto's thyroiditis), but in some cases the pituitary gland is not functioning properly. This is an autoimmune disease that affects women more than men (McCance 1998).

Spiritual/Emotional Strongholds: Self-hatred, guilt, fear, and anxiety.

Repent and renounce any of these strongholds, including unbelief, and break agreement with them. Take responsibility for them in your generations and break their power.

References:

Gerfo, Paul. *Hypothyroidism*. New York Thyroid Center, McConnell, Robert. Clinical Medicine

Thyroiditis. Merck Manual 16th Edition Ch. 87 p. 1083.

Headache Disorders

In the past ten years, the traditional medical view of the cause of headaches has undergone a fundamental revision. The traditional or orthodox view of tension headaches was that they resulted from a prolonged contraction of muscles in the neck and head, which stimulated nerves and reduced blood flow in the affected muscles. The traditional or orthodox view of migraine headaches (vascular model) believed that dilated blood vessels in the head were the cause. The traditional teaching was that the muscles and blood vessels were themselves the cause (Kendall 2002).

It is interesting to note that "in spite of recent advances in medicine, most individuals with a recurrent headache disorder—even a disorder that impairs functioning—do not have the means to effectively manage their headaches. In addition, a third of the patients who receive medical treatment for headache problems discontinue treatment because they are dissatisfied with the care they receive. Advances in drug therapy alone are unlikely to solve these problems. Rather, effective headache management may require that individuals be empowered to manage their own headache problems. Psychological treatment strategies can play a central role in empowering patients" (Kendall 2002). Let's look at these headaches individually and find how we can not only manage them, but be free of them.

TENSION-TYPE HEADACHES

Frequent tension-type headaches are now thought to be maintained primarily by a central nervous system dysfunction, not solely by input from peripheral nerves in the neck and shoulder muscles (Olesen 2000). As we have learned earlier, the CNS or our brain is the source of our thoughts. The "dysfunction" is primarily anxiety, fear, bitterness, worry, frustration and many other negative emotions. It is these negative emotions that cause the muscles to become tense and stiff causing the headaches.

Spiritual/Emotional Strongholds: Anxiety, fear, bitterness, worry, frustration, and many other negative emotions.

Repent and renounce any of these strongholds, including unbelief, and break agreement with them. Take responsibility for them in your life and generations, breaking their power over you.

MIGRAINE HEADACHES

Migraine headaches begin as a dull pain on the side of the head. It increases in severity and may throb with the pulse. Usually an aura, nausea, and sensitivity to light and noise precede or accompany a migraine. It is incapacitating and can last from hours to days, and is three times more prevalent in women. When histamine is released from anxiety, and serotonin is lowered from guilt and self-conflict, the cranial blood vessels dilate and put pressure on the cranial nerves causing pain. Histamine expands blood vessel size and serotonin regulates blood vessel size. The most common drug prescribed today is Imitrex. Imitrex is an antihistamine and an antidepressant that is designed to reduce blood vessel size, thus relieving the pain.

The sensory disturbances, or aura, that can precede a migraine, now are believed to result from a spreading depression (Lauritzen 1994). This substantiates our findings that thoughts and emotions such as guilt and self-conflict predispose to migraines.

All recent research confirms that mood and/or anxiety disorders are substantially elevated in migraine sufferers (Kendall 2002). The presence of a major depression increased the risk of developing a migraine. In one study, the onset of an anxiety disorder preceded the onset of a migraine in about eighty percent of the individuals (Merikangas 2000). As in many other diseases, science has discovered the true cause and then developed a drug to try to cover or mask the emotional or spiritual cause of the disorder.

We have also observed the tendency for asthma or allergy sufferers to breath very shallowly. In their fear of an airborne allergen or cold, they consciously or even unconsciously reduce the rate and depth of breathing. This can result in migraine headaches and/or brain fog. This is why migraines at times are treated with oxygen.

Spiritual/Emotional Strongholds: Guilt, anxiety, fears, self-conflict, pain, and depression.

Repent and renounce any of these strongholds, including unbelief, and break agreement with them. Take responsibility for your thoughts against yourself and break their power.

References:

Migraines and Serotonin Receptors. Brain Briefings Society for Neuroscience.

Migraine. Inteli-Health. Harvard Medical Schools.

REBOUND HEADACHES

The results of taking more and more medications for headaches. If medications are taken more than two to three times per week, it is the sign of a rebound headache. It is a headache actually caused by the medication itself. The cure is to get off the medications. The goal is get off as soon as possible. Most do it cold turkey at home, while others need a treatment center.

Spiritual/Emotional Strongholds: Dependence on drugs, anxiety, fear, and many other negative emotions.

Repent and renounce any of these strongholds, including unbelief, and break agreement with them. Take responsibility for your thoughts against yourself and break their power.

Reference:

ABC television program 20-20. *Rebound Headaches*. Friday, Jan. 10, 2003.

Hearing Loss

Hearing can be lost over time due to several causes such as stress, loud noises, trauma, medication, infection, and constriction of blood vessels. Dr. Russell Jaffe, an immunologist, teaches that excess cortisol and adrenaline levels in our blood, are immunologically toxic and lead to hearing damage.

Spiritual/Emotional Strongholds: Anxiety, fear, infirmity, trauma, and deaf and dumb spirit.

Repent and renounce any of these strongholds, including unbelief, and break agreement with them. Take responsibility for them in your generations and cast them out.

Reference:

Nutrition and Immunology. Presented by Russell Jaffe, MD, Ph.D. at the SHHH convention, Cherry Hill, NJ. June 2001.

Heart Disease—Coronary Heart Disease (CHD)

CHD is the leading cause of death in the United States. Each year about 450,000 people die from CHD, and a million experience an initial or recurrent coronary event (American Heart Association 2001). CHD is composed of several manifestations of one underlying condition, coronary artery disease (CAD). Initially, lipids (fats) and related cells (macrophages, foam cells) accumulate in microscopic amounts on the artery wall. These deposits grow into visible fatty streaks as early as middle childhood, and increase in prevalence with age (Strong 1999, Tuzca 2001).

Medical research is exploding with new evidence about the causes of heart disease. Let's look at some of the latest research.

This disease is examined in several ways in clinical research. One way is prevention through health behaviors. Modifiable behavioral risk factors (smoking, diet, and activity level) are important risk factors for the development of CHD (Stamler 1999). Behavioral change is an essential component of prevention. Others examine stress and other psychosomatic causes of CHD. "Psychological and social factors have a more direct effect on the development of CHD through the intervening psychobiological effects of stress and negative emotions. Perhaps the most important implication of research on psychological risk factors for coronary disease is that intervention, and targeting these factors, could reduce cardiac morbidity and mortality" (Kendall 2002).

Earlier we examined the direct effects of anxiety and fear in the release of adrenaline and cortisol in heart disease. Now let's look at other studies about negative emotions.

Hostility has been identified as the toxic component of the type-A pattern. Historically, the type-A coronary-prone behavior pattern has been the best known psychosocial risk factor. New research has identified individual differences in hostility as an important predictor of CHD as well as a cause of mortality. The emotional component of hostility involves anger, but it also includes contempt and scorn. The term hostility most accurately describes cognitive factors such as cynicism, mistrust, and the tendency to interpret others' actions as aggressive in intent (Kendall 2002, Miller 1996, Everson 1997). A facet of the type-A pattern is referred to as "social dominance." Social dominance has also proven to be a predictor of CHD (Siegman 2000).

Depression, anxiety, pessimism, job stress, social isolation, conflict, and other negative emotions are also a predictor of CHD (Kendall 2002). Over the past decade literally hundreds of studies have demonstrated the effect of negative emotions on many measures of health, including heart disease.

A November 6, 2002 Associated Press article reported about two new studies from the *Journal of the American Medical Association* (JAMA) that add to the rapidly growing body of evidence that inflammation in the bloodstream can be a powerful predictor of heart disease. These findings could help explain why people with no known risk factors such as high cholesterol or high blood pressure can still have heart attacks.

Myeloperoxidase (MPO) Levels

One of the JAMA studies found that patients with the highest levels of MPO, which is normally found in infection-fighting white blood cells, had a twenty fold greater risk of heart disease than those with the lowest levels. Inflammation is an indicator of infections. High levels were found even in people with no significant heart disease and with no risk factors such as high cholesterol and high blood pressure.

The JAMA study found that levels of MPO were elevated in people who had had heart attacks, heart bypass surgery, and narrowed coronary arteries. In recent years, doctors have come to suspect that inflammation, whether triggered by an infection or some other condition, can damage the walls of heart arteries, making them more prone to the fatty buildups that can lead to heart attacks.

Cleveland Clinic researchers said that this may help explain why heart attacks frequently occur in people previously thought to be healthy. "What is most exciting is that this marker appears to be significantly better at predicting risk for athlerosclerosis, or hardening of the arteries, than blood tests now used," including cholesterol tests, said Dr. Stanley Hazen, who coordinated the research. He noted that about fifty percent of heart attack patients have normal cholesterol levels.

Interleukin-6 Tied to Death Risk

The second JAMA study involved more than three thousand Scandinavian patients and found that high levels of Interleukin-6 increased the risk of death in patients hospitalized with chest pain and other heart attack symptoms. Interleukin-6 has been previously linked in other studies with inflammation and heart disease (Cohen 2000, Ershler 2000, Kendall 2002).

Patients whose blood tests showed high Interleukin-6 levels faced a more than threefold risk of dying within six to twelve months of initial hospitalization, compared with patients with low levels.

In November 2002 *The New England Journal of Medicine* reported on another study comparing C-reactive protein and low-density cholesterol (LDL, the "bad" cholesterol), in predicting first cardiovascular events. C-reactive protein and LDL cholesterol were measured in 27,939 apparently healthy American women who were then monitored for eight years for the occurrence of myocardial infarction (heart attack), stroke, coronary revascularization (bypass surgery), or death from cardiovascular causes.

The study revealed that seventy-seven percent of all events occurred among women with LDL cholesterol levels below 160 mg, and forty-six percent occurred among those with LDL cholesterol levels below 130 mg. The conclusion is that the C-reactive protein level is a stronger predictor of cardiovascular events than the LDL cholesterol level (Ridker 2002).

We have also seen in other studies that negative emotions such as depression or anxiety, can directly affect the cells of the immune system and either up or down regulate the secretion of proinflammatory cytokines including Interleukin-6 which causes inflammation (Kendall 2002).

This new evidence is completely changing how we look at heart disease. It is not all about cholesterol. It is really all about our thoughts and emotions. Now let's look at individual heart diseases.

ATRIAL FIBRILLATION (A-FIB)

A serious heart arrhythmia caused by an interference with the electrical activity in the heart's sinus node. This chaotic, rapid electrical signaling causes fibrillation (quivering) of the atria (upper chambers in the heart). The fibrillation leads to ineffective pumping action of the heart muscle, causing poor blood supply to the body. Fatigue, pallor, shortness of breath, fainting, and chest discomfort may occur.

Excessive adrenaline secreted because of anxiety, worry, fear, bitterness, and other stressors cause the heart to beat faster and erratically (Morady 1989, Toivonen 1997, Sun 1995, McCance 1998).

Spiritual/Emotional Strongholds: Fear of man, anxiety, fear, performance, self-hatred, hostility, bitterness, type-A behavior, and depression.

Repent and renounce any of these strongholds in your life and generations, taking responsibility for them and breaking agreement with them.

ANGINA (CHEST PAIN)

Cardiac pain and pressure precipitated by exertion and relieved by rest. Coronary artery disease and arteriosclerosis are the most common precursors. Psychological factors such as stress, fear, depression, and anger are contributors (Cohen H.J. 2000, Ershler 2000, Kendall 2002).

Spiritual/Emotional Strongholds: Fear, anxiety, anger, depression, bitterness, and hostility.

Repent and renounce any of these strongholds and break agreement with them. Take responsibility for them in your generations and break their power over you.

References:

Rosch, Paul J. *Stress and Heart Disease*. New York Medical College

Angina Pectoris, Merck Manual 16th Edition Ch. 25 p. 498-500.

BARLOW'S SYNDROME (BILLOWING MITRAL VALVE PROLAPSE)

A heart disorder characterized by one or both leaflets of the mitral valve protruding into the left atria, resulting in a backup of blood. Occasionally it is found in the tricuspid valve. It is more often found in women than in men. A clicking sound can be heard on auscultation. The main symptoms are stabbing chest pains, fatigue, shortness of breath and fainting.

Spiritual/Emotional Strongholds: Fear, anxiety, anger, hostility, and depression.

Repent and renounce generational fear and anxiety, taking responsibility for it in your generations. Come out of agreement with fear, doubt, and unbelief, and trust in the living God.

CARDIOMYOPATHY

An often fatal autoimmune heart disease characterized by weakening or thickening of the left ventricle (large pumping chamber of the heart). The heart becomes unable to pump effectively, resulting in an obstruction of blood flow to the rest of the body. Dilated cardiomyopathy is the most common type among middle aged men. Alcohol is known to suppress the heart and excessive intake can cause cardiomyopathy. Symptoms may include fatigue, weakness, swelling of the legs and feet, shortness of breath and cough.

Spiritual/Emotional Strongholds: Self-hatred, fear, anxiety, anger, hostility, depression, and addictions.

Repent and renounce any of these strongholds and break agreement with them. Take responsibility for them in your generations.

References:

Facts About Cardiomyopathy, Public Health Service. National Institute of Health National Heart, Lung and Blood Institute.

Seidman, Christine. *Brave Heart: Circle of Life*. Cardiovascular Genetics Lecture Series, Howard Hughes Medical Institute.

CONGESTIVE HEART FAILURE

Heart disease that is due to ineffective mechanical performance of the heart, result-ing in decreased cardiac output. Upon mild exertion, initially the symptoms include shortness of breath, fatigue, cough and fluid accumulation in body's tissues, especially the lungs and lower legs.

The heart is wearing out. Anxiety and fear are powerful emotions that cause the heart to work overtime. Scripture tells us that in the last days people's hearts will fail them because of fear (Luke 21:26).

Spiritual/Emotional Strongholds: Fear, anxiety, anger, self-bitterness, hostility, and depression.

Repent and renounce any of these strongholds, including unbelief, in your life and generations, and take responsibility for them. Take authority over them, breaking their power and cast them out.

References:

Data Fact Sheet Congestive Heart Failure in the United States: A New Epidemic. National Heart, Lung and Blood Institute

CORONARY ARTERY DISEASE (CAD)

A narrowing of the coronary arteries. It has been believed for years that it was caused by high levels of lipids (fats) in the blood, forming plaques or deposits in the arteries. Total cholesterol has been considered the one major indicator of this disease. The major symptom is angina (chest pain). CAD is the number one killer among Americans.

Now we are learning that inflammation is the major cause and that it can be measured by testing for C-reactive protein and Interleukin-6. Several studies show that negative emotions such as depression or anxiety can directly affect the cells of the immune system and either up or down regulate the secretion of proinflammatory cytokines such as Interleukin-6. Proinflammatory cytokines create inflammation in many parts of the body. Inflammation has recently been linked to several conditions or diseases including cardiovascular disease (Cohen 2000, Ershler 2000, Kendall 2002).

Also, two-thirds of all acute coronary events tend to occur when there is only mild to moderate obstructive plaque. The culprit does not appear to be the plaque itself, but the adrenaline surge that precipitates the crisis, which results from anger and rage (Shah 1997). Panic-like anxiety triples the risk of CHD (Haines 1987) while just "higher" levels of an anxiety double the risk (Kawachi 1994b).

Spiritual/Emotional Strongholds: Self-anger, anger, rage, anxiety, fear, hostility, type-A behavior, and depression.

Repent and renounce any of these strongholds and break agreement with them. Take responsibility for these in your generations and break their power over you.

References:

Cummings, Kenneth C. *Coronary Artery Disease and High Sensitivity C-Reactive Protein*. Clinical Pathology March, 2002.

Coronary Artery Disease, Merck Manual 16th Edition Ch.25 p 498.

Hepatitis (Chronic active Hepatitis)

This is an autoimmune disease that causes an inflammation of the liver due to a viral infection. Contact with blood, feces, or saliva, and sexual contact can spread it. Autoimmune hepatitis occurs when the body attacks and destroys its own liver. All types have symptoms that include fever, nausea, fatigue, jaundice and pain. Scarring of the liver (cirrhosis), liver cancer, and death are complications of this disease.

Spiritual/Emotional Strongholds: Infirmity, uncleanness, self-hatred, addictions, anxiety, and fear.

Repent and renounce any of these strongholds, including unbelief, if applicable, and break agreement with them. Take responsibility for them and break their power off you.

Reference:

McCance, Kathryn L. and Huether, Sue E. 1998. *Pathophysiology, The Biologic Basis for Disease in Adults and Children* (381-411). Third Edition, Mosby Inc. St. Louis, MO.

Hernia

A tear or weak spot in the abdominal wall where a part of the intestine or organ may protrude causing damage. Sometimes it occurs near the inguinal ring (inguinal hernia), causing a bulge in the groin. Another common site for a hernia is the umbilicus (belly button). Usually, there is no pain involved in this type.

Spiritual/Emotional Strongholds: Anger and rage.

Repent and renounce these strongholds in your life, including unbelief, and generations and break agreement with them. Parents take responsibility for them and break their power off of you.

Herpes Simplex Virus (HSV)

There are six types of herpes simplex viruses: Type 1 (cold sores or fever blisters on the mouth); Type 2 (sexually transmitted genital infections); cytomegalovirus (CMV) (sexually transmitted HSV without specific genital disease); varicell-zoster virus (chickenpox-shingles); Epstein-Barr virus (mononucleosis, kissing disease); and human herpes virus 6 (HHV-6) (roseola) (McCance 1998). Let's look at each of these in more detail:

HSV (TYPE 1)

Cold sores or fever blisters. It is estimated that up to eighty percent of the population is antibody positive for HSV type 1. But only about half of the population experiences oral outbreaks. Several studies have explored psychological variables that cause this. These studies have examined several stressors, including anxiety, stressful life events, personal relationships, job-related stress, frustrations, and daily hassles and found them to be significantly elevated in the patient prior to the recurrence of oral lesions (Friedman 1996, Schmidt 1985).

Spiritual/Emotional Issues: Anxiety, fear, bitterness, and self-hatred.

Repent and renounce any of these issues and break agreement with them. Take responsibility for them and break their power off of you.

GENITAL HERPES (TYPE 2)

A sexually transmitted disease caused by the herpes 2 virus (HSV 2). The virus remains in nerve cells for life, causing sores in the genital areas. The weaker the immune system, the more frequent the outbreaks.

The studies that I have cited for HSV 1, Epstein-Barr, and cytomegalovirus (CMV) also apply to HSV 2, for risk factors that cause an outbreak of the latent virus. But the causes of the initial infections are different. HSV 2 and cytomegalovirus are usually sexually transmitted, often by oral sex.

Spiritual/Emotional Issues: Anxiety, fear, bitterness, self-hatred, uncleanness, and fornication.

Repent and renounce any of these issues and break agreement with them. Take responsibility for them and break their power.

References:

Genital Herpes, Center for Disease Control.

Anderson, J. and Dahlberg, L. 1992. *High-risk sexual behavior in the general population*. Results from a national survey. 1988-90. Sex Transm. Dis. 19:320-325.

CYTOMEGALOVIRUS (CMV)

This is usually a sexually transmitted herpes virus. It is associated with a number of clinical syndromes in newborns, otherwise healthy adults, and immunosuppressed individuals. CMV does not cause a specific genital disease, but several severe syndromes. The incidence is high in individuals being treated for other sexually transmitted diseases. The virus is found in semen, cervical secretions, urine, blood, saliva, breast milk, and stool. Transmission is associated with close physical contact. It is more common in homosexual men and young women with multiple sexual partners.

Spiritual/Emotional Issues: Anxiety, fear, bitterness, self-hatred, uncleanness, and fornication.

Repent and renounce any of these issues and break agreement with them. Take responsibility for them and break their power.

SHINGLES

A disease caused by a herpes virus which affects nerve cells and extends to the skin leaving painful blisters. The waist and trunk are the most affected areas of the body.

This virus can remain dormant in the nerve for years. If shingles affects the eye, the cornea can become infected and lead to temporary or permanent blindness. Another complication of the virus is postherpetic neuralgia (PHN), a condition where the pain from shingles persists for months, sometimes years, after the shingles rash has healed. The elderly and those with compromised immune systems are at risk for this disease.

Spiritual/Emotional Strongholds: Anxiety and fear.

Repent and renounce any of these strongholds, including unbelief.

References:

Shingles. National Institute of Neurological Disorders and Stroke Facts Sheet

McCance, Kathryn L. and Huether, Sue E. 1998. *Pathophysiology, The Biologic Basis for Disease in Adults and Children* (381-411). Third Edition, Mosby Inc. St. Louis, MO.

EPSTEIN-BARR VIRUS (INFECTIOUS MONONUCLEOSIS OR KISSING DISEASE)

This is an acute infection of the B-cells. It is spread through close human contact, such as kissing, therefore the name "kissing disease." This disease is usually self-limiting and recovery occurs in a few weeks (McCance 1998).

There have been several studies examining the psychological risk factors associated with the development of a primary infection with EBV as the agent for infectious mononucleosis. The risk factors include poor academic performance, high motivation, overachieving father, inability to disclose emotional information, repressive coping styles, defensiveness, anxiety, depression, loneliness, and stress related to academic examinations. All of these risk factors were found to increase antibody titers, which show that the disease is active in the body and that the immune system is fighting it (Friedman 1996).

Spiritual/Emotional Issues: Anxiety, fear, bitterness, self-hatred, and uncleanness.

Repent and renounce any of these issues and break agreement with them. Take responsibility for them and break their power.

HUMAN HERPES VIRUS 6 (HHV-6, ROSEOLA)

Viral infection in children between 2 months and 2 years of age. It is a rash primarily over the trunk and neck. Children usually feel well, eat normally, and have few other symptoms (McCance 1998).

High Blood Pressure (Essential Hypertension)

Primary or essential hypertension (HTN) is elevation of blood pressure. HTN affects almost fifty million people in the United States (Burt 1995), placing them at risk of stroke, heart attack, congestive heart failure, kidney failure, and peripheral vascular disease (Blumenthal 1993, Waldstein 1991).

As blood is pumped through your body, it exerts pressure on the walls of your arteries. The systolic blood pressure is the pressure against these walls when the heart contracts or pumps, and the diastolic blood pressure is the pressure when the heart relaxes. HTN is defined as having systolic blood pressure over 140 mm Hg, or diastolic blood pressure consistently over 90 mm Hg, or taking medication.

Blood pressure is determined by the amount of blood pumped by the actions of the heart, and by the size and condition of the arteries. Many other factors can affect or predict high blood pressure including the water volume in the body, salt content of the body, condition of the kidneys, nervous system, blood vessels, and various hormone levels and stress levels in the body.

Many clinical studies have provided a thorough review of psychosocial factors and HTN, and have noted that lifestyle factors were linked to the development of HTN. The primary behavioral approaches for the treatment and prevention of HTN included exercise, diet, reduced calorie intake, and stress management (Shairo 1982). Secular stress management consists of techniques that reduce excessive stress arousal by changing cognitive and emotional responses to events (Kendall 2002). Several studies demonstrated a remarkable degree of success persisting over several years after the therapy ended (Patel 1997, Patel and Marmot 1988).

Medical textbooks refer to HTN as an anxiety and stress disorder. It is the result of too much adrenaline and cortisol being released because of our reactions to stressors (McCance 1998, Jacobson 2000). Negative thoughts and emotions create the "physiological distress" which in turn causes the high blood pressure. "Christian stress management" is learning to forgive and repent. When this is accomplished the anxiety, fear, anger, guilt, shame, bitterness, etc., that cause the fight-flight response, and raised the blood pressure, are gone.

Spiritual/Emotional Strongholds: Fear, anxiety, anger, and bitterness.

Repent and renounce these strongholds, including unbelief, and break agreement with them. Forgive those who have hurt you and repent for your failures.

References:

Essential Hypertension. Medical Encyclopedia. Medline.

Cohen, Debbie. University of Pennsylvania Medical Center, Philadelphia, PA.

Merck Manual 16th Edition Chapter 24 p 413-14.

Rutledge, Thomas. *Psychological Distress May Predict Hypertension.* Center for the Advancement of Health. Dr.tom@medscape.com.

High Cholesterol (Familial Hypercholesteremia)

Our bodies require cholesterol to function, but high levels have been associated with heart diseases. Recent research may change our view about cholesterol (see heart disease profile).

High cholesterol primarily is the result of excessive adrenaline, which increases cholesterol production (especially LDL, the "bad" cholesterol) and decreased cholesterol clearance. This results in increased formation of plaque on artery walls (Jacobson 2000, Hart 1996). Diet can affect cholesterol levels, but only to a minor degree.

Medical textbooks teach that increased cholesterol production (especially LDL, the "bad" cholesterol) is related to excessive adrenaline caused by anxiety and fears (McCance 1998). Every cell in the body needs cholesterol to function, but under stress some cells stop using cholesterol and start producing it.

Spiritual/Emotional Strongholds: Self-anger, guilt, anxiety, and fear.

Repent and renounce these strongholds, including unbelief, breaking agreement with them.

References:

Brown, M.S. and Goldstein, J.L. *A Receptor-mediated pathway for cholesterol homeostasis*. Science. 1986. 232: 34-47.

The Merck Manual of Diagnosis and Therapy. Sixteenth edition, 1992. Merck Research Laboratories, N.J.

Hives

Hives are red itchy bumps or "welts" on the skin that occur in response to an allergic reaction or the immunological release of histamine. Histamine is located in certain white blood cells called mast cells. When triggered, these mast cells release histamine, causing the cells of the blood vessels to contract and allowing fluid to leak out of the capillaries. Excess cortisol and adrenaline in the blood have been found to trigger histamine. Women are twice as likely to suffer from hives as men. Hives can also cause a serious reaction that involves the whole body, called anaphylaxis. There are several known factors that cause histamines to be released, and hives to form. These include: stress, allergies to medications or substances in the environment and acute or chronic infections. The American Academy of Allergy, Asthma and Immunology lists emotional stress as one of five causes for hives.

Spiritual/Emotional Strongholds: Fear and anxiety.

References:

West, Lynn. *Hives*. Discovery Health.com.

McCance, Kathryn L. and Huether, Sue E. 1998. *Pathophysiology, The Biologic Basis for Disease in Adults and Children* (381-411). Third Edition, Mosby Inc. St. Louis, MO.

Hyperparathyroidism

A disorder of the parathyroid glands in which too much parathyroid hormone (PTH) is produced. With elevated PTH, the bones lose calcium into the bloodstream and kidney stones are formed. Often there are benign growths causing this disorder. In some cases, there is no known cause. Some symptoms may include nausea and vomiting, pain, fatigue, depression, confusion, and muscle weakness. It is classified as an autoimmune disease (McCance 1998).

Spiritual/Emotional Strongholds: Fear, anxiety, self-bitterness, and depression.

Repent and renounce any of these strongholds, including unbelief, and break agreement with them. Take responsibility for these in your generations, and break their power.

Reference:

McCance, Kathryn L. and Huether, Sue E. 1998. *Pathophysiology, The Biologic Basis for Disease in Adults and Children* (381-411). Third Edition, Mosby Inc. St. Louis, MO.

Hypoglycemic Syndrome

A decrease of blood sugar resulting in a release of adrenal hormones, causing confusion, nervousness, fast heart rate, irritability, sweating, poor concentration, tremors, and hunger. This syndrome is more common in women than in men. The pancreas is involved in controlling the blood sugar level and, as in most endocrine disorders, there is an autoimmune component.

Spiritual/Emotional Strongholds: Self-bitterness, anxiety, fear, fear of abandonment, and lack of trust in God.

Repent and renounce any of these strongholds in your life and generations, and break agreement with them.

References:

Podell, Richard. 1997. *Hypoglycemia's Hormonal Origin*. Robert Wood Johnson Medical School, New Brunswick, N.J.

Immunologic Idiopathic Thrombocytopenia Purpura

An autoimmune blood disorder characterized by a decrease in blood platelets due to the immune system attacking and destroying them. Bleeding of the gums, bruising, and bleeding of the digestive and urinary tracts are common symptoms of this disease. Females are affected three times more frequently than males.

Spiritual/Emotional Strongholds: Broken heart, rejection, self-rejection, self-hatred, guilt, and fear of rejection.

Repent and renounce any of these strongholds. Forgive those who have hurt you and separate them from their sin. Take responsibility for these strongholds in your generations and break agreement with them.

References:

Caldwell, Stephen H. et al. *Guidelines for Idiopathic Thrombocytopenic Purpura*. Annals of Internal Medicine, October 1, 1997. University of Virginia, Charlottesville, VA 22908.

Immunologic Idiopathic Thrombocytopenic Purpura. Merck Manual 16th Edition Ch. 96 p. 1211.

Immunologic Idiopathic Thrombocytopenic Purpura. National Institute of Health Publication No. 90-2114 NIDDK.

Infertility

About 2.1 million American women meet the criteria for infertility. It is defined as the inability to conceive (no pregnancy for twelve months without contraceptive use).

The psychological model that has been taught for years is that a women's unconscious conflict causes fertility problems (Kipper and Zadik 1996). Research on the links between a variety of psychological variables (neuroticism, coping styles, depressive symptoms, distress, and intense and prolonged exercise) supports the association of these factors with infertility (Kendall 2002).

There are many factors that may contribute to this disorder such as, hormonal imbalance, infections (STDs), autoimmune diseases (hypothyroidism, endometriosis, diabetes), tumors, aging, cysts, scarring of fallopian tubes, alcohol, smoking, drugs, obesity, varicoceles in men (varicose veins in the scrotum), high prolactin in men and women, and anti-sperm antibodies. Forty percent of infertility is due to the male. Cigarette smoke, car exhaust, drugs, cocaine, marijuana, some antibiotics and antihypertensive medications, steroids, anti-gout medications and other substances decrease sperm counts. Infertility in male or female is considered to be an autoimmune condition (McCance 1998).

Spiritual/Emotional Strongholds: Fear, anxiety, addictions, fornication, self-hatred, guilt, and depression.

Repent and renounce any of these issues if applicable and break agreement with them. Take responsibility for them in your generations and break their power over you.

References:

Infertility. DS00310 August 08, 2001 © 1998-2002 Mayo Foundation for Medical Education and Research (MFMER).

Endocrinology and Male Infertility. The Hormone Foundation and The Endocrine Society.

Female Infertility. Sexual Health Channel Health Communities.

Insomnia

The inability to sleep even when tired. Often people suffering with depression and anxiety disorders have insomnia. Negative emotions can cause an imbalance in the hypothalamus and pineal gland, producing melatonin, thus causing insomnia. Caffeine, nicotine, alcohol, and some prescription medications contribute to insomnia. It is more common among the elderly and in women.

Spiritual/Emotional Strongholds: Fear, anxiety, depression, unforgiveness, occultism, and lack of trust in God. Unforgiveness and occultism open the door for night torments.

Repent and renounce these strongholds and break agreement with them. Take responsibility for these strongholds and cast them out.

References:

Bentley, Alice. *Insomnia*. Chairperson for Sleep Society of South Africa.

Insulin Resistance Syndrome

Insulin resistance is a reduced sensitivity in the tissues of the body to the action of insulin. Insulin brings glucose into tissues to be used as a source of energy. The pancreas works overtime to keep up with this high demand for insulin, and diabetes occurs when the pancreas fails to sustain this increased insulin secretion. One half of patients with essential hypertension are insulin resistant. Obesity and high cholesterol levels are also linked to this syndrome. (See diabetes profile.)

Spiritual/Emotional Strongholds: Fear, self-rejection, self-anger, and depression.

Repent and renounce any of these strongholds, including unbelief, and break agreement with them. Take responsibility for them and break their power over you.

References:

Marks, Jennifer B. *The Insulin Resistance Syndrome*. Wound Care Institute Miami FL. University of Miami School of Medicine.

Interstitial Cystitis (IC)

IC is a chronic autoimmune inflammatory condition of the bladder that causes frequent, urgent, and painful urination and pelvic discomfort. It occurs eight times more often in women than men. Onset is usually before the age of forty.

Spiritual/Emotional Strongholds: Self-bitterness, guilt, and insecurity.

Repent and renounce any of these strongholds, including unbelief, and break agreement with them.

Reference:

Interstitial Cystitis. Women Health Channel.

Carley, Michael E. *Urongynecology*. Mayo Clinic, Rochester, MN.

Intracranial Hemorrhage

A rupture of a cranial blood vessel (aneurysm) commonly due to hypertension. Congenital defects, tumors, blood clots, and trauma are some other causes. These hemorrhages (bleeding) usually begin abruptly with headache, neurologic deficits, and coma. The severity of the symptoms depends on the size of the area of the brain affected. Incidence increases in individuals over the age of 55.

Spiritual/Emotional Strongholds: Anger, fear, anxiety, and rage.

Repent and renounce any of these strongholds, including unbelief, and break agreement with them. Take responsibility for these strongholds in your generations and break their power off of you.

References:

Liebeskind, David S. *Intracranial Hemorrhage*. eMedicine.com. Department of Neurology, Comprehensive Stroke Center, University of Pennsylvania.

Iritis

Inflammation of the iris, the colored part of the eye. Symptoms are light sensitivity, severe eye pain, tearing, blurred vision, and red eye. Infections, autoimmune diseases and injury are a few of the causes of this disease.

Spiritual/Emotional Strongholds: Anxiety, fear, self-hatred, guilt, and critical spirit.

Repent and renounce any of these strongholds, including unbelief. Take responsibility for these in your life and generations and break agreement with them.

References:

Davis, Elizabeth A. *Iritis*. Massachusetts Eye and Ear Infirmary, Harvard Medical School, Boston, MA

Irritable Bowel Syndrome (IBS)

IBS is described as a functional disorder because there is no agreement on structural abnormality. It is clinically defined as recurrent abdominal tenderness. Accompanied by diarrhea, constipation, or alternating diarrhea and constipation that is present for at least three months or longer. It is diagnosed after medical tests have ruled out inflammatory bowl disease, lactose intolerance, malabsorption, intestinal parasites, and other rare gastrointestinal diseases (Kendall 2002).

Many psychological and psychiatric disturbances are found among IBS patients. It has long been recognized that IBS patients, as a group, are somewhat psychologically distressed and thus score higher on various anxiety or personality inventory tests (Kendall 2002). For the most part, these studies found primary affective disorder, anxiety and fears. A possible explanation for the high levels of psychological distress and psychiatric disorders found in IBS patients is the role of early physical and sexual abuse. Various studies have found that over fifty percent of IBS patients have suffered physical and/or sexual abuse (Drossman 1990). The more severe the IBS is, the more likely it is to find abuse and more severe psychological disturbances. Medical textbooks list this as an anxiety and stress disorder (McCance 1998).

Spiritual/Emotional Strongholds: Anxiety, fear, unforgiveness, bitterness, trauma, and depression.

RECURRENT ABDOMINAL PAIN (RAP) IN CHILDREN

RAP is usually a precursor to IBS. RAP is defined as at least three episodes of stomach pain occurring within three months that are severe enough to affect the child's activities (Apley 1958). Thirteen to seventeen percent of school age children experience abdominal pain at least weekly (Hymas 1995). A recent review article investigated the similarities between IBS and RAP and noted many common factors, including the prevalence of psychological and psychiatric family symptoms, and a family history of stressful life events (Burke 1999).

Spiritual/Emotional Strongholds: Anxiety, fear (especially fear of abandonment), fear of rejection, and insecurity.

Repent and renounce any of these strongholds, including unbelief, and break agreement with them. Take responsibility for these strongholds in your life and generations.

References:

Salt II, William B. *Irritable Bowel Syndrome and the Mind-Body/Brain-Gut Connection.* ISBN: 0965703894.

About Irritable Bowel Syndrome. International Foundation for Functional Gastrointestinal Disorders, Inc.

Kidney Stones

A stone formed in the kidney due to excess minerals, excess oxalates in the diet, metabolic and genetic disorders, addictive exercisering and dieting, dehydration (coffee, soda, and alcohol drinkers are prone to dehydration), and diuretics. Kidney stones are usually made mostly of calcium. They are extremely painful and more common in Caucasian men.

University of Kuopio physician Olavi Kajander's research shows that newly discovered microbes called nano-bacteria (extremely small) may be the cause of kidney stones. These bacteria sometimes grow a hard, grayish-brown shell composed of a compound of calcium. Calcium builds up, layer on layer, on the outer layer of the bacteria's lilliputian armor, forming a stone. The bacteria were found in every stone that he examined.

Spiritual/Emotional Strongholds: Self-bitterness, self-rejection, anxiety, and fear.

Repent and renounce any of these strongholds, including unbelief, and break agreement with them. Take responsibility for them and break their power over you.

References:

UCLA Kidney Stone Treatment Center.

Lactose Intolerance

The intolerance results in the inability to digest significant amounts of lactose, the predominant sugar of milk. Common symptoms are nausea, bloating, cramps and diarrhea, which occur about thirty minutes after eating or drinking foods that contain lactose. As many as seventy-five percent of African-Americans and American Indians are lactose intolerant. This is an allergy to milk and milk products. (See allergy profile)

Spiritual/Emotional Strongholds: Inherited rejection, fear of rejection and abandonment, and bitterness.

Repent and renounce any of these strongholds, including unbelief, and break agreement with them. Forgive those who have rejected you and separate them from their sins. Take authority over these strongholds and break their power over your life.

References:

Dr. Minocha, *Lactose Intolerance*, Division of Digestive Diseases, University of Mississippi Medical Center in Jackson, MS.

Leaky Gut Syndrome

A disorder of the intestinal wall where the epithelium becomes more permeable (porous) due to inflammation and irritation, allowing toxins and undigested proteins to flow into the blood stream. The inflammation that causes the leaky gut syndrome also damages the protective coating of the gut. This compromises the immune system, the lymphatic system, the endocrine system and the liver. This makes the body less resistant to viruses, bacteria, parasites, and candida. Additionally, the immune system makes antibodies against the molecules (foods) that leak through the gut into the bloodstream. This creates an inflammatory reaction when the specific food is consumed. Autoantibodies are thus created and inflammation becomes chronic, creating an autoimmune disease. For example, if the inflammation occurs at a joint, autoimmune arthritis (rheumatoid arthritis) develops. If it occurs in the brain, chronic fatigue syndrome may be the result. If the antibodies start attacking the gut, Crohn's disease may occur.

In this manner, LGS plays a role in chronic fatigue syndrome, Candidiasis, asthma, allergies, sinusitis, eczema, migraines, rheumatoid arthritis and inflammatory joint diseases, and others. Anxiety, fear, and the overuse of antibiotics and NSAIDS (non-steroidal anti-inflammatory drugs), alcohol, coffee, and refined carbohydrates all have contributed to the breakdown of the intestinal wall.

Spiritual/Emotional Strongholds: Self-hatred, fear, anxiety, and unbelief (i.e., Pharmakeia, dependence on drugs).

Repent and renounce any of these strongholds, including unbelief, and break agreement with them. Take responsibility for them in your generations and break their power over you.

References:

Fratkin, Jake Paul. *Leaky Gut Syndrome*. Great Smokies Diagnostic Laboratory (1998-2002).

Altered Immunity and The Leaky Gut Syndrome, Zoltan P Rona MD, Website.

Lewy Body Disease

Dementia caused by deposits (lewy bodies, named after Dr. Lewy in 1912) in the brain. These are eosinophilic (type of white blood cell) structures within the cytoplasm of neurons. Memory, language, the ability to judge distances, reasoning, and the ability to carry out simple tasks are affected. It progresses more quickly than Alzheimer's.

The main component in nervous system disease is really autoimmunity, which is a inappropriate immune response to the body's own organs (Singh 1994, 1997).

Spiritual/Emotional Strongholds: Fear, self-hatred, guilt, and occultism.

Repent and renounce any of these strongholds, including unbelief, and break agreement with them. Forgive yourself and others and separate them from their sin.

References:

Forno, L.S. *Pathology of Parkinson's disease: the importance of the substantia nigra and Lewy bodies.* Parkinson's Disease. Johns Hopkins University Press, 1990, p. 185-238

Lichen Planus

An autoimmune skin disorder producing flat purplish bumps with white lines or spots. They can be found anywhere on the body but are usually found on the ankles and wrists. Women are affected more than men. More severe forms of this disease are oral lichen planus, where there are painful, open sores in the mouth. Another type affects other mucous membranes such as the vagina. Lichen planus in the mucosal areas has a higher risk of becoming cancerous.

Spiritual/Emotional Strongholds: Bitterness, self-hatred, and guilt.

Repent and renounce these strongholds, including unbelief, and break agreement with them. Forgive those who have hurt you and separate them from their sins. Take authority over these strongholds and break their power off of you.

References:

Tsu-Yi Chuang, *Lichen Planus.* eMedicine.com.

Lupus

An autoimmune disease where the body's immune system attacks various connective tissues. The body lines up in agreement with the thoughts one has about themselves and seeks to attack and destroy itself. There are two types: discoid lupus, which only affects the skin, and SLE. SLE, or systemic lupus erythematosus, which affects multiple systems in the body including vital organs, joints, skin and the nervous system. It is ninety percent more common in women (especially, minority women), than in men. It is more prevalent among African-American, Hispanic and Asian populations. Hypertension is a risk factor.

Spiritual/Emotional Strongholds: Self-hatred, self-conflict, guilt, and performance.

Renounce and repent for any of these strongholds including unbelief, in your life and generations. Forgive those who have hurt you and separate them from their sins. Take responsibility for your responses and come out of agreement with these strongholds.

References:

Lahita, Robert G. *Lupus Cause and definition.* Lupus Foundation of America. St. Vincent's Medical Center. New York Medical College 153 West 11th Street New York, NY 10011.

Lyme Disease

A disease carried by a tick-borne spirochete, BB (Borrelia Burgdorferi). It transmits bacteria, resulting in a multi-system inflammatory disease. It begins with a large bull's-eye red rash, fever, fatigue, facial paralysis, headache, tremors and swollen lymph nodes. The spirochete infects macrophages, binds to platelets and can hide in joints, tendons, white blood cells, skin and the brain. It can set off an autoimmune response, causing more damage. The blood brain barrier blocks white blood cells from entering the brain, and if the spirochete has a chance to enter the brain, it can cause encephalitis (brain infection). Later symptoms may include joint pain, cardiac, and brain symptoms.

Spiritual/Emotional Strongholds: Fear, anxiety, self-hatred, and guilt.

Repent and renounce these strongholds including unbelief and break agreement with it. Take authority over it and break its power over you.

References:

Why Is Chronic Lyme Borreliosis Chronic? Pub Med Clinical Infectious Diseases 1997; 25 (supp. 1): 564-70.

Malabsorption

The inability of the stomach and intestines to absorb enough nutrients. An alarm or fight-flight reaction results in nerve impulses being sent from the brain that stimulate the adrenal glands to release the neurotransmitters, stimulating the sympathetic nervous system. When the sympathetic nervous system is stimulated, blood sugar is raised to make it readily available for fuel. In addition, the heart beats faster, the lungs breathe more rapidly, the eyes dilate, and blood is sent to organs such as the brain and muscles that are essential for fight or flight. Organs that are not needed in such an emergency are essentially shut down. These would include the liver, spleen, and digestive organs (Jacobson 2000). When the GI system shuts down it receives less blood and therefore absorption of nutrients is diminished.

Spiritual/Emotional Strongholds: Fear and anxiety.

Repent and renounce any of these strongholds. Take responsibility for not taking better care of your temple. Take authority over these strongholds and break their power over you. Trust in the living God and walk in peace.

Masturbation

While we do not attribute a specific disease to this behavior, we believe that it is a sin, primarily because of the guilt and shame that almost always follows the action.

We have learned that there are at least three entry points for this sin into our lives. First, a child growing up in an atmosphere full of tension and strife will get temporary relief by masturbating, but what comes in behind it are the feelings of uncleanness and guilt. Thus we have a vicious cycle of release and condemnation. Masturbation and cocaine are very similar in their spiritual implications; there is a release, fulfillment and guilt. And both are psychologically addicting. Second, Some children learn through abuse. Sometimes the abuse is overt for the satisfaction of the abuser and other times it is less overt. Some parents masturbate their children to quiet or soothe them. As disgusting as this may sound, the parent probably learned it from their parents. The child then learns to do it himself. A third entry point is from the sin of the parents. If they are involved in this activity, the spirits or sins are passed on to the children.

The remedy is a two-step process. First the parents must deal with the sin in their lives. They need to repent for this sin in their life and in their generations, break the soul tie with themselves, and cast out the spirits of sexual perversion. Then the parent can help their child. In doing this, they need to repent to the child for the generational sin (in appropriate words), cast out the spirits of sexual perversion, and then bless the child with a father's and a mother's blessing if possible.

Memory Loss

Short term memory loss due to acute or chronic stress which releases an over-secretion of cortisol. High levels of cortisol damage the neurons in the hippocampus (memory center of the brain), which causes memory loss.

Spiritual/Emotional Strongholds: Fear, anxiety, worry, and severe trauma.

Repent and renounce these strongholds in your lives and break agreement with them. Take responsibility for them and break their power over you.

References:

Flood, J.F. and Roberts, E. *Dehydroepiandrosterone sulfate improves memory in aging mice.* Brain Res 1988 448(1):178-181.

Jacobson, M.D. 2000. *The Word on Health.* Moody Press, Chicago, Ill.

Menière's Disease

A disorder of the inner ears that causes dizziness, ringing in the ear, pressure in the ear and hearing loss. Hereditary factors, viruses, and allergies are some contributors to this disease. There also is an autoimmune component involved. There is an increase of immunoglobulins found in the endolymphatic fluid.

Spiritual/Emotional Strongholds: Fear, anxiety, self-hatred, and occultism.

Repent and renounce any of these strongholds, including unbelief, in your lives and generations and break agreement with them. Take responsibility for these and break their power over you.

References:

Dickens, J. and Graham, S.S. *Menière's disease—1983-1989.* American Journal of Otology 1990 11: 51-65.

Menopause

During menopause, estrogen production in the ovaries ceases. Throughout the fertile part of a woman's life the ovaries are the primary source of estrogen and proges-terone. In addition, the adrenal glands produce both. When a woman enters menopause, the ovaries dramatically reduce the production of estrogen and progesterone. Then, as in men, the adrenal glands become the primary source for estrogen and progesterone. The adrenal glands are also a principal stress organ. Under prolonged stress, the adrenal glands produce excessive amounts of adrenaline and cortisol, and do so at the expense of estrogen and progesterone (Jacobson Jan. 2001). The resulting reduction in estrogen can lead to symptoms such as hot flashes, sweating, pounding of the heart (palpitations), increased irritability, anxiety, depression, and brittle bones (osteoporosis).

Perimenopause refers to the hormonal changes that take place in some women in the ten years prior to menopause. Hormonal changes and fluctuations affect brain chemicals (serotonin), causing mood changes. Symptoms include irregular periods, breast tenderness, sleep changes, depression, worsening PMS, and decreased libido. If a woman has had PMS, then she will probably have menopause troubles. See the PMS profile.

The administration of estrogen hormone replacement therapy (HRT) has been thought to alleviate those symptoms. Recent studies show that hormone replacement therapy increases the risk of heart disease and certain types of cancer (breast and endometrial).

The Women's Health Initiative (WHI), begun in 1991 by the National Institutes of Health, is one of the largest studies of women's health ever undertaken. More than 160,000 post-menopausal women, ages 50 to 79, were recruited into a variety of trials designed to find the best ways to prevent heart disease, breast and colorectal cancers, and osteoporosis.

Thanks to the study's rigid design, most doctors view the WHI as the definitive word on women's health. Final results were due out—and eagerly awaited—in 2005. But one part of the study, involving more than 16,000 women was stopped early. These women were taking a combination of estrogen and progestins.

Researchers concluded that the risks of HRT clearly outweighed the benefits. WHI reported a twenty-two percent increase in heart disease and a twenty-six percent greater risk of breast cancer. Though HRT may still be appropriate as a short-term therapy for menopausal distress, women cannot expect it to protect them in the long term against aging-related diseases (*Time Magazine*, "The Truth about Hormones," July 22, 2002).

More recent conclusions drawn from the WHI demonstrate even more dramatic results. The *Journal of the American Medical Association* reported on June 25, 2003, that in addition to stimulating breast cancer, HRT so make tumors harder to detect, leading to dangerous delays in diagnosis. In women using HRT 25.4 percent had cancers that had begun to spread, compared with only sixteen percent in the placebo group (WHI 2002, 2003).

Women are also more likely to have changes in their breast tissue that lead to abnormal mammograms. 9.4 percent of those on HRT had abnormal mammograms. It is estimated that about 120,000 women each year, in the general population, have abnormal mammograms because of HRT. This leads to many additional mammograms, biopsies and other tests, not to mention the emotional strain.

The WHI study also found that hormone replacement therapy increased the risks of heart attack and stroke, which they were once thought to prevent. HRT also increased the likelihood of blood clots (*Anchorage Daily News*, "Hormones up cancer risk," June 25, 2003).

God designed the female body to enter menopause. He also designed the adrenal glands to produce an adequate amount of the necessary female hormones for this time of life. The problem is not menopause, but the anxiety and fear that many live in, that overwork the adrenal glands stopping or hindering the production of these hormones.

Spiritual/Emotional Strongholds: Fear, anxiety, worry, resentment (of being female), fear of aging, abandonment, self-hatred, guilt, and self-condemnation.

Repent and renounce any of these strongholds in your life and generations. Take responsibility for them and break their power over you.

References:

Chiang, Jeanne. *What is perimenopause?* The Healing Center for Perimenopause.

Green, Laurie. *Perimenopause.* WebMD

Menorrhagia (Heavy Uterine Bleeding)

Heavy uterine bleeding has many different causes including hereditary diseases. Other causes are stress, fibroids, IUDs, obesity, thyroid disease, an imbalance of progesterone and estrogen, an increase in vasodilators and endothelins, decrease in vitamin K, smoking, and excessive alcohol use.

Spiritual/Emotional Strongholds: Anxiety, fear, self-conflict about female issues, performance, addictions, and guilt.

Repent and renounce any of these strongholds, including unbelief, and come out of agreement with them. Take responsibility for not taking better care of your temple. Take responsibility for these strongholds in your life and generations and break their power over you.

References:

Menstrual Disorders Menorrhagia: When periods are too much. Gynecological Health Center.org.

Miscarriage (recurrent) or Recurrent Spontaneous Abortion (RSA)

About fifteen to twenty percent of all pregnancies result in miscarriage, and the risk of pregnancy loss increases with each successive pregnancy loss. For example, in a first pregnancy the risk of miscarriage is eleven to thirteen percent. In a pregnancy immediately following that loss, the risk of miscarriage is thirteen to seventeen percent. But the risk to a third pregnancy after two successive losses nearly triples to thirty-eight percent.

New research indicates that as many as eighty percent of "unexplained" losses may be attributable to immunological factors.

There are two major reasons for recurrent spontaneous abortion (RSA), or miscarriage. One is that there is something wrong with the pregnancy itself, such as a chromosomal abnormality that curtails embryonic development. The other cause of RSA, and the category into which immunological problems fall, is an environmental barrier to pregnancy (something wrong with the environment in which the fetus grows). These are the autoimmune factors.

The immunologic causes for pregnancy loss and implantation failure are the result of abnormalities in antibody responses. These responses fall into two categories: autoimmune and alloimmune.

There are four different autoimmune problems that can cause RSA. A woman may have one or more of these underlying problems: antiphospholipid antibodies, antithyroid antibodies, antinuclear antibodies, or lupus-like anticoagulant. Thirty percent of women with "unexplained" RSA will test positive for an autoimmune problem.

There are two possible reasons that women with alloimmune problems may lose their pregnancy in miscarriage: Either their immune system is not recognizing the pregnancy, or they develop an abnormal immunologic response to the pregnancy.

Alloimmune diseases occur when the immune system of one individual produces an immunologic reaction (antibodies) against tissues of another individual. Examples would be blood transfusions, skin grafts, or to a developing baby during pregnancy (Rh incompatibility) (McCance 1998).

Spiritual/Emotional Strongholds: Self-hatred, bitterness, resentment (of being pregnant), hatred (toward the baby), and guilt.

Repent and renounce any of these strongholds in your life or generations. Forgive those who have hurt you and separate them from their sins. Forgive yourself for hurting yourself and your child, and believe what God says about you.

Reference:

Coulam, Carolyn B. and Hemenway, Nancy P. *Immunology May Be Key To Pregnancy Loss*.1999 The International Council on Infertility Information Dissemination, Inc. P.O. Box 6836 Arlington, Virginia 22206. Phone: (703) 379-9178. FAX: (703) 379-1593. Email: mailto:nancy@inciid.org.

Mixed Connective Tissue Disease

An autoimmune disease with an "overlap" to other connective tissue disorders such as lupus, rheumatoid arthritis, scleroderma and polymyositis. This disorder may be caused by heredity, hormones, or an over-active immune system. It is more common in females.

Spiritual/Emotional Strongholds: Severe self-hatred, bitterness, resentment, and guilt.

Repent and renounce any of these strongholds in your life or generations and come out of agreement with them. Forgive those who have hurt you and separate them from their sins. Forgive yourself for hurting yourself and believe what God says about you.

Reference:

Klein-Gitelman, Marisa S. *Mixed Connective Tissue Disorder*. EMedicine.com., Department of Pediatrics, Northwestern University and Children's Memorial Hospital.

Multiple Sclerosis

A progressive autoimmune central nervous system disorder where the body's immune system attacks and destroys the myelin sheath. Myelin is the insulating sheath surrounding and protecting the nerves. Symptoms may include numbness of the feet and legs, memory loss, blurred vision, loss of bladder control, and spastic muscles. Some contributing factors for this disorder may be vitamin B-12 deficiency, heredity, and viruses. It usually occurs between the ages of 20-40 and affects women twice as much as men.

The main component in nervous system disease is really autoimmunity. If you examine central nervous system diseases closely, you will find that for almost each condition there is a suspicion of autoimmune process involvement. In some diseases such as MS, there is a large body of research to support this (Singh 1994, 1997).

Spiritual/Emotional Strongholds: Rejection (often by the father), self-hatred, guilt, and depression.

Repent and renounce any of these strongholds and break agreement with them. Take responsibility for them in your generations and break their power over you. Forgive those who have hurt you and separate them from their sins.

References:

Charcot, J.M. and Sigerson, G. *Lectures on the diseases of the nervous system* (delivered 1988). London: New Sydenham Society, 1st series, lect 6.

Myasthenia Gravis

An autoimmune neuromuscular disorder resulting from a genetic abnormality characterized by muscle weakness and fatigue. The body's immune system attacks its own acetylcholine receptors, interrupting nerve transmissions to the muscles. Ten percent of the patients with myasthenia gravis have a tumor on their thymus gland. MG occurs in men more often than in women. Onset is usually past age 50. Initial symptoms are posies (drooping eyelids), difficulty swallowing, and fatigue.

Spiritual/Emotional Strongholds: Self-bitterness, guilt, grief, fear, and anxiety.

Repent and renounce any of these strongholds in your life, including unbelief, and break agreement with them. Forgive those who have hurt you and separate them from their sins.

Reference:

Howard, James F. Jr. *Myasthenia Gravis–A Summary*. Department of Neurology The University of North Carolina at Chapel Hill.

Narcolepsy

A neurological disorder that affects the control of sleep. There is an intrusion of REM sleep during wakefulness (i.e., drowsiness and sleep during daytime). About 125,000 people in the U.S. suffer from this disease. There may also be cataplexy (a sudden loss of muscle tone brought on by strong emotions such as, laughter, anger or surprise) and hallucinations (Taber 1997). Recently researchers have found two neuro-transmitters, hypocretin 1 and 2, that are deficient in this disorder. The main component in nervous system disease is really autoimmunity, which is an inapproriate immune response to the body's own organs (Singh 1994, 1997).

Spiritual/Emotional Strongholds: Anxiety, fears, self-bitterness, occultism (Free-masonry), and deaf and dumb spirit.

Repent and renounce any of these strongholds, including unbelief, in your life or generations and break agreement with them. Take responsibility for them and break their power over you.

References:

Mignot, Emmanuel. *Narcolepsy Caused by Damage to Hypocretin System.* Stanford University Medical School.

Narcolepsy. Sleep Channel. Harvey A.J. Hopkins, Alegent Health Sleep and Breathing Disorder Laboratory Omaha, NE.

Osteoporosis

A chronic disorder that is characterized by low bone mass and fragility fractures. In women over 50, it is often due to depletion of estrogen postmenopausally. Other risk factors include smoking, alcohol, poor diet, and lack of exercise. Younger women can have osteoporosis due to lack of vitamin D and calcium in their diets, thyroid and parathyroid imbalances. The negative emotions of envy and depression play a large role (Michelson 1996).

Spiritual/Emotional Strongholds: Anxiety, fear, envy, self-bitterness, low self-esteem, and depression.

Repent and renounce any of these strongholds in your lives or generations. Take responsibility for them and break their power over you.

References:

Oncken, Cheryl. *Study Zeros in on Smoking's Bone Thinning Link.* Reuters Health University of Connecticut Health Center in Farmington.

Osteoporosis in Young Women. Gannett Cornell University Health Services.

Pancreatitis (Chronic)

An inflammation of the pancreas, usually due to pancreatic enzymes auto-digesting the gland. It is usually due to long term alcohol abuse, gallstones blocking a duct, or it can be inherited. The result is the destruction of the pancreas. Severe abdominal pain, fever, jaundice, swelling, and nausea are the main symptoms. The inflammation and the auto-digesting indicate an autoimmune response.

Spiritual/Emotional Strongholds: Addictions, self-bitterness, pride, and insecurity.

Repent and renounce any of these strongholds, including unbelief, and break agreement with them. Take responsibility for them in your generations and break their power over you.

References:

Khoury, Ghattas. *Pancreatitis*, eMedicine., American University of Beirut.

Parasites

Parasites are organisms that obtain food and shelter by living on or within another organism. Parasites that live within the body are called endoparasites. Individuals with compromised immune systems are most susceptible. Parasite infections typically stimulate more than one immunological defense mechanism depending upon the kind of parasite involved (Roitt 1985). Amebiasis is an infestation of an intestinal parasite resulting in abdominal pain, bloody stools, and weight loss. The infection is acquired by the fecal-oral route, either by person-to-person contact or indirectly, by eating or drinking fecally contaminated food or water. In some cases, the parasites invade the intestinal mucosa, entering the blood stream and affecting the liver. Parasites can cause other diseases such as meningitis.

Spiritual/Emotional Strongholds: Fear, anxiety, and other negative emotions or thoughts.

Repent and renounce any of these strongholds and break agreement with them.

References:

Parasitology Department of Pathology and Microbiology University of South Carolina School of Medicine.

Parkinson's Syndrome

A chronic progressive disorder of the nervous system resulting in motor system dysfunction. It is caused by the lack of dopamine with a subsequent increase in acetyl-choline in the brain. Dopamine is a neurotransmitter responsible for transmitting messages in the brain that control movement of the body. Glutamate and nitric oxide are two neurotransmitters that cause radical stress on dopaminergic neurons. People with Parkinson's have difficulty walking, talking and performing simple tasks. Early onset Parkinson's is the more rare form which occurs before the age of 50 and is usually inherited. Late onset Parkinson's is much more common and is usually not inherited.

The main component in nervous system disease is really autoimmunity, which is an innappropriate immune response to the body's own organs (Singh 1994, 1997).

Spiritual/Emotional Strongholds: Inherited rejection (usually by the father), fear of rejection, occultism, and hopelessness.

Repent and renounce any of these strongholds in your life, including unbelief, and break agreement with them. Take responsibility for these strongholds in your generations and break their power over you.

References:

Parkinson's Disease, National Institute of Neurological Disorders and Stroke.

Pericarditis (Idiopathic)

An inflammation of the pericardium which is the thin fibrous sac around the heart. In most patients, no specific cause can be found. An autoimmune response is a factor. Symptoms include chest pain that radiates to the shoulder and neck, difficulty breathing, swelling of the ankles, fatigue, anxiety, and fever with increased white blood cells. It is more common in men than women. Inflammation can be a marker for an improper immune response (Singh 1994, 1997).

Spiritual/Emotional Strongholds: Anxiety, fear of failure, self-hatred, and guilt.

Repent and renounce any of this strongholds, including unbelief, in your life. Take responsibility for these in your life and generations and break their power over you.

References:

Pericarditis. Asia Medicine.net Wearnes Biotech and Medicals 1998 Pte Ltd.

Phobic or Fear and Anxiety Disorders

In an earlier chapter, we listed many different diseases caused by anxieties and fears. They are not to be confused with the specific phobic, or fear and anxiety disorders discussed in this section. Those diseases are the result of these phobias and many other forms of anxiety and fear. The description of these disorders is taken from Healthandage.com.

A phobic or anxiety disorder is an excessive inappropriate aroused state characterized by feelings of apprehension, uncertainty, or fear. The word is derived from the Latin word, *angere*, which means to choke or strangle. The anxiety response is often not attributable to a real threat; nevertheless it can still paralyze the individual into inaction or withdrawal. The threat or stressor can be removed simply by how we choose to react or respond. Forgiveness resolves and removes most threats.

Anxiety disorders have been classified according the severity and duration of their symptoms and specific behavioral characteristics. The categories include:

- Generalized Anxiety Disorder (GAD), which is long-lasting and low-grade.
- Panic disorder or panic attacks, which have more dramatic symptoms.
- Phobias.
- Obsessive-compulsive disorder (OCD).
- Post-traumatic stress disorder (PTSD).
- Separation anxiety disorder (nearly always in children).

Let's look at each of these individually.

GENERALIZED ANXIETY DISORDER (GAD)

Generalized Anxiety Disorder or GAD is the most common and least severe anxiety disorder. It affects about five percent of Americans over the course of their life. It is characterized by a constant state of worry. While not as severe as that in panic attacks, sufferers may experience anxiety physically, such as stomach complaints, in addition to the mental worry.

A diagnosis of GAD is confirmed if three or more of the following symptoms are present (only one for children) on most days for six months: being on edge or very restless, feeling tired, having difficulty concentrating, being irritable, having muscle tension, or experiencing sleep disturbances.

PANIC DISORDER OR PANIC ATTACKS

Panic disorder is characterized by periodic attacks of anxiety or terror. They usually last fifteen to thirty minutes although residual effect can persist much longer. The frequency and severity of the anxiety determine the diagnosis. A diagnosis of panic disorder is made under the following conditions: A person experiences at least two recurrent, unexpected panic attacks and there is a fear that another one will occur.

The symptoms of a panic attack include a rapid heart beat, sweating, shakiness, shortness of breath, a choking feeling, dizziness, nausea, feelings of unreality, numbness, hot flashes or chills, chest pain, fear of dying, and fear of going insane. Panic attacks can be triggered spontaneously or in response to a particular situation. Recalling or re-experiencing even harmless circumstances surrounding an original attack may trigger subsequent attacks.

PHOBIAS

Phobic disorders are manifested by overwhelming and irrational fears. In most cases, people can overcome them, but often they are incapacitating. There are several kinds of phobias:

Agorophobia is the fear of open spaces. In its severest form, it is a paralyzing terror of being in places or situations from which there neither escape nor help.

Social phobia (also known as Social Anxiety Disorder) is the fear of being publicly scrutinized and humiliated and is manifested by extreme shyness and discomfort in social settings.

Specific phobias (or Simple Phobias) are an irrational fear of specific objects or situations. Specific phobias are among the most common medical disorders. They would include fear of confined spaces, dentists, storms, tunnels, animals, snakes, etc.

OBSESSIVE-COMPULSIVE DISORDER (OCD)

Obsessive-Compulsive Disorder, or OCD, has been described as an over-inflated sense of responsibility in which a person's thoughts center on possible dangers and an urgent need to do something about it. The obsessions are recurrent or persistent mental images, thoughts, or ideas. The thoughts or images can range from mundane worries about whether one has locked a door, to bizarre and frightening fantasies. Obsessive behaviors are repetitive, rigid, and self-prescribed routines. These acts might include the repeated checking to see that the door was locked, stove shut off, calling a loved one, washing of the hands, or continued cleaning.

Recent research is also referring to OCD as an autoimmune disease. When treated with immune enhancing drugs, the OCD effect diminishes or even completely subsides for a time (Singh 1997). Dr. Singh's work with OCD includes the work of Dr. Susan Swedo's group regarding strep infection. They were administering an immune therapy known as plasmapheresis, when they observed an association between group A streptococcus infection and OCD. While providing therapy to address the infection, it was found that the patient's OCD symptoms were reduced by plasmapheresis. Subsequent studies with intravenous immunoglobulin treatment (IVIG) have also shown positive responses.

Dr. Singh also reports on a pilot study of OCD patients he conducted with a psychiatrist, Dr. Gregory Hanna, at the University of Michigan. They found that patients with OCD may have antibodies to brain serotonin receptors. Dr. Singh's research shows that the main component in all nervous system disease is really autoimmunity, which is an inappriapriate immune response to the body's own organs (Singh 1994, 1997). Other research is demonstrating that the cause is related to peer pressure, family factors such as criticism, low self-esteem, and identity problems (Polivy 2002).

References:

Obsessive Compulsive Disorder. National Institutes of Health (NIH). 9000 Rockville Pike, Bethesda, Maryland 20892.

OCD profile includes several disorders:

BODY DYSMORPHIC DISORDER (BDD)

People with Body Dysmorphic Disorder or BDD are obsessed with the belief that they are ugly, or part of their body is abnormally shaped. There is extreme self-consciousness over some perceived physical flaw, seen often in adolescents. Recent research shows that there is a chemical imbalance in the brain (serotonin) that has been found to cause this obsession (Polivy 2002). Self-hatred, guilt, and shame restrict the production of serotonin. Multiple surgeries and excessive weight lifting are common with this disorder. In some cases, it may interfere with normal functioning in school and on the job. In more severe cases, there can be major depressive episodes and suicide attempts.

Spiritual/Emotional Strongholds: Inherited self-hatred, self-mutilation (tattoos and body piercing), low self-esteem, self-deception, and fear of rejection.

Repent and renounce the thoughts these strongholds bring, and break agreement with them. Take responsibility for your wrong beliefs and break their power over you.

References:

Thompson, K. 1990. *Exacting Beauty: Theory, Assessment, and Treatment of Body Image Disturbance*. Pergamon Press.

Phillips, K.A. *Body Dysmorphic Disorder: Clinical Aspects and Treatment Strategies*. Butler Dysmorphic Disorder Program, Butler Hospital, Providence, RI.

TRICHOTILLOMANIA

People with trichotillomania continually pull their hair, leaving bald spots.

TOURETTE'S SYNDROME

Symptoms of Tourette's Syndrome include jerky movements, tics, and uncontrollably uttering obscene words. Dr. Singh teaches that OCD, autism, Tourette's syndrome, and many other neurological disorders are related an autoimmune response. His research shows that the main component in nervous system disease is really auto-immunity, which is a inappropriate immune response, to the body's own organs (Singh 1997).

References:

A Description of Tourette's Syndrome. National Institute of Neurological Disorders and Stroke. National Institutes of Health, Bethesda, MD 20892, NIH Publication No. 95-2163

OBSESSIVE-COMPULSIVE PERSONALITY (OCP)

Obsessive-Compulsive Personality, or OCP, should not be confused with obsessive-compulsive disorder (OCD). OCP is defined by certain character traits such as perfectionism, excessive self-consciousness, moral rigidity, or preoccupation with rules and order. These traits do not necessarily occur in people with OCD.

POST-TRAUMATIC STRESS DISORDER (PTSD)

Post-Traumatic Stress Disorder or PTSD is an extreme and usually chronic, emotional reaction to a traumatic event that severely impairs one's life. It is classified as an anxiety disorder because of the similarity of symptoms. PTSD is triggered by violent or traumatic events that are usually outside the norm of human experience. The symptoms are the same whether the triggering event is a violent action or natural disaster. The event may include sexual assaults, accidents, combat, natural disaster, and unexpected deaths. PTSD may also occur in people who have serious illnesses and receive aggressive treatments, or who have close family member or friends with such conditions.

ACUTE STRESS DISORDER

This is a mild form of PTSD. Warning symptoms for acute stress disorder usually occur within two days to four weeks after exposure to a traumatic event. The response is one of fear, helplessnes, or horror. It is also followed by emotional numbness, being in a daze, a sense of losing contact with reality, a feeling of loss of self or identity, or the loss of ability to remember aspects of the event. These symptoms indicate a psychological state known as dissociation.

People with this disorder persistently re-experience the trauma in images, thoughts, flashbacks, dreams, or feelings. They avoid reminders of the event, such as thoughts, people, or other reminders. They have symptoms of anxiety or heightened awareness of danger which may involve sleeplessness, irritability, being easily startled, or becoming overly vigilant. Their emotional state impairs normal functioning and relationships.

Symptoms of full-blown PTSD can occur months after the event. They last beyond a month, are much more severe, and they are chronic. Other symptoms include withdrawal, extreme avoidance of any reminder of the event, hopelessness, self-destructive behavior, personality changes, mood swings, difficulty sleeping, other anxiety disorders, and guilt over surviving the event.

References:

Post Traumatic Stress Disorder. National Mental Health Association.

Post Traumatic Disorder (PTSD). American Academy of Child and Adolescent Psychiatry (AACAP).

Facts About Post Traumatic Stress Disorder. National Institute of Mental Health.

The roots to all phobic or fear disorders are very similar. The root is unbelief, because fear is the opposite of faith. In these and many other fears, we have chosen not to trust God. God has not given us a spirit of fear, but of love, peace, power, and a sound mind (II Timothy 1:7). An unsound mind is the fruit of disobedience. The fear that is associated with these disorders is the opposite of faith. Fear and faith are opposites. One will always replace the other. Satan is the master counterfeiter and he will always take what God has meant for good and distort it for his purposes.

The dictionary defines fear as, "the emotion of being afraid, of feeling that danger or evil is near, an uneasy or anxious thought." Synonyms are dread, alarm, or worry. Dread is defined as "a great fear."

Fear can warn us of danger so that we can protect ourselves. If we are standing next to a cliff, it warns us to be careful. In times of danger, fear also creates a fight-flight response in our bodies in which the adrenal glands secrete large amounts of adrenaline and cortisol causing several different physiological responses in our bodies. The primary one is an increase in strength. But many live in a constant state of fight-flight, as they think about the things that have happened to them. The oversecretion of adrenaline and cortisol will destroy the immune system and damage the body in many ways. Dwelling on the memories from the past can lead to panic attacks and other phobic disorders.

Scripture teaches us that we are to fear God. This does not mean that we are to be afraid of Him. The Hebrew word used for this kind of fear is *yir'ah* (Strong's, 3374).

It means "to have reverence for God". He is the giver of every good and perfect gift. But all too many of us are afraid of Him. The Hebrew word for this kind of fear is *yare* (Strong's, 3372). It means "to cause to be frightened or to make afraid, or dread."

God the Father is love. In Matthew 22:37 Jesus said, "Thou shalt love the Lord thy God with all thy heart, and with all thy soul, and with all thy mind." We are to love God the Father, not be afraid of Him. God is the only one that loves each of us perfectly.

The Greek word *deilos,* translated "fear" in the New Testament, means "to dread; timid." By implication it means "faithless or fearful." Fear is equated with being faithless in Matthew 8:26, Mark 4:40, II Timothy 1:7, and Revelation 21:8. Matthew 8:26 illustrates this meaning. "And He saith unto them, Why are ye fearful, O ye of little faith? Then He arose, and rebuked the winds and the sea; and there was a great calm." Mark 4:40 says, "And He said unto them, Why are ye so fearful? How is it that ye have no faith?"

In my book, *Biblical Foundations of Freedom,* I establish the fact that this kind of fear is a sin and teach how to defeat it. We demonstrate what fear has done, and is doing to us, and how it functions. Being "afraid, uneasy, or anxious, and having great fear" can cause extreme problems spiritually, physically and mentally.

Spiritual/Emotional Strongholds: Trauma, fear, anxiety, worry, self-hatred, depression, guilt, and shame.

Repent for any and all fears. Command the various fears to go in Jesus' Name. Renounce any of these strongholds, including unbelief, and break agreement with them. Take responsibility for these in your life. Often the mind will bring back old memories from past traumas. Command the traumas to leave in the name of Jesus and ask the Holy Spirit to cleanse your mind of all the sights, sounds, feeling, smells, or tastes that are associated with the traumas in your life.

Polycystic Ovarian Syndrome

A complex hormonal disturbance affecting the entire body. There are usually high levels of male hormones (testosterone). Often there are high levels of prolactin and low levels of thyroid hormones. The resulting disorders include infertility, diabetes type 2, high cholesterol, hypertension, obesity, excessive hair growth, acne and menstrual cycle disturbances. These women are often in conflict over their femininity, and suffer low self-esteem.

Spiritual/Emotional Strongholds: Fear, victimization, self-conflict, guilt, and low self-esteem.

Repent and renounce any of these strongholds, including unbelief, and break agreement with them. Take responsibility for them and break their power over you.

References:

Polycystic Ovarian Syndrome (pcos). Mt. Auburn Obstetrics and Gynecologic Assoc.

Post-Lyme Disease Syndrome

A chronic inflammatory disease thought to be due to a "post-infectious immune phenomena" causing an over-reactive immune system without any evidence of the spirochetal infection. Symptoms include joint pain, fatigue, memory loss, headache, malaise, light sensitivity, stiff neck, and dizziness. Inflammation is evidence of an autoimmune response (Singh 1997).

Spiritual/Emotional Strongholds: Fear, doubt, unbelief, and self-hatred.

Repent and renounce any of these strongholds and break agreement with them. Take responsibility for these in your generations and break their power over you.

Reference:

Chronic Lyme Disease/Post-Lyme Syndrome. American Lyme Disease Foundation, Inc.

Postpartum Depression

The period following childbirth necessitates a range of psychological, social, and physical adjustments. The three depressive-spectrum phenomena in the postpartum period include postpartum blues, which involves mild symptoms; postpartum psychosis, which involves a psychotic episode, often with depressive features; and postpartum depression, with symptoms of a major depressive period (O'Hara 1990). The strongest predictors of postpartum depression are a history of mood disturbances before or during pregnancy, poor marital relationship, low social support, and the occurrence of stressful life events (Miller 1999, Nonacs and Cohen 1998). The long-held assumption that hormonal changes following childbirth cause postpartum depression is not supported (O'Hara 1994, Steiner 1998).

The major source of postpartum depression is the guilt and shame that some women feel when they do not experience idealized emotions about motherhood and feel they do not measure up to the selfless and sacrificing model of motherhood in our culture (Taylor 1996).

Spiritual/Emotional Strongholds: Anxiety, fear, insecurity, self-hatred, shame, guilt, and depression.

Repent and renounce any of these strongholds, including unbelief, and break agreement with them. Take responsibility for them and break their power over you.

Preeclampsia

Preeclampsia, also known as toxemia, is one of the most challenging problems facing pregnant women. The expectant mother may develop high blood pressure, the spilling of protein in the urine, edema (excess fluids), or a hyper-irritable central nervous system resulting in seizures, or any combinations of these symptoms. The standard treatment is a high intravenous dose of magnesium. The only known cure is to deliver the baby.

Several recent studies may give us a clue to the real cause. One study demonstrated a more than threefold increase of preeclampsia for women employed in high stress jobs. This same study also demonstrated that working women had a twofold higher risk of developing preeclampsia compared to non-working women (Klonoff-Cohen 1996). Another study found that women who performed regular exercise were thirty-three percent less likely to develop preeclampsia. Also, the more exercise the woman obtained, the lower the risk. Thus, women with high energy expenditure cut their risk of preeclampsia by forty-three percent (Marcoux 1989).

The real issue is anxiety and fear. Anxiety, worries, and fear cause the cells of the body to become rigid and trap the toxins. Also, these and other stressors tend to inhibit the production of digestive enzymes from the pancreas that are necessary to cleanse the cells of our bodies.

Spiritual Emotional Strongholds: Fear or conflict (with being female, being pregnant, over the baby), anxiety, fear of abandonment, depression, self-bitterness, anger, and guilt.

Repent and renounce any of these strongholds, including unbelief, and break agreement with them.

Premenstrual Syndrome (PMS)

Premenstrual Syndrome PMS is described as an increase in negative psychological and physical symptoms prior to menses (Kendall 2002). The early beginning of menses, negative attitude toward menstruation, greater physical problems at onset, and insufficient preparation predict more negative responses (Anson 1999, Brooks-Gunn 1988, Koff 1996). Some common emotional symptoms are depression, anxiety, irritability, inability to concentrate, aggression, feeling overwhelmed, and food cravings. Physical symptoms include breast pain, bloating, fatigue, abdominal pain, or cramping and headaches (Tucker and Whalen 1991). Symptoms usually disappear when menses begin. It is typical to blame PMS on hormones, but the role of biological factors has not been confirmed (Schmidt 1991, Walker 1992).

Psychological studies have focused on the quality of interpersonal relationships, self-esteem, attitudes or expectations about menstruation, stress, and coping abilities. My studies show that, spiritually, PMS is the result of shame or guilt associated with being a female. Somehow the woman has learned to resent being a female or at least the monthly cycle. She has developed a fear and/or resentment about how God created the female body to function. We have observed that this can come from several sources. She has been taught that she will have pain, that she just has to put up with it. Often, there has been abuse that would not have happened, if she were not a girl. The parents got a girl when they wanted a boy and thus the girl feels rejected. An overbearing mother causing resentment toward the female role; and the girl feeling shame from early development.

Spiritual Emotional Strongholds: Conflict (with being female), anger with God for how he made the female body to function, anxiety, fear of abandonment, depression, self-bitterness, anger, and guilt.

Forgive those who have hurt you in the past. Make sure that there is no resentment or other emotional pain in any situation listed above. Repent for any fear about the coming cycle and for any resentment toward God in how He chose to make the female body to function. Repent and renounce any of these strongholds and break agreement with them. Take responsibility for them in your generations and break their power over you. Enter into a paradigm shift in your thinking and choose to look forward to the cycle because it is how God chose to create life and it is also how the female body cleanses itself.

Psoriasis

Psoriasis is a chronic autoimmune skin disorder that generally appears as patches of raised red skin, covered by a flaky white buildup. Emotional stress and cold climates cause most flare-ups.

Spiritual/Emotional Strongholds: Self-hatred, guilt, and fear of abandonment.

Repent and renounce any of these strongholds, including unbelief, and break agreement with them. Take responsibility for them and break their power over you.

References:

About Psoriasis, What is Psoriasis? National Psoriasis Foundation.

Pulmonary Fibrosis (Idiopathic)

Inflammation of the lungs that results in scarring or fibrosis. Over time the fibrosis builds up to the point where the lungs are unable to provide oxygen to the rest of the body. It usually occurs between the ages of 40-70. It develops over time. An autoimmune response is suspected. Symptoms include dry cough and shortness of breath and fatigue. It can lead to death. Inflammation is evidence of an autoimmune response (Singh 1994, 1997).

Spiritual/Emotional Strongholds: Insecurity, self-rejection, and self-hatred.

Repent and renounce any of these strongholds, including unbelief, and break agreement with them. Take responsibility for them and break their power over you.

References:

What is Idiopathic pulmonary fibrosis? Pulmonary Fibrosis Foundation NIH Publication No. 95-2997, "Idiopathic Pulmonary Fibrosis," September 1995.

Reflux (Acid Reflux Disease)

Gastroesophageal Reflux Disease, or GERD, is the return of the stomach contents back up into the esophagus. Chronic anxiety and fear cause a malfunctioning of the lower esophageal sphincter of the stomach. Obesity, alcohol, caffeine, and some medications (progesterone, calcium channel blockers) are all contributors to this disorder.

Spiritual/Emotional Strongholds: Fear and anxiety.

Repent and renounce any of these strongholds, including unbelief, and break agreement with them.

References:

Gastroesophageal Reflux. eMedicine.com.

Reiter's Syndrome

An inherited autoimmune disease that is a chronic form of inflammatory arthritis. This can also include the inflammation of the eyes, genital, urinary, or gastrointestinal systems. It is more common among white males between the ages of 20 to 40.

Spiritual/Emotional Strongholds: Inherited self-hatred, guilt, self-accusation and insecurity, and low self-esteem.

Repent and renounce any of these strongholds including unbelief and break agreement with them. Take responsibility for them in your generations and break their power over you.

References:

Reiter's Syndrome. The University of Washington Orthopedics and Sports Medicine. Edited by Frederick A. Matsen, III, M.D.

Resting Tremor

Shaking of the hands, when the hands are stationary and the arms are limp. Anxiety, low blood sugar, metabolic disorders and exhaustion usually trigger it.

Spiritual/Emotional Strongholds: Fear and anxiety.

Repent and renounce these strongholds and break agreement with them

Restless Leg Syndrome

A disorder of the nervous system where there are creepy-crawly sensations in the legs. These symptoms usually occur at night during inactivity, and cause sudden jerking movements that keep the person awake at night causing fatigue. A chemical imbalance in the brain has been implicated in this disorder, especially dopamine and serotonin. RLS has been associated with alcoholism, high caffeine intake, iron and folic acid deficiencies, osteoarthritis (seventy percent of RLS patients have osteoarthritis) diabetes and varicose veins. It is more common in women than in men.

The main component in nervous system disease is really autoimmunity, which is a inappropriate immune response, to the body's own organs (Singh 1997).

Spiritual/Emotional Strongholds: Fear, anxiety, oppression, self-bitterness, and guilt.

Repent and renounce any of these strongholds and break agreement with them. Take responsibility for these in your generations and break their power over you.

References:

Leg Disorders (Restless Legs Syndrome and Nocturnal Leg Cramps) September 2001 Harvey Simon, M.D. Harvard Medical School

Rosacea

A skin disorder characterized by inflammation of the face. The disorder involves enlargement of the blood vessels just under the skin. It occurs most often in fair skinned people of Northern European descent. Women are more commonly affected, but men are usually more severely affected. It usually begins between ages 30-50.

Spiritual/Emotional Strongholds: Anxiety, fear, anger and insecurity.

Repent and renounce any of these strongholds, including unbelief, and break agreement with them. Take responsibility for them and break their power over you.

References:

Lehrer Michael, *Rosacea*. Medline Plus Updated Department of Dermatology, University of Pennsylvania Medical Center, Philadelphia, PA.

Reflex Sympathetic Dystrophy (RSD)

A chronic neurological syndrome characterized by severe burning pain, pathological changes in bone and skin, excessive swelling and extreme sensitivity to touch. Minor injuries, such as a sprain or a fall, are frequent causes of RSD which can start immediately after the injury or later. One characteristic of RSD/CRPS is that the pain is more severe than expected for the type of injury that occurred. In ten to twenty-six percent of cases, no precipitating factor can be found. There are two types: Type 1 which has no nerve injury, and Type 2, which does involve nerve injury (see the chronic pain profile).

The main component in nervous system disease is really autoimmunity, which is a inappropriate immune response, to the body's own organs (Singh 1997).

Spiritual/Emotional Strongholds: Self-bitterness, oppression, hatred, self-pity and fear of pain.

Repent and renounce any of these strongholds, including unbelief, and break agreement with them. Forgive those who have hurt you and separate them from their sins.

References:

What is RSD? Reflex Sympathetic Dystrophy Syndrome Association of America.

Sarcoidosis

Sarcoidosis is a rare, chronic, autoimmune disease due to inflammation. It can appear in almost any body organ, but most often starts in the lungs or lymph nodes. Small granulomas develop and, sometimes clear up and disappear. When they do not heal, they cause fibrosis or scarring of the lungs. It occurs in the 20-40 age group and the highest risk group is African-American females.

Spiritual/Emotional Strongholds: Broken heart, self-hatred, self-bitterness, and fear of abandonment.

Repent and renounce any of these strongholds, including unbelief, and break agreement with them.

References:

Sarcoidosis, American Lung Association.

Schizophrenia

A mental illness characterized by a disturbance of the brain's functioning. Major symptoms include hearing voices, delusions, disorganized speech, social withdrawal, apathy, depression, and suicidal thoughts. It occurs in the teenage years and early 20s, and affects women and men equally. There are chemical imbalances among the brain's neurotransmitters especially serotonin, dopamine, and glutamate. Physical and emotional trauma from childhood experiences plays a significant role.

Dr. Singh research connects schizophrenia to an immune response along with other diseases such as autism, obsessive compulsive disorder (OCD), Multiple Sclerosis (MS), Alzheimer's disease, and major depression. He teaches that the main component in nervous system disease is really autoimmunity, which is an inappropriate immune response to the body's own organs (Singh 1994, 1997).

I believe that at times all humans hear voices. The key is found in understanding the source of the thoughts, impressions, or voices. We need to understand that not all thoughts are our own. We need to be able to discern the source and then deal with it appropriately. When we do not understand the voices, a great deal of self-hatred can result, which can create a severe autoimmune response. For a more in depth discussion of this topic read the chapter on discernment in *Biblical Foundations of Freedom*.

Spiritual/Emotional Strongholds: Self-hatred, rejection, double-mindedness, insanity and confusion (coming out of deaf and dumb spirit), rebellion, fear, inability to discern good from evil, depression, and trauma.

Repent and renounce any of these strongholds, including unbelief, and break agreement with them. Take responsibility for these strongholds in your generations and break their power.

Reference:

Schizophrenia. NARSAD Diagnostic and Statistical Manual of Mental Disorders, Fourth Edition. Copyright 1994 American Psychiatric Association.

Scleroderma

A rare autoimmune connective tissue disease. Scleroderma means "hard skin" and usually involves the hands, face, arms, and trunk. It is eight times more common in women than in men, and usually occurs in mid-life. The more serious form can affect the lungs and GI tract. Hispanics and African-Americans have a higher incidence of diffuse scleroderma.

Spiritual/Emotional Strongholds: Self-hatred, guilt, and unforgiveness.

Repent and renounce any of these strongholds, including unbelief, and break agreement with them. Forgive yourself and those who have hurt you and separate them from their sin.

References:

Scleroderma, American College of Rheumatology.

Scleroderma, Arthritis Foundation.

McCance, Kathryn L. and Huether, Sue E. 1998. *Pathophysiology, The Biologic Basis for Disease in Adults and Children*. Third Edition, Mosby Inc. St. Louis, Missouri.

Scoliosis (Idiopathic)

Curvature of the spine. It is more common among teenage girls than boys. It develops gradually, and is often diagnosed around 12-14 years of age. If it gets severe, it can cause pain, fatigue, and breathing difficulty.

Spiritual/Emotional Strongholds: Inherited self-conflict, anger, fear, and rebellion, resulting in tension in the muscles on one side of the back causing an imbalance in the vertebrae.

Repent and renounce any of these strongholds, including unbelief, and break agreement with them. Take responsibility for these in your generations and break their power over your children.

Reference:

Brayden, Robert. *Scoliosis*. University of Colorado School of Medicine.

Seizures (see Epilepsy)

Shingles (see Herpes)

Sinusitis (Chronic)

Chronic sinusitis is a persistent inflammation of the sinus passages in the forehead, and behind and on either side of the nose, or in the cheeks. About fifteen to twenty percent of the population, has chronic sinusitis (meaning lasting longer than three weeks.) Allergies trigger the release of histamine and other chemicals that cause swelling and pain. The inflammation is indicative of an abnormal or autoimmune response (Singh 1994, 1997).

Spiritual/Emotional Strongholds: Fear, anxiety, self-hatred, and insecurity.

Repent and renounce any of these strongholds, including unbelief, and break agreement with them. Take responsibility for them and break their power over you.

References:

Kennedy Elicia, *Sinusitis*, eMedicine, Clinical Assistant Professor, Department of Emergency Medicine, University of Arkansas for Medical Sciences

Sjogren's Syndrome

Sjogren's syndrome is an autoimmune disease causing a person's immune system to attack and destroy salivary (saliva-producing) glands, and lacrimal (tear-producing) glands. Nine out of ten patients are women and onset is usually past 40. Symptoms may include dry mouth and eyes, making it difficult to eat or speak. In a more severe form of the disease called Systemic Sjogren's, other organs are affected such as the kidneys, arteries, GI tract, liver, pancreas, and lungs (McCance 1998).

Spiritual/Emotional Strongholds: Self-hatred, guilt, and grief.

Repent and renounce any of these strongholds and break agreement with them. Take responsibility for these and break their power over you.

References:

What is Sjogren's Syndrome? Sjogren's Syndrome Foundation.

Sleep Apnea

Sleep apnea is a central nervous system disorder and is not caused by an obstruction. This type is due to a neurological problem or interference in the brain stem's signaling system that controls the respiratory muscles. Symptoms include: cessation of breathing during sleep, weakness, numbness, and difficulty swallowing. It is more common in men than in women. Breathing pauses until high carbon dioxide level and low oxygen levels cause the brain to force breathing.

Dr. Singh teaches that the main component in nervous system disease is really autoimmunity, which is a inappropriate immune response to the body's own organs. If you examine central nervous system diseases closely, you will find that for almost each condition there is a suspicion of autoimmune process involvement (Singh 1997).

Doctors typically advise people to lose weight (for persons who are overweight, losing even as few as twenty pounds can reduce the severity of sleep apnea), to sleep on either side (for some people, this position greatly improves breathing as opposed to sleeping on the back), and to quit smoking. In addition, avoiding alcohol and medications such as antihistamines and sleeping pills before bedtime may prevent episodes of sleep apnea.

Spiritual/Emotional Strongholds: Self-hatred, fear, and occultism.

Repent and renounce any of these strongholds, including unbelief. Take responsibility for these in your generations.

References:

Sleep Apnea. National Sleep foundation. www.sleepfoundation.org.

Stevens Johnson Syndrome

A rare, very serious inflammatory, autoimmune disease characterized by lesions in the mouth, eyes, and mucosa, conjunctivitis, seizures, fever, headache, rapid heart rate, and fatigue. Involvement in the mucous membranes of the mouth can be so severe that patients may not be able to eat and drink. Drugs and malignancies most often are implicated as the etiology in adults and the elderly. Respiratory involvement can lead to respiratory failure. It is twice as common in men as in women.

Spiritual/Emotional Strongholds: Self-hatred, guilt, bitterness, and accusation.

Repent and renounce any of these strongholds, including unbelief and break agreement with them. Take responsibility for these in your generations on both sides of your family tree and break agreement with them.

References:

Stevens-Johnson Syndrome. eMedicine.com.

Strabismus

Misalignment of the eyes (crossed eyes) due to a neurological cause, often resulting in double vision. Strabismus is common in children. The brain controls the muscles that control the eye. When the nerve impulses in the visual pathway are interrupted, disturbances in normal visual perception and muscle control result.

Dr. Singh teaches that the main component in nervous system disease is really autoimmunity, which is a inappropriate immune response to the body's own organs. If you examine central nervous system diseases closely, you will find that for almost each condition there is a suspicion of autoimmune process involvement (Singh 1997).

Spiritual/Emotional Strongholds: Inherited self-hatred, occultism, double mindedness, and deaf and dumb spirit.

Deaf and dumb spirit often comes out of homes where there are matriarchal control issues; explore this possibility.

Repent and renounce any of these strongholds and break agreement with them. Parents, take responsibility for these in your generations and break their power over you and your children.

Stroke

A "brain attack" or a lack of oxygen to the brain, which results in the death of brain cells. The majority of strokes are caused by blood clots. The severity of the stroke depends on the size of the area of the brain affected. Often symptoms include sudden headache, visual disturbances, numbness in an arm or leg, slurred speech, and memory disturbances. Stress can induce strokes (Jacobson 2000).

According to a study published in *Neurology*, the scientific journal of the American Academy of Neurology, some researchers believe that the anger and aggression stroke victims display is a result of the brain injury suffered during the stroke. We disagree. We believe that the anger, aggression and self-hatred are the cause of the stroke. Research in heart disease shows that it is the anger and rage that result in the adrenaline surge that precipitate the crisis (Shah 1997). We believe that is also the primary cause of a stroke.

Additionally, Alzheimer's and other dementia patients may also display worsening anger, as they lose the ability to control their emotions. The anger has always been there, but as they lose control it manifests. Scientists call this "emotional incontinence." The Womens Health Initiative has shown that the use of hormones in women increased this risk of heart attack, strokes and blood clots.

Spiritual/Emotional Strongholds: Anger, rage, and self-bitterness.

Repent and renounce any of these strongholds and break agreement with them. Take responsibility for them in your generations and break their power over you.

References:

The National Institute of Neurological Disorders and Stroke. National Institutes of Health, Bethesda, MD.

Stuttering

A speech disorder resulting in hesitation of speech and disruption in fluency of speech. Heredity, stress, and interference in neurological speech pathways are some possible factors. Emotional traumas (divorce, moves) make it worse. The amygdala and hippocampus in the brain contribute to fear programming.

Spiritual/Emotional Strongholds: Self-hatred, insecurity, fear of failure, and performance.

Repent and renounce any of these strongholds and break agreement with them. Take responsibility for them and break their power over you.

References:

Johnson, Valerie. *What causes stuttering?* Overton Speech and Language Center, Inc., 4763 Barwick Drive, Suite 103 Fort Worth, TX.

Suicide

The desire to kill oneself is the most severe level of self-bitterness. In working with people who have attempted or are talking about or planning suicide, there will be extreme guilt, shame, regret, sadness, self-condemnation, etc. about something that they have done. Sometimes they have been victims, but they are blaming themselves for what happened.

Spiritual/Emotional Strongholds: Extreme self-hatred, self-bitterness, hopelessness, and depression.

Identify the specific events or circumstances that you are condemning yourself for, forgive those who have hurt you, and repent for your sins. Receive God's forgiveness in each one. Remember that there is nothing that God cannot and will not forgive. Make sure that all the shame and guilt is gone in each issue. After this process is completed the spirit of death must be cast out.

Synovitis

Inflammation of the synovial membrane of the joints (sliding surfaces in joints), which is not due to injury, but to the proliferation of white blood cells. This chronic inflammation leads to tissue destruction and fibrosis (scar tissue) of the joint. The inflammation and presence of white blood cells indicate an autoimmune response (Singh 1994, 1997).

Spiritual/Emotional Strongholds: Self-hatred, guilt, and fear.

Repent and renounce any of these strongholds, including unbelief and break agreement with them. Take responsibility for these and break their power over you.

Tinnitus

This is a ringing in the ears without any observable signs of disease, trauma, metabolic illness, vascular disease, or side effects of medications. It is often referred to as "subjective" tinnitus, and a muscle spasm in the stapedial muscle is suspected.

Spiritual/Emotional Strongholds: Anxiety, fear, occultism, and deaf and dumb spirit.

Repent and renounce any of these strongholds including unbelief and break agreement with them. Take responsibility for them and break their power over you.

References:

Tinnitus, National Organization of Rare Disorders.

Fortune, D. Scott. Hayes, David S. and Hall, Jay W. *Tinnitus, Current Evaluation and Management*. Vanderbilt University Medical Center, Nashville, Tennessee.

Transient Ischemic Attacks (TIAS)

A temporary blockage of an artery in the brain, resulting in a "mini-stroke" or temporary neurological symptoms (numbness, loss of speech, loss of memory, and visual disturbances). Transient Ischemic Attacks, or TIAS, are precursors or warnings of an imminent stroke. TIAS usually last only minutes and leave no permanent damage. Some contributors to TIAS are athlerosclerosis, high blood pressure, diabetes, migraines, epilepsy, estrogen, smoking, and arrhythmias.

Spiritual/Emotional Strongholds: Anxiety, fear, self-bitterness, performance, and anger.

Repent and renounce any of these strongholds, including unbelief, and break agreement with them. Take responsibility for these in your generations and break their power over you.

References:

Transient Ischemic Attack (TIA), NINDS Information Page.

Trigeminal Neuralgia (Tic Douloureux)

Facial pain along the fifth cranial nerve, usually affecting adults over 50. The "electric-like shocks" are debilitating and intense. Abnormal vessels, aneurysms, tumors, chronic inflammation, or other lesions may irritate the nerve roots. It is often associated with a specific sensory trigger (cold, wind, touch or talking). The sensory trigger indicates a fear of the trigger and chronic inflammation indicates and autoimmune response.

Spiritual/Emotional Strongholds: Anxiety, fear, self-hatred, anger, pain, and oppression.

Repent and renounce any of these strongholds, including unbelief, and break agreement with them. Forgive those who have hurt you and separate them from their sins. Take authority over any strongholds and cast them out.

References:

Huff, Steven J. *Trigeminal Neuralgia*, eMedicine, University of Virginia Health System.

Upper Respiratory Illness (URI)

Nationwide annual surveys regularly indicate that URI is the single most common cause of physician visits and missed days of work among all acute medical conditions (Couch 1990). Couch estimated that the common cold and influenza accounted for 165 million significant illnesses resulting in an average of 3.2 days of restricted activity, and 1.6 days in bed. Half of those illnesses received medical attention. The incidence of common colds is highest in infants and children who suffer from four to eight colds each year. Adults typically get two to five colds (Hall 1994).

There are numerous studies that indicate that psychological stress can affect upper respiratory illness. One approach studies environmental causes. These studies look at major life events such as the death of a spouse, change in employment, and major purchases. These studies also look at daily minor events such as an argument with the spouse, problems at work, or issues with the children (Boyce 1990). The emotional approach studies the experience of negative emotions such as anxiety or sadness and their connection to URI (Cohen 1991). The integrative approach studies the ability of individual people to cope with the various forms of stressors (Lazarus 1984).

All of these studies show a direct relationship between the various stressors and susceptibility to URI. Our ability to cope and deal with the stressors dictates the result in our health. (See the allergy and asthma profiles.)

Spiritual/Emotional Strongholds: Anxiety, fear, anger, self-bitterness, insecurity, over work, frustration, and any other negative emotions.

Repent and renounce any of these strongholds and break agreement with them. Take responsibility for them and break their power over you.

Ulcers

Stress induces increased secretion of stomach acid, leading to an increased risk of ulcers (Seyle 1996). In a recent example, the occurrence of gastric ulcers was noted to increase dramatically in Japanese residents who survived the devastating Hanshin-Awaji earthquake (Aoyama 1998). The presence of another significant disease further increases the likelihood that stress will cause gastric ulcers (Suzuki 1989).

For years the medical community believed that stress and anxiety caused an irritation in the stomach, which eventually caused the oversecretion of stomach acids and the ulceration. Recently they have begun to prescribe antibiotics and are telling us that a bacteria or viruses cause ulcers.

People who have ulcers also have compromised immune systems because of anxiety and stress. When you have a compromised immune system, you don't have the ability to defeat bacteria and viruses. The fear and anxiety come first and the bacteria and viruses show up after the immune system is compromised.

Spiritual/Emotional Strongholds: Anxiety, fear, self-bitterness, and insecurity.

Repent and renounce any of these strongholds and break agreement with them. Take responsibility for them and break their power over you.

References:

Jacobson M.D., (2000). *The Word on Health*. Moody Press, Chicago, Ill.

Ulcerative Colitis

A chronic, inherited, inflammatory disease of the large bowel due to anxiety and an overactive immune system. There is a risk of developing colon cancer, especially if the disease begins in childhood. Symptoms include: bloody stools, abdominal pain, and diarrhea and sometimes affects other parts of the body (arthritis, inflammation of the eyes, hepatitis and blockage of the bile duct).

Spiritual/Emotional Strongholds: Anxiety, self-bitterness, and insecurity.

Repent and renounce any of these strongholds and break agreement with them. Take responsibility for them and break their power over you.

References:

Ulcerative Colitis, Jackson Gastroenterology 423 North 21st Street, Suite 100 Camp Hill, PA 17011 gicare.com.

Uterine Fibroids

Benign tumors that grow from the muscular wall of the uterus. Heavy bleeding and pelvic pain are the main symptoms. It is two times more common in African-American women than in other ethnic groups. Elevated hormone levels contribute to fibroid growth.

Spiritual/Emotional Strongholds: Self-bitterness, and fear of abandonment.

Repent and renounce any of these strongholds and break agreement with them. Forgive yourself and anyone else who has hurt you (often female family members).

References:

Uterine Fibroids, The Merck Manual of Diagnosis and Therapy Ch. 240.

Varicose Veins

Varicose veins are abnormally dilated, twisted veins that have ineffective valves, causing reverse bloodflow. They can occur anywhere in the body. Blood clots sometimes form. Obesity, hereditary, pregnancy, hormonal imbalances, and standing long hours all contribute to varicose veins. A woman is more likely to develop varicose veins than a man.

Spiritual/Emotional Strongholds: Anger and self-anger.

Repent and renounce any of these strongholds and break agreement with them. Take responsibility for these strongholds in your generations and break their power over you.

References:

Varicose Veins. Intelihealth. Harvard Medical School.

Vitiligo

A skin condition where there is loss of pigment, resulting in irregular white spots. It is thought to be an autoimmune disorder, and often runs in families. Its incidence is higher in people with thyroid conditions and some other metabolic diseases.

Spiritual/Emotional Strongholds: Self-hatred, guilt, anxiety, and fear.

Repent and renounce any of these strongholds, including unbelief, and break agreement with them. Take responsibility for these in your generations and break their power over you.

References:

A Handbook for Patients with Vitiligo. National Vitiligo Foundation 611 South Fleishel Ave. Tyler, TX 75701.

Vitiligo. American Autoimmune Related Diseases Association Inc.

Vulvodynia

Vulvodynia is the universal term now used to describe vulvar discomfort lasting six months or longer. It is characterized by the patient's complaint of persistent burning, stinging, irritation, or excoriation (Hawkins, et.al. 1995, Lynch 1986). The cause of vulvodynia is unknown. However some predisposing factors that contribute to chronic vulvar pain are recurrent systemic and/or cutaneous candidiasis infection, vulvar dermatoses (erosive lichen planus), contact irritant dermatitis, genital herpes, and allergic reactions.

Spiritual/Emotional Strongholds: Fear, trauma, unforgiveness, and fornication.

Repent and renounce any of these strongholds, including unbelief, and break agreement with them. Take responsibility for them in your generations.

References:

Thomas, Jessica. *Vulvodynia: Causes, Diagnosis and Modern Therapy*, University of Wisconsin Medical School, Madison, Wisconsin.

Lecks, Karen J. *Continuing Education Forum. Vulvodynia: Diagnosis and Management*. Journal of the American Academy of Nurse Practitioners 10, no. 3 (March 1998): 129-134.

Wegener's Granulomatosis

A rare, inflammatory, autoimmune disease of the blood vessels mainly affecting the upper respiratory tract although any organ can be affected. The symptoms may include nose bleeds, fever, fatigue, ear infections with hearing loss, coughing up blood, shortness of breath, inflammation of the eyes, skin lesions, joint pain, weight loss, and sinusitis. In severe cases, meningitis, chronic renal failure, and heart attacks may occur. There is no causative agent found in this disease. It usually attacks individuals in their early 40s, and affects men and women equally. It is more common in Caucasians than African-Americans.

Spiritual/Emotional Strongholds: Self-anger, perfectionism, and insecurity.

Repent and renounce any of these strongholds, including unbelief, and break agreement with them. Take responsibility for these strongholds in your life and generations and break their power over you.

References:

Types of Vasculitis Wegener's Granulomatosis, John Hopkins Vasculitis Center.

Wegener's Granulomatosis Fact Sheet, Institute of Allergy and Infectious Disease.

Wilson's Syndrome

A sluggish metabolism due to thyroid hormones malfunctioning. Severe stress causes interference with thyroid hormones. The thyroid gland produces enough thyroid hormones but there is not proper conversion of T4 to T3, slowing cellular metabolism. When cortisol levels are high, deiodinase (an enzyme that converts T4 to T3) is blocked. Some symptoms may include anxiety, fatigue, dry skin and hair, constipation, hair loss, poor memory, low sex drive, psoriasis, slow healing, depression, PMS, CFS, infertility, and fluid retention.

Spiritual/Emotional Strongholds: Anxiety, fear, abuse, and depression.

Repent and renounce this stronghold and break agreement with it. Take responsibility for it in your generations and break its power over you. Take authority over it and cast it out.

References:

Cathcart, Robert F. *Symptoms of Wilson's Syndrome*, 415-949-2822 This list of symptoms was taken from the Table of Contents of E. Denis Wilson, M.D. *Wilson's Syndrome: The Miracle of Feeling Well*, Cornerstone Publishing Company, Orlando, FL. Third Edition, 1996.

Wilson Denis, *Wilson's Syndrome*, Med Facts, Provident Medical Institute.

Manual for Wilson's Syndrome, 1991 Muskeegee Medical Publishing Co.

A Discussion of Treatment Options

I want to briefly discuss some of the common treatment modalities (methods) that are available today. This is not intended to be a thorough discussion, but something to provoke further thought. (For a more complete discussion read my book, *Biblical Foundations of Freedom*.) Often we accept the words of a "medical professional" as gospel. I want to suggest to you that you need to think about, and study for yourself, what you are being told to do. You have a responsibility before God to take care of His temple.

I Corinthians 3:16: "Know ye not that ye are the temple of God, and that the Spirit of God dwelleth in you?"

I Corinthians 6:19: "What? Know ye not that your body is the temple of the Holy Ghost which is in you, which ye have of God, and ye are not your own?"

ALLOPATHIC MEDICINE (WESTERN MEDICINE)

We wouldn't want to live in a world without doctors but a few words of caution are in order. I believe that a brief look at the history of medical practices will quickly bring us to a place of caution.

First let's look at Scripture. The first mention of doctors in Scripture is found in Genesis 50:2. Joseph was commanding them to embalm his father. The next reference is in II Chronicles 16:12 where King Asa made a mistake by not seeking the Lord but going to the doctors. In Job 13:4, Job said that his friends were "physicians of no value." They had come to Job to console him, but nothing they had said helped him in the least.

Mark 5:25-26 tells the story of "a certain woman which had an issue of blood twelve years, And had suffered many things of many physicians, and had spent all that she had, and was nothing bettered, but rather grew worse." But let's also remember Luke, the beloved physician (Colossians 4:14).

Now let's look at medical practices of the past.

Whenever medicine and mankind have violated the simple truths of God's Word, there has been a great price to pay. Some estimate that over sixty million people died in the plagues of the Middle Ages. The plagues spread mostly because of poor hygiene. Even before man discovered bacteria, God told us to wash after the touching a dead body (Leviticus 22, Numbers 19, Haggai 2). Why? Many have thought that it was just for ceremonial purposes, but God knew about germs, bacteria and viruses. He knew that washing would cleanse and prevent the spread of disease.

Not many years ago, twenty to twenty-five percent of pregnant women died of infection when birth took place in a teaching hospital. The doctors were examining the women without washing their hands after dissecting cadavers, thus transferring bacteria and infection from the anatomy lab. When a doctor recognized the problem, and demonstrated that washing prevented the infections, his colleagues scorned him and refused to change the practice.

It wasn't very many years ago that the best medical advice was to drain most of the blood from a patient. George Washington consulted the best doctors for a sore throat. He died a few hours later from what was probably dehydration, from the letting of most of his blood (Jacobson 2000).

Dr. Jacobson also tells of an experience on his first day of medical school. The dean had the following to say to the incoming students: "In the next fours years, fifty percent of what you are about to learn will be incorrect! However, we do not yet know where the inaccuracies are. So, you are going to need to learn it all, master it, then continue to study after you leave here so that, as new discoveries are made, that which is no longer relevant will be discarded" (Jacobson 2000).

Medical practices of the past are barbaric to us today. But I sometimes wonder if we won't feel the same way about many of today's medical practices a hundred years from now? We often think that we are so advanced and so knowledgeable, but people of a hundred fifty years ago thought that they were equally advanced.

Today, doctors are giving drugs for everything, even drugs to counteract the side effects of other drugs. According to a report filed by Michael Berens, a reporter for the *Chicago Tribune*, in 2000 more than 103,000 people died from infections they received in the hospital (*Anchorage Daily News,* July 22, 2002). Deaths linked to hospital germs represent the fourth leading cause of death among Americans, behind heart disease, cancer, and strokes, according to the federal Centers for Disease Control and Prevention (*Anchorage Daily News,* July 22, 2002). The Institute of Medicine reports that as many as 98,000 people die each year in the U.S. from medical mistakes (Vergano 2003). When you add all these causes of deaths together, we learn that well over one half of all deaths are caused by the medical profession. I wonder if in a hundred fifty years, we won't look at the hospitals and medical practices of today in the same light as we do the ones of a hundred fifty years ago.

Today, some advertising agencies own medical research laboratories. A November 2002 episode of Bill Moyers' television program "Now" exposed the fact that "launching" advertising agencies own the medical research laboratories that are developing the drugs and performing the clinical trails. It is incredible to me that an advertising agency could own the research company that develops the drugs that they are selling on the radio and TV. Does this give you confidence in the medications? It scares me.

To me this translates into greed and huge profits at the public's expense. No wonder we are seeing new diseases invented every week. There is a huge pressure to sell more and new drugs for the exorbitant profits. New diseases are invented daily, such as "social anxiety disorder," all just to sell a medication.

Western medicine, or allopathic medicine, is very good at dealing with symptoms. In fact that is what the word allopathic means: treating symptoms. This works very well for a broken arm or medical emergency, but leaves much to be desired in most chronic diseases. As we have seen in this book, medicine and psychology are good at identifying many true root causes of disease, but they do not and cannot treat them effectively. Western medicine is not very good at treating the root cause, because the true answer is found in obedience to God, and not in a drug or surgery that covers up or disguises the root cause.

"The problem is that medicine has a long history of ignoring the Word of God. Countless theories and practices have been proposed and implemented that are contrary to Biblical teaching or principle. And medicine stubbornly clings to these until overwhelming evidence forces it to change" (Jacobson 2000).

Again, I want to emphasize that I am not a medical doctor. The only medical advice that I can legally give you is, "consult your medical doctor." But as you talk to your doctor, remember that your doctor can only treat you for some illnesses. There are only two true healers, God and yourself. You can choose to obey God and deal with all the negative emotions, or not.

In Hosea 4:6, God says, "My people are destroyed for lack of knowledge: because thou hast rejected knowledge, I will also reject thee, that thou shalt be no priest to me: seeing thou hast forgotten the law of thy God, I will also forget thy children." Let's not be like those that ignored His Word and His promises. Let's remember God's promises and obey Him.

ALTERNATIVE MEDICINE

Almost every treatment method (modality) in alternative medicine involves balancing the "energy" in our bodies. Other names for this "energy system" include yin and yang (which means good and evil), positive and negative, chi or chakras, etc. Eastern medicine and eastern religions both teach that our "energy" must be balanced, that "imbalance" will create a disorder or disease. The foundation of this belief is that good and evil are equal, and therefore, our only option is to balance them. Bad karma must be replaced with good karma.

A New Age writer and practitioner has this to say: "Though karma often does not appear merciful to us, it is the most compassionate and effective way to restore, balance, and teach the soul. However painful to the individual, karma is the greatest aid in clearing the way for the self-directed evolution which leads to the open spaces of freedom, and finally makes of man a god." "Nor is there any forgiving God, who takes away the sins we have committed" (Jansma 2002). I know better because the shame and guilt from my sins are gone.

Eastern religions cannot be separated from eastern medicine and most forms of alternative medicine, or their underlying belief that good and evil are equal, and that we have to replace the evil with good. As Christians, we know that evil is not equal with God. We know that through Jesus, we have power to destroy the works of the devil. The only way to get it right is through His forgiveness and the power of His Holy Spirit.

Western medicine does not recognize these so-called "energy systems" that alternative or eastern medicine does. But the real point is why would a Christian want to balance evil with good? Why would a Christian allow evil in himself in any form? We do, because we are deceived and do not understand the power and authority we have in Jesus.

When I was so sick and desperate, I clung to any thread of hope. I tried many, many alternative practices. Some forms of alternative medicine, did help me. But it was superficial and ineffective, compared to the help I received by truly dealing with the root causes, in the power of Jesus.

Allergy elimination treatments such as NAET or full body modification did help, but I was never completely healed of an allergy, even though I spent thousands of dollars and even learned to do the treatments myself. These types of treatments only superficially treated the fears (classical conditioning) of many allergens that I had. That is why they healed me only slightly. When I learned to deal with bitterness and fear in God's way, I was completely healed of more than one hundred allergies. Only God can erase the conditioning from the spirit of fear (II Timothy 1:7). I have also helped hundreds of others to become completely free of allergies and asthma through the power of God.

God is the only true healer. Let's do it His way and get rid of the evil, instead of tolerating it in our lives through some form of balancing. For a more complete discussion of this subject see *Biblical Foundations of Freedom*.

PSYCHOLOGY

Most forms of treatment in psychology involve some type of talk therapy or behavioral modification. Sometimes it is good to talk about issues, but there must be closure to the hurts and pains in this life. There must be closure to bitterness, anger, hatred, shame, guilt, regret or sorrow. There must be victory over the fear. Many times talking about it will help in the short run, but when there is no closure, people become discouraged. Digging up the hurts of the past without closure becomes discouraging and humiliating. Digging up the things from the past only makes people worse if there is no closure.

Only Jesus can heal the broken heart and take the pain from the negative events in life. Only Jesus can forgive you of your sins and take the shame, guilt, regret and sorrow from the mistakes that you have made. Only Jesus can bring closure and peace and cleanliness and righteousness. Only Jesus can give you the authority and power to change your behaviors. Only Jesus can give you authority over fear. Turn to the true healer and let Him take the pain and heal your broken heart. The methods of man cannot do this.

NUTRITION

Excellent nutrition is critical. It is very important that we eat well and take care of our bodies, which are the temple of the Lord. But in my opinion, nutrition is only a very small part of the problem. Almost every nutritional problem (malabsorption, stomach and gut issues, etc.) is rooted in anxiety, fear, and other stress-related negative emotions.

We need to remember the instruction of Jesus in Matthew 15:11, 17-20: "Not that which goeth into the mouth defileth a man; but that which cometh out of the mouth, this defileth a man. Do not ye yet understand that whatsoever entereth in at the mouth goeth into the belly, and is cast out into the draught? But those things which proceed out of the mouth come forth from the heart; and they defile the man. For out of the heart proceeds evil thoughts, murders, adulteries, fornications, thefts, false witness, blasphemies: These are the things which defile a man: but to eat with unwashen hands defileth not a man."

There are also times when eating can be sin. Romans 14:12-23 says:

So then every one of us shall give account of himself to God. Let us not therefore judge one another any more: but judge this rather, that no man put a stumblingblock or an occasion to fall in his brother's way. I know, and am persuaded by the Lord Jesus, that there is nothing unclean of itself: but to him that esteemeth any thing to be unclean, to him it is unclean. But if thy brother be grieved with thy meat, now walkest thou not charitably. Destroy not him with thy meat, for whom Christ died. Let not then your good be evil spoken of: For the kingdom of God is not meat and drink; but righteousness, and peace, and joy in the Holy Ghost.

For he that in these things serveth Christ is acceptable to God, and approved of men. Let us therefore follow after the things which make for peace, and things wherewith one may edify another. For meat destroy not the work of God. All things indeed are pure; but it is evil for that man who eateth with offence. It is good neither to eat flesh, nor to drink wine, nor any thing whereby thy brother stumbleth, or is offended, or is made weak. Hast thou faith? Have it to thyself before God. Happy is he that condemneth not himself in that thing which he alloweth. And he that doubteth is damned if he eat, because he eateth not of faith: for whatsoever is not of faith is sin.

This passage suggests several ways that eating, or how we look at it, can be sin. Verses 12 and 13 command us not to judge. "So then every one of us shall give account of himself to God. Let us not therefore judge one another any more." Whether some choose to eat vegetables or meat is not the issue. It is not our place to judge them. The real sin or offense is judging a brother. This concept is taught in many other passages such as the Lord's Prayer in Matthew 6. Jesus taught us to pray by asking God the

Father to forgive us in the same manner that we forgive others. Do you really want to do this? We need to think about what we are praying.

Verse 15 teaches that we should not offend others but be considerate. Even if one believes that he is perfectly free to eat meat we should be careful not to offend our brother who lacks the faith to do so. We are to love our neighbor as our self.

Verse 17 teaches that the "kingdom of God is not meat and drink; but righteousness, and peace, and joy in the Holy Ghost." The kingdom of God does not consist of meat, drink, and outward religion. It consists of three things here:

1. Righteousness (Romans 3:21-31, Romans 4:1-25, Romans 8:4)
2. Peace (Romans 2:10, Romans 5:1, Romans 8:6, Romans 10:15)
3. Joy (Romans 5:11, Galatians 5:22, I Peter 1:8)

Verse 20 again instructs us that meat cannot destroy the work of God. What could be clearer than this—that meat itself does not destroy God's work? (Also see Colossians 2:14-17, I Timothy 4:1-6, I Corinthians 8:8-13, 10:23-31.) It is the bickering over meats and doubtful things which destroy the soul, and liberty in using them may also cause an offense.

Verse 20 continues to say that "all things indeed are pure; but it is evil for that man who eateth with offence." All edible things are pure and lawful, but they become sinful to the man who eats with offense and with a defiled conscience. The negative emotion of guilt causes great harm to our bodies. We are to enjoy what God has given us. Guilt is really saying that God is a liar.

Romans 14:21 again reinforces the command not to offend a brother. It is better to deny a personal pleasure than to cause an offense.

Verses 22 and 23 are very interesting verses in how they relate to our health. "Hast thou faith?" The word faith here means the full persuasion that one is right, lawful, and sanctioned by God in this act. God has created all plants and animals for our food. But I have seen many condemn themselves because of food. They condemn themselves for eating too much, or too little, or the wrong kinds of food. Others become afraid to eat certain foods that God has created for us. All food allergies are a fear of that food and of the one who created it. This kind of fear is the opposite of faith and is a sin.

The verse continues by saying, "Happy is he that condemneth not himself in that thing which he alloweth." Unhappy is the person who condemns himself for eating what God has given.

Verse 23 sums this up by saying "for whatsoever is not of faith is sin." Eating is a sin when it is not done in faith. Eating is a sin, if we are doing it to self-medicate. Not eating is a sin if we are in fear or, in other words, afraid of the food. God created it; it is not bad for you. This is the first realization that all serious allergy suffers must understand. It is the fear of the food, along with anger and resentments that weakened the immune system, and created the allergies. We can have victory over allergies.

Food, supplements, and vitamins can become idols. We must always remember that Jesus is the healer. No diet, food, or supplement can heal you. Where is your faith? Diet programs usually are a substitute for Jesus.

Food can also become an addiction. God has given each of us a healthy desire and need for food. Without food obviously we would die. When our bodies need food, we become hungry and then we eat to satisfy the physical need. But sometimes our "appetite" is governed by more than physical need.

True physical need can be satisfied, but an appetite that is governed by psychological need cannot be satisfied. For example, God says that the mouth of the righteous will be satisfied with good things (Psalms 103:5). He promises to provide bread that satisfies the poor (Psalms 132:15). God has promised that the meek, the one who trusts God, will eat and be satisfied (Psalms 22:26).

But the appetite that comes through the flesh (sin) cannot be satisfied just as cocaine or alcohol never satisfies. There is only a craving for more. The mouth is a contact point for security. As little babies we put our thumbs in our mouth to suck on to satisfy ourselves. As we become older we learn to put food, cigarettes, alcohol, or drugs in our mouth, in an attempt to satisfy or cover up our psychological needs. In other words, we chose to self-medicate with these things to cover the pain from situations and events in this life.

Only Jesus can take the pain and truly bring satisfaction and peace. Food used in this manner is an addiction and is also a form of idolatry. We use it in an attempt to have peace when only the Prince of Peace can bring true peace. Just as the blessing of the Lord brings satisfaction from food, so also is the failure of food to satisfy a warning that we need to deal with something in our life. We need to forgive those who have hurt us. We need to repent for the things that we have done that bring shame. We need to let Jesus heal our broken heart so we do not have to self-medicate.

WHAT DO WE DO WHEN WE GET SICK?

The first question that we should ask is, "what does the Word of God say we should do?" "In today's language, the answer is to get the proper diagnosis. In other words, first determine the root cause of the illness. Establishing the diagnosis is the goal of every western-trained doctor as well. The problem is that he is usually focused on only the physical realm. But Scripture gives three legitimate avenues to pursue in establishing the diagnosis: (1) Seek the Lord; (2) Call for the elders; (3) Recognize when there is need for a physician" (Jacobson 2000).

According to Dr. Jacobson, the first thing we should do is "seek the Lord." Do not make the same mistake that King Asa or the woman with the issue of blood did. As we have seen in our study, most of our diseases have a spiritual root. First, let's go to our creator, the One who fearfully and wonderfully made our bodies. Let's consult with the Great Physician, because He is the only one that knows the true diagnosis.

The second step according to Dr. Jacobson is to call for the elders. Steps one and two are part of the same process, the process of identifying issues of our heart that might be the cause of the disease.

James 5:14-16 says, "Is any sick among you? Let him call for the elders of the church; and let them pray over him, anointing him with oil in the name of the Lord: And the prayer of faith shall save the sick, and the Lord shall raise him up; and if he has committed sins, they shall be forgiven him. Confess your faults one to another, and pray one for another, that ye may be healed. The effectual fervent prayer of a righteous man availeth much."

The elders (mature believers) who are praying the prayer of faith need to be "in faith" (fully persuaded) in the Lord and his ability to heal. James also commands us to confess our faults to one another and pray for one another, so we can be healed. Could it be said in any clearer language? In many different passages Jesus teaches that there is a connection between sin and disease. He even asked the question "is it easier to say take up your bed and walk, or your sins are forgiven?" (Matthew 9:5).

The first step when we get sick is to seek the Lord and examine the issues of our hearts. Are we stressed out or overwhelmed? Is there bitterness, jealousy and envy, rejection, fear, or occult activities? Is there any anger, resentment, retaliation, hatred, violence, and murder (with the tongue)? Is there any shame, guilt, regret, or sorrow? If so, then we have issues to take to the Lord in repentance and forgiveness.

Dr. Bruce Thompson, a physician who developed the counseling schools for YWAM (Youth With A Mission) states in his book, *Walls of My Heart*: "medicine is to complement the primary ministry of counseling." Sometimes we need help in this process. None of us is good at taking the log out of our own eyes. That is why we need to call on the elders, or counselors, for help in recognizing our sins.

If we have worked through the issues of heart and we are still sick, then is the time to see a doctor. In a medical emergency, it only takes an instant to first seek the Lord. Pray! Ask the Great Physician for His diagnosis and His healing. If the healing does not happen, see the doctor.

The following is a more extensive list of the issues of our heart that stop the hand of God in our lives.

WHY WE ARE NOT HEALED

There can be many reasons or blocks to His healing in our lives. The question is: "Have the conditions for God's promises of health been met?" Here are some of the blocks to His healing that we have experienced in ministry.

Ignorance of God's Precepts

Hosea 4:6 says, "My people are destroyed for lack of knowledge: because thou hast rejected knowledge, I will also reject thee, that thou shalt be no priest to me: seeing thou hast forgotten the law of thy God, I will also forget thy children."

Jesus said the same thing in a different way:

- If you continue in My word, then are you My disciples indeed (John 8:31).
- Whosoever committeth sin is the servant of sin (not a son). And the servant abideth not in the house forever: but the Son abideth ever (John 8:34-35).
- My sheep hear My voice, and I know them, and they follow Me (John 10:26-27).
- If a man love Me he will keep My words (John 14:21-23).
- If a man abide not in Me, he is cast forth as a branch, and is withered; and men gather them, and cast them into the fire, and they are burned (John 15:6).
- If you keep My commandments you shall abide in My love (John 15:10-13).
- You are My friends, if you do whatsoever I command you (John 15:14).

God's law was given to show us our sin and also to identify what sin is. If we do not know or understand what sin is, we will be destroyed. If we do not know who our enemy is, we'll be taken advantage of. This is why *Biblical Foundations of Freedom* defines sin in the first chapter.

We are also ignorant concerning the healing power of the Word of God. Proverbs 4:20-22 says, "My son, attend to my words; incline thine ear unto my sayings. Let them not depart from thine eyes; keep them in the midst of thine heart. For they are life unto those that find them, and health to all their flesh." The Word of God cannot be health to either the soul or body before it is heard, received, and attended to. The words of God are life only to those that "find" them. If you want to receive life and healing from God, take time to find the words of Scripture, which promise these results.

In this passage God tells us exactly how to "attend" to His Words. He says, "Let them not depart from thine eyes, keep them in the midst of thine heart." Instead of having your eyes on your symptoms and being occupied with them, let not God's Words "depart from thine eyes." The only way a seed can do its work is to be kept in the ground, so the only way that God's "imperishable seed" can effectually work in us is by being kept in the midst of our hearts (Bosworth 1973).

When your eyes are upon your symptoms, and your mind is occupied with them more than with God's Word, you have in the ground the wrong kind of seed for the harvest that you desire. You have sown the seeds of doubt (James 1:6-8).

Lack of Discernment

Hebrews 5:14 says, "But strong meat belongeth to them that are of full age, even those who by reason of use have their senses exercised to discern both good and evil."

We must be able to distinguish between good and evil. This is the mark of Christian maturity. When we become mature or "full of age" in Christ, and through the hard work of using all our senses, we will be able to discern or thoroughly distinguish, or separate, good from evil.

Not Understanding How Satan Attacks or Tempts

We must learn the difference between the voice of God and the voice of the devil. This is another facet of discernment that we discuss in *Biblical Foundations of Freedom*.

We Must Learn to Resist the Devil

James 4:7 says to "Submit yourselves therefore to God. Resist the devil, and he will flee from you." If we do not resist the devil, he will not flee.

Bitterness Toward Others

Bitterness includes any Unforgiveness, Resentment, Retaliation, Anger, Hatred, Violence, Murder.

Bitterness is the root cause of many diseases and stops God from healing. The only righteous anger is directed at evil. It is never to be directed at another person. We must be very careful of the words that come from our mouths. We will answer for every idle word. In the manner that we judge others, is the manner that we will be judged. The manner or way that we forgive others is the standard that we establish for receiving forgiveness from God (Matthew 6:9-15).

Self-bitterness

This is any way that we put down or condemn ourselves and includes: Self-unforgiveness, Self-resentment, Self-retaliation, Self-anger, Self-hatred, Self-violence, Self-murder.

God looked at His creation and said that it was very good. This applies to man that He created in His image. Thus any way that we put ourselves down is a form of self-bitterness. Additionally since we are created in His image we also curse Him when we curse ourselves.

Jealousy and Envy

This involves anyway we compare ourselves to others and what they have. It also involves competing with others to get more than they have. The result is always bitter-ness. Proverbs 6:34 says, "For jealousy is the rage of a man." Proverbs 27:4 says, "Wrath is cruel and anger is outrageous but who can stand before envy?" Mark 15:10 says, "For he knew that the chief priests had delivered him because of envy."

Rejection

We must learn not to be afraid of rejection. If we are in fear of rejection, we have fallen into idolatry by putting more importance on the words or actions of others, instead of God. We must also learn not to reject others.

Fear

Fear is a form of unbelief. Synonyms are anxiety, worry, feeling overwhelmed or stressed, etc. These emotions all represent an area of our lives in which we have chosen not to trust God.

Occult Activities

Our Father is a jealous God. He will not let us worship another god. He is zealous for each of us. There are many forms of occultism in the Christian church today. For a full discussion, read *Biblical Foundations of Freedom* and *Continuing Works of Christ*.

Unbelief

What prevented Jesus from doing the works that He was sent to do when He was on the earth? Only one thing: Unbelief! This issue is the same today as it was in Nazareth. In Mark 6:4-6 Jesus returns to His hometown of Nazareth and says to them: "A prophet is not without honour, but in his own country, and among his own kin, and in his own house. And he could there do no mighty work, save that he laid his hands upon a few sick folk, and healed them. And he marvelled because of their unbelief. And he went round about the villages, teaching."

Jesus "could do no mighty work" in His hometown because the people did not believe. It is not that He didn't want to teach and heal and save everyone. He did. But the unbelief of the people prevented Him. Even God cannot and will not override our free will. John 12:40 says, "He [Satan] hath blinded their eyes, and hardened their heart; that they should not see with their eyes, nor understand with their heart, and be converted, and I should heal them."

There are many different ways that unbelief can come into our lives. We need to examine all that we have been taught in our schools, churches, and in our generations to make sure that it lines up with the Word. Only the Word of God is the final authority. It is my opinion that many of the commonly taught doctrines of many Christian churches do not line up with His Word and are nothing more than the traditions of men that bring death to the Church.

The Traditions or Precepts of Men

Isaiah 29:13 warns about the precepts of men, "Wherefore the Lord said, Forasmuch as this people draw near me with their mouth, and with their lips do honour me, but have removed their heart far from me, and their fear toward me is taught by the precept of men." Here are some of the modern precepts of men that bring us unbelief and steal the power of the Gospel.

Cessationism: Many seminaries teach that the gifts or manifestations of the Holy Spirit listed in I Corinthians 12 are not for today. Those who hold to this doctrine teach that they passed away with the last original apostle. I was taught this in college and seminary. I am sure glad that it is a false teaching; if it were true, I would still be sick. God has healed me and hundreds of others.

Many also teach that His healing miracles or the "age of miracles" has ceased or passed away. God has not changed; we have. We have allowed unbelief into our lives and accepted a form of godliness that denies His power. In doing this we have built a doctrine based in our failures and not in Scripture.

Some teach that we do not have to confess past, present, or future sins. Once we accept Jesus all of our sins are automatically forgiven. If this were true, why is there so much pain in past memories? Why are our hearts still broken from the past failures or abuses?

Some teach that once we are saved, the devil does not have any more influence over us. Are you not still tempted? Of course, we all are. It is time to stop being ignorant of the wiles of the devil. Evil spirits can and do bring disease (Mark 9).

Another tradition is that God is the author of disease and that He wills sickness on some people. The book of Job is usually taught in this manner. If sickness is ever the will of God, then every physician, nurse or those that go to them is breaking His law. If God wants someone to be sick then it is a sin to want to be well. What an absurd position for anyone to take. To accuse God of this is to accuse Him of sin because disease is the work of the devil. He has promised that we will reap what we sow and that He will not be mocked in this. Job reaped what he sowed or God is a liar. Job opened the door to Satan in his sin, but even in his sin God limited what the devil could do to him.

Along this same line of thought are those who believe that we can glorify God more by remaining sick and exhibiting patience than we can by being divinely healed. How could the evil of sickness glorify Him? He says that He is the giver of every good and perfect gift (James 1:16-17). Disease only came into this world through sin and is the fruit of Satan. So how can we glorify God in the works of the devil?

Some teach that it is not God's will to heal all our diseases. Psalm 103:2-3 says, "Bless the Lord, O my soul, and forget not all his benefits: Who forgiveth all thine iniquities; who healeth all thy diseases." Many Scriptures plainly teach that it is His will to heal all disease.

Others teach that we should ask God to heal us "if it be Thy will." This is a statement of unbelief that actually calls God a liar. He simply states that it is His will to heal all our diseases. Jesus also demonstrated His will to heal by healing everyone that came to Him. He never turned anyone away.

The modern teaching that Paul's thorn in the flesh was a physical disease has caused many to doubt God. It is often taught used as an example of God choosing not to heal. II Corinthians 12:7 says, "And lest I should be exalted above measure through the abundance of the revelations, there was given to me a thorn in the flesh, the messenger of Satan to buffet me, lest I should be exalted above measure." This verse simply says that Paul's thorn in the flesh was a messenger of Satan. What is a messenger of

Satan? The English word "messenger" is the Greek word, *agello* (GSN-32). It is translated "angel" 179 times and "messenger" seven times. It is never translated, nor does it ever mean, disease or physical infirmity. The simple explanation of the thorn in the flesh is that an angel of Satan, one of the spirit beings, which fell with him, followed Paul and buffeted him when he was tempted to become exalted. The word buffet means, "to cuff on the ears." In other words, to tempt with words and thoughts.

Paul asked for the "thorn" to be removed three times and God refused. There are two very important reasons why God refused. First, this proves that the thorn was not a disease. Every person that came to Jesus for healing was healed. He never refused. Scripture plainly teaches that it is God's will to heal all our diseases (Psalms 103:3).

Second, it also proves that the thorn was the devil, or one of his evil spirits. Satan will not be bound in hell until the Lord comes again. Until then, the devil has the ability to buffet or tempt us. In our Savior's love and mercy, it is His will that none should perish; thus He will delay His Second Coming until the time is right.

Another tradition that has hindered God's ability to heal is the teaching that Jesus healed the sick as the Son of God and not as a man. The Scriptures teach us that Jesus, the Son God, emptied Himself and became like each of us, except He did not sin. Jesus did His miracles only through the power of the Holy Spirit. That same power is available to each of us to do even greater works (John 14:12).

For a full discussion of these and many more similar subjects, read *Continuing Works of Christ*.

Religious Spirit

This is a trap that says we have to do things a certain way. The religious spirit ties us to the traditions of men. The religious spirit makes us afraid of what is new or different from our experience or worldview. The religious spirit desires to make our relationship with God one of obligation and duty instead of passion. The religious spirit focuses on the letter of the law. The religious spirit says we have to look good on the outside, never mind what is in the heart. The religious spirit keeps us from the things of the spirit. The religious spirit says, "you have to." The religious spirit makes people doctrinally obsessed. The religious spirit breeds confusion. The religious spirit breeds rebellion, unforgiveness, and judgment.

Needing to "See a Miracle"

Some refuse to believe His written word and expect an instant miracle and then curse or blame God by saying He dosen't care about me. We need to understand the difference between the gift of miracles and the gift of healing. We see far more healings than miracles. Most diseases are healed in the gift of healing, which is a process of time as we repent for our sins that are really the cause of most disease.

The Way of Cain

Demanding that God heal us our way. Cain refused to obey God's command to bring the proper sacrifice. He was determined to worship God on his own terms. Jude warns us of this sin.

Refusing to Take Personal Responsibility

We do this in any way we blame God for the calamities of this life. God forbids terrorism, murder, stealing, abuse, and every other horrible thing that can happen in this world. Only man has allowed or permitted these horrible events to happen in our disobedience to God. Mankind must accept full and complete responsibility. God the father is the giver of every good and perfect gift (James 1:16-17); therefore, if it is not good and perfect, it is from the devil.

Some Have No Purpose and No Diligence When Seeking God for Healing

God rewards those who diligently seek Him. We have seen many turn to the doctors and spend everything they have, without any promise or hope. Yet they will not look to God who promises to heal.

Lack of Obedience

The church, for the most part, has refused to teach that obedience and being set apart are required, if we want to be a "vessel of honor fit for his service" (II Timothy 2:20-21). Instead, we allow and condone worry, fear, anxiety, unforgiveness, resentment, anger, hatred, violence, murder, shame, guilt, regret, and sorrow, by saying that is "just how I am." Or we teach a brand of grace that says it doesn't really matter how we live, and if we have said a few magic words we are going to heaven. I do not believe that this is what is taught in James chapter 2. We refuse to believe that under the New Covenant, there are consequences for our sins, just as there were under the Old Covenant. We refuse to accept the plain truth that most of our diseases are the consequence of our own choices. Obedience is required.

Bob Gass, in his publication *Word For Today*, dated December 21, 2002, lists seven of the church's all-time biggest blunders:

1. We've made unbelief a doctrine. While third-world nations believe God for New Testament results, we teach our seminary students that God doesn't do miracles any more.

2. We've tolerated division. Who needs the devil when we're so adept at hating one another in the name of denominational loyalty?

3. We've cultivated a religious spirit. We've taught that Christianity is about avoiding things. As a result we've lost our joy because intimacy with God cannot be achieved through performance.

4. We've encouraged "superstars." Consequently, some of our preachers have stopped modeling servanthood, and have forgotten that Jesus washed feet and rode on a donkey.

5. We've equated money with success. We've found a way to "theologize" greed, instead of using our God-given prosperity to feed the poor and reach the world with the Gospel.

6. We've stayed in the pews and become irrelevant. We freak out when somebody uses rap or rock music to reach the younger generation. Instead of engaging the culture, we're hiding from it!

7. We've taught people to be escape artists. Instead of "occupying till He comes," we'd rather be astronauts and fly away. We read rapture novels when we should be praying for those living on the verge of martyrdom. Why can't we have their kind of faith? We can—if we're willing to pay the price and commit ourselves fully to God!

It is time to grow and mature as individuals and as a church. It is time to move on to perfection as Paul commanded us in Hebrews. It is time to become holy, as He is holy. God commanded us to do these things, so therefore it must be possible. The indwelling power of His Holy Spirit empowers us to defeat sin.

Hebrews 5:11-6:2: "Of whom we have many things to say and hard to be uttered, seeing ye are dull of hearing. For when for the time ye ought to be teachers, ye have need that one teach you again which be the first principles of the oracles of God; and are become such as have need of milk, and not of strong meat. For every one that useth milk is unskilful in the word of righteousness: for he is a babe. But strong meat belongeth to them that are of full age, even those who by reason of use have their senses exercised to discern both good and evil.

"Therefore leaving the principles of the doctrine of Christ, let us go on unto perfection; not laying again the foundation of repentance from dead works, and of faith toward God, Of the doctrine of baptisms, and of laying on of hands, and of resurrection of the dead, and of eternal judgment."

CONCLUSION

The purpose of this book is to expose the reader to the fact that negative emotions such as anxiety, fear, bitterness, jealousy, envy, rejection, etc., do cause most of our diseases. We have taught this from psychology, medicine, and from Scripture.

Our purpose is to give the reader only a brief overview of these negative emotions and experiences. Also, our purpose was not to teach you how to have victory over them in this book. If you want to learn the full extent of what these negative emotions and experiences are, and how to defeat them in you life, read and study *Biblical Foundations of Freedom*. For an extensive teaching on unbelief and other blocks to healing and our relationship with God, I recommend that you read and study *Continuing Works of Christ*.

—Art Mathias Ph.D.

Index

End Notes

Ader, R. and Cohen, N. 1975. Behaviorally Conditioned Immunosuppression. *Psychosomatic Medicine*, 37, 333-340.

Ader, R. and Cohen, N. 1993. Psychoneuroimmunology: Conditioning and stress. *Annual Review of Psychology*, 44, 53-85.

Affleck, G. et al. 1987. Attributional processes in rheumatoid arthritis patients. *Arthritis and Rheumatism*. 30, 927-931.

Amaral, J.R. and Sabbatini, R. 1999. Placebo Effect: The Power of the Sugar Pill. www.epub.org.br/cm/n09/mente/placebo1_htm.

Anson, O. 1999. Exploring the bio-psycho-social approach to premenstrual experiences. *Social Science and Medicine*, 49, 67-80.

Aoyama, N. 1998. Peptic Ulcers After the Hanshin-Awaji Earthquake: Increased Incidence of Bleeding Gastric Ulcers. *American Journal of Gastroenterology* 93, no. 3 (1998): 311-316.

Arck, P.C. et al. 1995. Stress-Triggered Abortion: Inhibition of Protective Suppression and Promotion of Tumor Necrosis Factor-Alpha (TNF-Alpha) Release as a Mechanism Triggering Resorptions in Mice. *American Journal of Reproduction Immunology* 33, no. 1: 74-80.

Associated Press. 2002. Protein-heart disease link backed. Inflammation may prove better predictor than cholesterol. Associated Press, Nov. 6, 2002.

Baltrusch, H.J., Stangel, W., and Titze, I. 1991. Stress, Cancer and Immunity. New Developments in Biopsychosocial and Psychoneuroimmunologic Research. *Acta Neurologica* (Napoli) 13, no. 4: 315-27.

Basha, I. et al. 1989. Atypical Angina in Patients with Coronary Artery Disease Suggests Panic Disorder. *International Journal of Psychiatry in Medicine* 19, No. 4: 341-46.

Bechara, A. et al. 1994. Insensitivity to future consequences following damage to human prefrontal cortex. *Cognition*, 50, 7-15.

Beecher, H.K. 1961. Surgery as placebo. *JAMA*; 176:1102-07.

Benedersky, M., and Lewis, M. 1994. Environmental risks, biological risks, and developmental outcome. *Developmental Psychology*, 30, 484-494.

Berk, L.S. et al. 2001. Modulation of Neuroimmune Parameters During the Eustress of Humor-Associated Mirthful Laughter. *Altern. Ther. Health Med.* 7 (2) 62-76.

Blumenthal, J.A. et al. 1993. Hypertension affects neurobehavioral functioning. *Psychosomatic Medicine*, 55, 44-50.

Boothby, J.L. et al. 1990. *Coping with chronic pain. Psychological factors in pain: Critical perspectives*. pp. 343-359. New York: Guilford Press.

Bosworth, F.F. 1973. *Christ the Healer*. Revell, P.O. Box 6287, Grand Rapids, Michigan.

Boyce, W., and Jemerin, J. 1990. Psychobiological differences in childhood stress response. I. Patterns of illness and susceptibility. *Development and Behavioral Pediatrics*, 11, 86.

Bovjberg, D.H. et al. 1990. Anticipatory immune suppression in women receiving cyclic chemotherapy for ovarian cancer. *Journal of Consulting and Clinical Psychology*, 58. 153-157.

Brooks-Gunn, J. 1988. Antecedents and consequences of variations in girls' menstrual timing. *Journal of Adolescent Health Care*, 9, 365-373.

Burt, V.L. et al. 1995. Prevalence of hypertension in the US adult population. Results from the Third National Health and Nutrition Examination Survey. 1988-91. *Hypertension*, 25, 305-315.

Burton, A.K. et al. 1995. Psychosocial predictors of outcome in acute and subacute low back trouble. *Spine*, 20, 722-728.

Burton, R. 1893. *1621 The Anatomy of Melancholy*, Vol. I, ed. AR Shilleto. London: Bell and Sons.

Busse, W.W., and Reed, C.E. 1988. Asthma: Definitions and pathogenesis. *Allergy: Principles and Practice* pp. 969-998. St. Louis, MO: Mosby.

Bussing, R. et al. 1996. Prevalence of anxiety disorders in a clinic-based sample of pediatric asthma patients. *Psychosomatics*, 37, 108-115.

Carney, R.M. et al. 1990. Major Depression, Panic Disorder, and Mitral Valve Prolapse in Patients Who Complain of Chest Pain. *American Journal of Medicine* 89, No. 6 (1990): 757-60.

Caspi, A., and Moffitt, T.E. 1991. Individual differences are accentuated during periods of social change. The sample case of girls at puberty. *Journal of Personality and Social Psychology*, 61, 157-168.

Coe, C.L. et al. 1992. Early rearing conditions alter immune responses in the developing infant primate. *Pediatrics*, 90, 505-509.

Cohen, H.J. 2000. Editorial: In search of the underlying mechanisms of frailty. *Journal of Gerontology: Biological Sciences and Medical Sciences*, 55A, M706-M708.

Cohen, S. et al. 1997. Social ties and susceptibility to the common cold. *JAMA* 277; 1940-44.

Cohen, S., and Herbert, Tracy B. 1996. *Annual Review, Psychology*. Health Psychology: Psychological Factors and Physical Disease from the Perspective of Human Psychoneuroimmunology. Department of Psychology, Carnegie Mellon University, Pittsburgh, PA.

Cohen, S., Tyrrell, D.A., and Smith A.P. 1991. Psychological Stress and Susceptibility to the Common Cold. *New England Journal of Medicine* 325, no. 9 (1991): 606-12.

Cohen, S., and Williamson, G. 1991. Stress and infectious disease in humans. *Psychological Bull*. 109,54.

Crombez, G. et al. 1999. Fear of pain is disabling than the pain itself: Further evidence on the role of pain-related fear in chronic back pain disability. *Pain*, 80, 529-539.

Costello, N. et al. 1998. Coping and emotional expression effects upon distress, illness burden, and cytokines in CFS patients after Hurricane Andrew. *Psychosom. Med.* 60:121-22.

Couch, R. 1990. *Respiratory diseases, in Antiviral agents and viral diseases of man*. Raven Press, NY pp. 327-372.

Cousins, N., 1989. Proving the power of laughter. *Psychology Today*. 20 (3): 22-26.

Crosby, L.J. 1998. Stress Factors, Emotional Stress and Rheumatoid Arthritis Disease Activity. *Journal of Advanced Nursing* 13, no. 4 (1988): 452-61.

Croiset, G. et al. 1987. Modulation of the immune response by emotional stress. *Life Sciences*, 40. 775-782.

Dahanukar, S.A. et al. 1996. The Influence of Surgical Stress on the Psychoneuro-Endocrine-Immune Axis. *Journal of Postgraduate Medicine* 42, no. 1: 12-14.

Dake's Annotated Reference Bible. Finnis Jennings Dake, Atlanta, Georgia. 1961.

Dentino, A.N. et al. 1999. Association of interleukin-6 and other biologic variables with depression in older people living in the community. *J. Am. Geriatr. Soc.* 47:6-11.

Devaraj, S. 2000. Alpha Tocopherol Supplementation Decreases Serum C-Reactive Protein and Monocyte Interleukin-6 levels in Normal Volunteers and Type 2 Diabetic Patients. *Free Radic Biol Med* 29, no. 8: 190-2.

Diagnostechs Lab Manual, 1991. Objective Evaluation of Stress. Kent, Wash. Diagnos-Techs, Inc.

Discovery Channel 2003. Placebo: Cracking the Code. www.discoveryhealth.co.uk.

Dunn, A.J. 1988. Nervous System-Immune System Interactions: An Overview. *Journal of Receptor Research* 8, nos. 1-4: 589-607.

Eaker, E.D., Pinsky J., and Castelli W.P. 1992. Myocardial infarction and coronary death among women: psychosocial predictors from a 20-year follow-up of women in the Framingham Study. *Am. J. Epidemiol.* 135:854-64.

Ershler, W. and Keller E. 2000. Age-associated increased interleukin-6 gene expression, late-life diseases, and frailty. *Annu. Rev. Med.* 51:245-70.

Everson, S.A. et al. 1997. Hostility and increased risk of mortality and acute myocardial infarction: the mediating role of behavioral risk factors. *Am. J. Epidemiol.* 146:142-52.

Fawzy, F.L. et al. 1990. A structured psychiatric intervention for cancer patients: I. Changes over time in methods of coping and affective disturbance. *Archives of General Psychiatry*. 47, 720-725.

Fawzy, R.L. et al. 1993. Malignant melanoma: Effects of a structured psychiatric intervention, coping, affective state, and immune parameters of recurrence and survival six years later. *Archives of General Psychiatry*. 50, 681-689.

Felitti, V.J. et al. 1998. Relationship of childhood abuse and household dysfunction to many of the leading causes of death in adults: The Adverse Childhood Experiences (ACE) Study. *American Journal of Preventive Medicine*, 14, 245-258.

Felton, D.L., Acherman, K.D., Wiegand, S.J., and Felten, S.Y. 1987. Noradrenergic sympathetic innervation of the spleen: I. Nerve fibers associated with lymphocytes and macrophages in specific compartments of the splenic shite pulp. *Journal of Neuroscience Research*, 18, 28-36.

Felton, D.L., Felton, S.Y., Carlso, S.L., Olschowka, J.A., and Livant S. 1985 Noradrenergic Sympathetic innervation of lymphoid tissue. *J. Immunol.* 135:755S-65S.

Felten, S.Y. and Felten, D.L. 1991. Innervation of lymphoid tissue. *Psychoneuroimmunology* (2nd ed., pp.27-71). Academic Press, San Diego, Cal.

Fleshner, M. et al. 1992. Specific changes in lymphocyte subpopulations: A mechanism for stress-induced immunomodulation. *Neuroimmunology*, 41, 131-142.

Frasure-Smith, N., Lesperance, F., and Talajic M. 1993. Depression following myocardial infarction: impact on 6-month survival. *JAMA* 270:1819–25.

Friedman, H., Klein, T., Friedman, Angrea L. 1996. *Psychoneuroimmunolgy, Stress, and Infection* (153). CRC Press Inc. Boca Raton, Florida.

Gatchel, R.J. et al. 1999. Psychosocial predictors of chronic pain and response to treatment. *Psychosocial factors in pain: Critical perspectives* pp. 412-434, New York: Guilford Press.

Gerencser, A., and Kovacs, K.J. *The Vagus Nerve: A Link Between Immune and Neuroendocrine System During Anaphylaxis.* Laboratory of Molecular Neuroendocrinology, Institute of Experimental Medicine, Budapest, Hungary.

Glaser, R. and Kiecolt-Glase, J.K. 1994. *Handbook of human stress and immunity.* Academic Press, San Diego, CA.

Glassman, A.H., and Shapiro P.A. 1998. Depression and the course of coronary artery disease. *Am. J. Psychiatry* 155:4–11.

Goadsby, P.J. 2001. Migraine, aura, and cortical spreading depression: Why are we still talking about it? *Annals of Neurology*, 49, 4-6.

Goldberg, A.L. et al. 1980. Hormonal Regulation of Protein Degradation and Synthesis in Skeletal Muscle. *Federation Proceedings* 39, no. 1: 31-36.

Goldsmith, H.H. et al. 1997. *Epidgenetic approaches to developmental psychopathology.* Development and Psychopathology, 9, 365-388.

Goliszek, A.G. *Breaking The Stress Habit.* Winston-Salem, NC: Carolina Press, 14.

Green, T., Neinemann, S.F., and Gusella, J.F. 1998. Molecular neurobiology and genetics: Investigation of neural function and sysfunction. *Neuron*, 20, 427-444.

Gunnar, M.R. 1992. Reactivity of the hypothalamic-pituitary-adrenocortical system to stressors in normal infants and children. *Pediatrics*, 90, 491-497.

Haines, A.P., Imeson, J.D., and Meade T.W. 1987. Phobic anxiety and ischemic heart disease. *Br. Med. J. Clin. Res. Educ.* 295:297–99.

Hall, C. and McBride, J. 1994. Upper respiratory tract infections: The common cold, pharyngitis, croup, bacterial tracheitis and epiglottis, in Respiratory infections. *Diagnosis and Management*, Third edition, Raven Press, NY, 1994.

Hart, A.D. 1986. *Adrenaline and Stress.* Waco: Word, 1986, p.67.

Hasenbring, M. et al. 1999. The efficacy of a risk factor-based cognitive behavioral intervention and electromyographic biofeedback in patient with acute sciatic pain: An attempt to prevent chronicity. *Spine*, 24, 2525-2535.

Hassed, C. 2001. How humor keeps you well. *Aust. Fam. Physician.* 30 (1): 25-28.

Haudek, C. et al.1999. The role an ethnicity and parental bonding in the eating and weight concerns of Asian-American and Caucasion college women. *Int. J. Eating Disorders.* 24:425-33.

Haworth-Hoeppner, S. 2000. The critical shapes of body image: the role of culture and family in the production of eating disorders. *J. Marriage and Family.* 62:212-27.

Health, October 1998. An Itsy-Bitsy Cause of Kidney Stones. Vol. 12. No. 7.

Heim, C. et al. Neuro-Endocrine and Immune Alterations In Adult Women After Childhood Abuse: Implications for the Pathophysiology of Physical Complaints. Dept. of Psychiatry and Behavioral Sciences, Emory University School of Medicine, Atlanta, GA, USA.

Herrmann, C. et al. 1998. Diagnostic groups and depressed mood as predictors of 22-month mortality in medical inpatients. *Psychosom. Med.* 60:570–77.

Hiller-Sturmhofel, Susanne and Bartke, A. 1998. The Endocrine System, an overview. *Alcohol Health and Research World* Vol. 22 No.3, 1998. Susanne Hiller-Sturmhofel, Ph.D. is a science editor of Alcohol Health and Research World. Andrzej Bartke, Ph.D. is professor and chairman of physiology at Southern Illinois University School of Medicine, Carbondale, Ill.

Huang, M.H., Ebey, J., and Wolf, S. 1989. Responses of the QT Interval of the Electrocardiogram During Emotional Stress. *Psychosomatic Medicine* 51, no. 4: 419-27.

Ingvar, D.H. 1985. Memory of the future: An essay on the temporal organization of conscious awareness. *Human Neurobiology*, 4, 127-136.

Iribarren, C. et al. 2000. The CARDIA Study. *JAMA.* 2000; 283: 2546-2551.

Jacobson, M.D. 2000. *The Word on Health.* Moody Press, Chicago, Ill.

Jacobson, M.D. June 2001. Diabetes Disease Activity may be related to Inflammation. *Vital Signs*, Vol. 3, no. 6.

Jacobson, M.D. Jan. 2001. Why Menopause Symptoms? *Vital Signs.* Vol. 3 no. 1.

Jansma, R. 2002. Karma: Key to Understanding Disease. *Sunrise Magazine.* December 2001/January 2002.

Johansson, E. et al. 2000. Low back pain patients in primary care. Subgroups based on the Multidimensional Pain Inventory. *International Journal Behavioral Medicine*, 7, 340-352.

Johnson-Laird, P.N. 1983. *Mental models: Towards a cognitive science of language, inference, and consciousness*. Cambridge, MA: Harvard University Press.

Kandel, E.R. 1998. A new intellectual framework for psychiatry. *American Journal of Psychiatry*, 155, 457-469.

Kandal, E.R. et al. 1992. *Principles of Neural Science* (2nd. ed.). New York: Elsevier.

Katon, W. 1998. The effect of major depression on chronic medical illness. *Semin. Clin. Neuropsychiatry* 3:82–86.

Katz, I.R. 1996. On the inseparability of mental and physical health in aged persons: lessons from depression and medical comorbidity. *Am. J. Geriatr. Psychiatry* 4:1–16.

Kawachi, I., Colditz, G.A., Ascherio, A., Rimm E.B. and Giovannucci, E. et al. 1994a. Prospective study of phobic anxiety and risk of coronary heart disease in men. *Circulation* 89:1992–97.

Kawachi, I., Sparrow, D., Vokonas, P.S., and Weiss, S.T. 1994b. Symptoms of anxiety and risk of coronary heart disease. The Normative Aging Study. *Circulation* 90:2225–29.

Kelly, J.A., and Kalichman, S.C. 2002. Behavioral Research in HIV/AIDS Primary and Secondary Prevention: Recent Advances and Future Directions. *Journal of Consulting and Clinical Psychology*. 2002, Vol. 70, no. 3, 629-639.

Kendall, P.C. et al. 2002. *Journal of Consulting and Clinical Psychology*, Special Issue: Behavioral Medicine and Clinical Health Psychology. June, 2002.

Kendler, K.S., Eaves, L.S. 1986. Models for the joint effect of genotype and environment on liability to psychiatric illness. *American Journal of Psychiatry*, 143, 279-289.

Kiecolt-Glaser, J.K. et al. 1987. Chronic stress and immunity in family caregivers of Alzheimer's disease victims. *Psyhcosomatic Medicine*, 29, 523-533.

Kiecolt-Glaser, J.K., Page G.G., Marucha, P.T., MacCallum, R.C., and Glaser, R. 1998. Psychological influences on surgical recovery: perspectives from psychoneuroimmunology. *Am. Psychol.* 53:1209–18.

Kiecolt-Glaser, J.K., McGuire, L., Robles, T.F., and Glaser, R. 2002. Emotions, Morbidity, and Mortality: New Perspectives from Psychoneuroimmunology. *Annual Review, Psychology*, 53:83-107.

Kida, H. et al. 1988. Facilitation of Tumor Metastasis to the Lung by Operative Stress in the Rat – Influence of Adrenocortical Hormones and Preoperative Administration of OK – 432 (Abstract). *Nippon Geka Gakkai Zasshi* 89, no.10: 1692-98.

Kleiger, R.E. et al. Decreased Heart Rate Variability and Its Association with Increased Mortality After Acute Myocardial Infarction. *American Journal of Cardiology* 59: 256-62.

Klonff-Cohen. 1996. Job Stress and Preeclampsia. *Epidemiology* 7: 245-249.

Korneva, E.A. 1967. The effect of stimulating different mesencephalic structures on protective immune response patterns. Sechenov *Physiological Journal of the USSR*, 53, 42-50.

Larsen, P.M. et al.1988. Future trends in cervical cancer. *Cancer Letters*, 41,123, 1988.

Lauritzen, M. 1994. Pathophysiology of the migraine aura: The spreading depression theory. *Brain*, 117, 199-210.

Lazarus, R., Folkman, S. 1984. *Stress, appraisal and coping*. Springer, NY, 1984.

Leary, W.P., and Reyes, A.J. 1993. Magnesium and Sudden Death. *South Africa Medical Journal* 64, no. 18:697-98; Mildred S. Seelig, Interrelationship of Magnesium and Estrogen in Cardiovascular and Bone Disorders, Eclampsia, Migraine and Premenstrual Syndrome. *Journal of American College of Nutrition* 12, no. 4: 442-58.

Lecomte, D., Fornes, P., Nicolas, G. 1989. Stressful Events as a Trigger of Sudden Death: A Study of 43 Medico-Legal Autopsy Cases. *Forensic Science International* 79, no.1 (1996): 1-10.

Lehman, C.D. et al 1991. Impact of Environmental Stress on the Expression of Insulin-Dependent Diabetes Mellitus. *Behavioral Neuroscience* 105, no. 2 (1991): 241-45.

Leventhal, H., Patrick-Miller, L., Leventhal, E.A., and Burns, E.A. 1998. Does stress-emotion cause illness in elderly people? In *Annual Review of Gerontology and Geriatrics*, Vol. 17. Focus on Emotion and Adult Development, ed. KW Schaie, MP Lawton, p. 138–84. New York: Springer.

Levine, M.P. et al.1994. Normative developmental challenges and dieting and eating disturbances in middle school girls. *Int. J. Eating Disorders*. 15:11-20.

Liebeskind, J.C. 1991. Pain can kill. *Pain* 44:3–4.

Lysle, D.T. et al. 1990. Characterization of immune alterations produced by a conditioned aversive stimulus. *Psychobiology*, 18, 220-226.

Lysle, D.T. et al. 1990. Stressor-induced alteration of lymphocyte proliferation in mice: Evidence for enhancement of mitogen responsiveness. *Brain, Behavior, and Immunology*. 4, 269-277.

Lutgendorf, S.K., Garand, L., Buckwalter, K.C., Reimer, T.T., Hong, S., and Lubaroff, D.M. 1999. Life stress, mood disturbance, and elevated interleukin-6 in healthy older women. *J. Gerontol. A Biol. Sci. Med. Sci.* 54A:M434–39.

Macris, N.T., Schiavi, R.C., Camerino, M.S., and Stein, J. 1970. Effect of hypothalamic lesions on immune processes in the guinea pig. *American Journal of Physiology*; 219,1205.

Maes, M., Bosmans, E., De Jongh, R., Kenis, G., Vandoolaeghe, E., and Neels, H. 1995. Increased serum IL-6 and IL-1 receptor antagonist concentrations in major depression and treatment resistant depression. *Cytokine* 9:853–58.

Maes, M., Lin, A., Delmeire, L., Van Gastel, A., and Kenis, G. et al. 1999. Elevated serum interleukin-6 (IL-6) and IL-6 receptor concentrations in posttraumatic stress disorder following accidental man-made traumatic events. *Biol. Psychiatry* 45:833–39.

Maes, M., Song, C., Lin, A., De, J.R., and Van, G.A. et al. 1998. The effects of psychological stress on humans: increased production of pro-inflammatory cytokines and a Th1-like response in stress-induced anxiety. *Cytokine* 10:313–18.

Marcoux, S. et al. 1989. The effect of leisure time physical activity on the risk of pre-eclampsia and gestational hypertension. *J. Epidemiol Community Health* 43 (2): 147-157.

Magarinos, A.M., Verdugo, J.M., and McEwen, B.S. 1997. Chronic Stress Alters Synaptic Terminal Structure in Hippocampus. *Proceedings of National Academy of Science USA* 94, no. 25: 14002-8.

Maier, S.F., and Laudenslager, M.L. 1988. Commentary: Inescapable shock, shock controllability, and mitogen stimulated lymphocyte proliferation. *Brain, Behavior, and Immunity.* 2, p. 87-91.

Maier, S., Watkins, L.R., and Flesher, M. 1994. Psychoneuroimmunology. *American Psychologist*, December.

Main, M., and Hesse, E. 1990. Parents' unresolved traumatic experiences are related to infant disorganized status: Is frightened and/or frightening parental behavior the linking mechanism? In Greenberg, M.T. et al. *Attachment in the preschool years: Theory, research, and intervention*, p. 161-182. Chicago: University of Chicago Press.

Mason, J.W. 1971. A re-evaluation of the concept of "non-specificity" in stress theory. *Journal of Psychiatric Research.* 8, 123-140.

Mathias, A.C. 2000. *Biblical Foundations of Freedom.* Wellspring Publishing, Anchorage, AK.

Mathias, A.C. 2002 *The Continuing Works of Christ.* Wellspring Publishing, Anchorage, AK.

McCance, Kathryn L., and Huether, Sue E. 1998. *Pathophysiology, The Biologic Basis for Disease in Adults and Children* (381-411). Third Edition, Mosby Inc. St. Louis, Missouri.

McCracken, L.M. et al. 1993. Prediction of pain in patients with chronic low back pain. Effects of inaccurate prediction and pain-related anxiety. *Behavioral Research and Therapy*, 31, 647-652.

McCraty, R. 1995. The Effects of Emotions on Short-Term Power Spectrum Analysis of Heart Rate Variability. *American Journal of Cardiology* 76, no.14: 1089-93.

McCraty, R. 1996. Stress and Emotional Health. Steroid Hormones Clinical Correlates: Therapeutic and Nutritional Considerations, Chicago: February 25, 1996.

Merikangas, K.R. et al. 2000. Migraine comorbidity. *The Headaches* 2nd ed. pp. 325-242. Philadelphia: Lippincott Williams and Wilkins.

Michelson, D., Stratakis, C., Hill, L., Reynolds, J., and Galliven, E. et al. 1996. Bone mineral density in women with depression. *N. Engl. J. Med.* 335:1176–81.

Miller, L.J. 1999. *Postpartum mood disorders.* Washington DC: American Psychiatric Press.

Miller, T.Q., Smith, T.W., Turner, C.W., Guijarro, M.L., Hallet, A.J. 1996. A meta-analytic review of research on hostility and physical health. *Psychol. Bull.* 119:322–348.

Miller, T.R. 1977. Psychophysiologic Aspects of Cancer: The James Ewing Lecture. *Cancer* 39, no. 2: 413-18.

Morady, F. et al. 1989. Epinephrine-Induced Reversal of Verapamil's Electrophysiologic and Therapeutic Effects in Patients with Paroxysmal Supraventricular Tachycardia. *Circulation* 79: 783-90.

Nance, D.M., Rayson, D., Carr, I. 1987. The effects of lesions in the lateral septal and hippocampal areas on the humoral immune response of adult female rats. *Brain, Behavior, and Immunity.* 1, 292-300.

National Heart, Lung, and Blood Institute NHLBI 1997. *Expert panel Report 2: Guidelines for the diagnosis and management of asthma.* National Asthma Education and Prevention Program. Washington DC: U.S. Department of Health and Human Services.

Neumark-Sztainer, D. et al. Disordered eating among adolescents: associations with sexual/physical abuse and other familial/psychosocial factors. *Int. J. Eat. Disord.* 28:249-58.

Nichols, G. 2003. Diabetes researcher with Portland, Or. Based Kaiser Permanente Center for Health Research. www.diabetes.org/enews/041901_depression.asp.

Nonacs, R., and Cohen, L.S. 1998. Postpartum mood disorders: Diagnosis and treatment guidelines. *Journal of Clinical Psychiatry*, 59, 34-40.

Nortan, W.W. 1980. Health-giving laughter. *British Medical Journal.* 280(6231): 1609-1610.

O'Hara, M.W. 1994. *Postpartum depression: Causes and consequences.* New York: Springer Verlag.

O'Hara, M.W. et al. 1990. Controlled prospective study of postpartum mood disorders: Comparison of childbearing and nonchildbearing women. *Journal of Abnormal Psychology*, 99, 3-15.

Olesen, J., and Schoenen, J. 2000. Synthesis of tension-type headache mechanisms. *The Headaches* (2nd ed. pp. 615-618). Philadelphia: Lippincot Williams and Wilkins.

Pate, C. 1997. Stress management and hypertension. *Acta Physiologica Scandinavica*, 640 (suppl.), 155-157.

Patel, C., Mormot, M. 1988. Can general practitioners use training in relation and management of stress to reduce mild hypertension? *British Medical Journal*, 296, 21-24.

Penninx, B.W.J.H., Guralnik, J.M., Pahor, M., Ferrucci, L., Cerhan J.R. et al. 1998b. Chronically depressed mood and cancer risk in older persons. *J. Natl. Cancer Inst.* 90:1888.

Penninx, B.W.J.H., Guralnik, J.M., Ferrucci, L., Simonsick, E.M., Deeg, D.J.H., Wallace, R.B. 1998a. Depressive symptoms and physical decline in community-dwelling older persons. *JAMA* 279:1720–26.

Penninx, B.W.J.H., Leveille, S., Ferrucci, L., van Eijk, J.T.M., Guralnik, J.M. 1999. Exploring the effect of depression on physical disability: longitudinal evidence from the established populations for epidemiologic studies of the elderly. *Am. J. Public Health* 89:1346–52.

Plaut, M. 1987. Lymphocyte hormone receptors. *Annual Review of Immunology*, 5, 621-669.

Polivy, J., and Herman, P.C. 2002. Cause of Eating Disorders. *Annual Review of Psychology*. 2002. 53:187-213.

Pratt, L.A., Ford, D.E., Crum, R.M., Armenian, H.K., Gallo, J.J., Eaton, W.W. 1996. Depression, psychotropic medication, and risk of myocardial infarction. *Circulation* 94:3123.

Perry, B.D. 1997. Incubated in terror: Neurodevelopmental factors in the "cycle of violence." In J. Osofsky (Ed.) *Children in a violent society* (pp. 124-149. New York: Guilford Press.

Rakic, P. et al. 1994. Synaptic development of the cerebral cortex: Implications for learning memory and mental illness. *Progress in Brain Research*, 102, 227-243.

Ramsey, J.M. 1982. *Basic pathophysiology: modern stress and the disease process.* Addison-Wesley Publishing Co., Menlo Park, Ca.

Rantanen, T., Penninx, B.W.J.H., Masaki, K., Lintunen, T., Foley D., Guralnik J.M. 2000. Depressed mood and body mass index as predictors of muscle strength decline in old men. *J. Am. Geriatr. Soc.* 48:613–17.

Research Update. Institute of HeartMath, Boulder Creek, Colo: Institute of HeartMath, 1995.

Ridker P.M. et al. 2002. Comparison of C-Reactive Protein and Low-Density Lipoprotein Cholesterol Level in the Prediction of First Cardiovascular Events. *The New England Journal of Medicine*. Vol 347:1557-1565. Nov. 14, 2002 No. 20.

Rinner, I. et al. 1992. Opposite effects of mild and severe stress on in-vitro activation of rat peripheral blood lymphocytes. *Brain, Behavior, and Immunity*. 6, 130-140.

Roitt, I.M. et al. 1985. *Immunology*. Churchill Livingstone, Edinburgh, 1985.

Rosenblum, L.A. et al. 1994. Adverse early experiences affect noradrenergic and sero-tonergic functioning in adult primates, *Biological Psychiatry*, 35, 221-227.

Roszman, T.L., Cross, R.J., Brooks, W.H., and Markesbery, W.R. 1985. Neuroimmuno-modulation: Effects of neural lesions on cellular immunity. *Neural Modulation of Immunity* pp. 95-111. Raven Press, New York.

Russell, J. 1996. Systemic Lupus Erythematosus: The disease and its Patients. *Lupus Letter* Volume 1, no. 1.

Rutter, M. et al. 1997. Integrating nature and nurture: Implications of person-environ-ment correlations and interactions in developmental psychopathology, *Development and Psychopathology*, 9, 335-364.

Sapolsky, R.M. 1992. *Stress: The aging brain and the mechanisms of neuron death.* Cambridge, MA: MIT Press.

Schmidt, D.D. et al. 1985 Stress as a precipitating factor in subjects with recurrent herpes labialis. *J. Fam. Practice*, 20, 359.

Seaward, B.L. 1992. Humor's healing potential. *Health Prog.* 73 (3): 66-70.

Selye, Hans. 1956. *The Stress of Life*. McGraw-Hill, New York, p. 78.

Selye, Hans. 1974. *Stress Without Distress*. J.B. Lippincott, Philadelphia and New York, p. 20.

Selye, H. 1974. *Stress of Life*, 176; Y. Tache, J. Tache, and Hans Selye, Antifertility Effect of CS-1 in the Rat. *Journal of Reproduction and Fertility* 37, no. 2: 257-62; K.H. Cui, 1996 The Effect of Stress on Semen Reduction in the Marmoset Monkey (Callithrix Jacchus). *Human Reproduction* 11, no. 3: 568-73; R. Alonso-Uriarte, I. Sojo-Aranda, and V. Cortes-Gallegos, 1991 Role of Stress in Male Fertility. *Archives de Investigacion Medica* (Mexico) 22, no. 2: 223-28.

Selye, Hans. 1996. *Stress of Life*, 1956. 43, 181; G. Riesso 1996. Effects of Different Psychophysiological Stressors on the Cutaneous Electrogastrogram in Healthy Subjects. *Archives of Physiology and Biochemistry* 104, no. 3: 282-86.

Selye, Hans. 1998. A Syndrome Produced by Diverse Nocuous Agents 1936, classical article. *Journal of Neuropsychiatry and Clinical Neurosciences* 10, no. 2: 230-31.

Shah, P.K. 1997. Plaque Disruption and Coronary Thrombosis: New Insight into Patho-genesis and Prevention. *Clinical Cardiology* 20, no. 11, suppl. 2: 38-44.

Shario, D. and Goldstein, I.B. 1982. Biobehavioral perspectives on hypertension. *Journal of Consulting and Clinical Psychology* 50, 841-858.

Shavit, Y., Lewis, J.W., Terman, G.W., Gale, R.P., Liebesking, J.C. 1984. Opioid peptides mediate the suppressive effect of stress on natural killer cell cytotoxicity. *Science* 223:188.

Sheridan, J.F. et al. 1994. Psychoneuroimmunology: Stress Effects on Pathogenesis and Immunity During Infection. *Clinical Microbiology Review* 7, no. 2: 200-212.

Shoebridge, P., and Growers, S.G. 2000. Parental high concern and adolescent-onset anorexia nervosa—a case-control study to investigate direction of causality. *Br. J. Psychiatry* 176: 132-37.

Siegel, D.J. 1999. *The Developing Mind, Toward a Neurobiology of Interpersonal Experience.* The Guilford Press, New York and London.

Siegman, A.W. et al. 2000. A prospective study of dominance and coronary heart disease in the normative aging study. *American Journal of Cardiology*, 86, 145-149.

Siegel, S.S. 1998. *Love, Medicine and Miracles.* Harper Perennial, A division of Harper Collins Publishers.

Singh, V.K. 1994. Autoimmunity and Neurologic Disorders. *Medical Sciences Bulletin,* September.

Singh, V.K. 1997. Immunotherapy for Brain Disease and Mental Illnesses. *Progress in Drug Research*, Monograph Series vol. 48, p. 129-146.

Smith, G.R., and McDaniels, S.M. 1983. Psychologically Mediated effect on the delayed hypersensitivity reaction to tuberculin in humans. *Psychosomatic Medicine*, 45, 65-70.

Solvason, H.B., Ghanta, V.K., Hiramoto, R.N. 1988. Conditioned augmentation of natural killer cell activity: Independence from nociceptive effect and dependence on interferon-beta. *Journal of Immunology*, 140, 661-665.

Spiegel, D. 2001. Mind matter: Group therapy and survival in breast cancer. *New England Journal of Medicine*, 345, 1767-1768.

Spiegel, D., and Bloom, J.R. 1983. Group therapy and hypnosis reduce metastatic breast carcinoma pain. *Psychosomatic Medicine*, 45, 333-339.

Speigel, D., et al. 1999. Effect of psychosocial treatment on survival of patients with metastatic breast cancer. *Lancet*, 8888-901.

Spinhoven, P. et al. 1994. The prevalence of respiratory disorder in panic disorder, major depressive disorder, and V-code patients. *Behavior Research and Therapy*, 32, 647-649.

Staats, P.S. 1999. Pain, depression and survival. *Am. Fam. Physician* 60:42–43.

Stamler, J. et al. 1999. Low risk-factor profile and long-term cardiovascular and noncardiovascular mortality and life expectancy: Findings for 5 large cohorts of young adult and middle-aged men and women. *JAMA*, 282, 2012-2018.

Stanford, S.C. and Salman, P. 1993. *Stress: From Synapse to Syndrome.* Academic Press, London.

Stein, N.L., and Trabasso, T. 1992. The organization of emotional experience: Creating links among emotion, thinking, language, and intentional actin. *Cognition and Emotion*, 6, 225-244.

Steiner, M. 1998. Perinatal mood disorders: A position paper. *Psycho-pharmacology Bulletin*, 34, 30-306.

Sternberg, E.M. 1997. Emotions and disease: from Balance of humors to balance of molecules. Dept. of Psychiatry and Behavioral Sciences, Emory University School of Medicine, Atlanta, GA, USA.

Stress, immune function, and health: The connection. New York: Wiley—Liss and Sons.

Stone, A.A. and Bovbjerg, D.H. 1994 Stress and Humoral Immunity: A Review of the Human Studies. *Advances in Neuroimmunology* 4, no.1: 49-56.

Strong, J.P. et al. 1999. Prevalence and extent of atherosclerosis in adolescents and young adults: Implication for prevention from the pathobiological determinants of atherosclerosis in youth study. *JAMA*, 281, 727-735.

Sun, A. et al. 1995. Restraint Stress Changes Heart Sensitivity to Arrhythmogenic Drugs. *Chung Kuo Yao LI Hsueh Pao* 16, no 5: 455-59; V. Elharrar et al. 1979 Adrenergically Medicated Ventricular Fibrillation in Probucol-Treated Dogs: Roles of Alpha and Beta Andregenic Receptors. *Pacing Clinical Electrophysiology* 2, no 4: 435-43.

Suzuki, Y. 1989. Pathogenesis of Water-Immersion Stress-Induced Gastric Ulcers in Rats with Renal Failure. *Scandinavian Journal of Gastroenterology*, Supplement 162: 127-30.

Taber's Medical Cyclopedic Dictionary. 18th Edition, 1997. F.A. Davis Company, Philadelphia.

Takahashi, K. et al. 2001. The elevation of natural killer cell activity induced by laughter in a crossover study. *Int. J. Mol. Med.* 8(6) 645-650.

Taylor, Kemeny, Reed. *American Psychologist* vol. 55, no. 1.

Teicher, M.H., et al. 1997. Preliminary evidence for abnormal cortical development in physically and sexually abused children using EEG coherence and MRI. *Annals of the New York Academy of Sciences*, 821, 160-175.

Tiller, W.A. et al. Cardiac Coherence: A New Noninvasive Measure of Autonomic Nervous System Order. *Alternative Therapies* 2, no. 1: 52-56.

Thompson, B. 2000. p.17 *Walls of My Heart.* Crown Ministries, Colorado Springs, CO.

Toivonen, L., Helenius, K., Viitasalo, M. 1997. Electrocardiographic Repolarization During Stress from Awakening on Alarm. *Cal. Journal of American College of Cardiology* 30, no. 3: 774-79.

Tucker, J.S. et al. 1991. Premenstrual syndrome. *International Journal of Psychiatry in Medicine*, 21, 311-341.

Turk, D.C. and Melzack, R. 1992. The measurement of pain and the assessment of people experiencing pain. In *Handbook of Pain Assessment*, ed. DC Turk, R Melzack, p. 3–12. New York: Guilford.

Tuzca, E.M. et al. 2001. High prevalence of coronary atherosclerosis in asymptomatic teenagers and young adults: Evidence from intravascular ultrasound. *Circulation*, 103, 2705-2710.

Ursin, H., Olff, M. 1993. *Stress from synapse to syndrome*. Academic Press, London. p.4-24.

Vahtera, J., Kivimaki, M., Koskenvuo, M., Pentti, J. 1997. Hostility and registered sickness absences: a prospective study of municipal employees. *Psychol. Med.* 27:693–701.

Van der Kolk, B.A. et al. 1996. *Traumatic stress: The effects of overwhelming experience on mind, body, and society*. New York: Guilford Press.

Van Doornen, Orlebeke K., *Journal of Human Stress* December 1982, 25-26.

Vergano, D. 2003. Teen has 2nd chance after mismatch forces 2nd transplant. *USA Today*, Feb. 21-23.

Verny, T. 1981. *The Secret Life of the Unborn Child*. Dell Publishing Company, New York, NY.

Vila, G. et al. 1999. Assessment of anxiety disorder in asthmatic children. *Psychosomatics*, 40, 404-413.

Wamboldt, M.Z. et al. 1998. Genetic association between atopy and behavioral symptoms in middle childhood. *Journal of Child Psychology and Psychiatry*, 39, 1007-1016.

Waldstein, S.R. et al. 1991. Neuropsychological correlates of hypertension: Review and methodologic considerations. *Psychological Bulletin*, 110, 451-468.

Watt, D.F. 1998. Affect and the limbic system: Some hard problems. *Journal of Neuropsychiatry and Clinical Neurosciences*, 10, 113-116.

Weiss, J.M. et al. 1989. Behavioral and neural influences on cellular immune responses: Effects of stress and interleukin-1. *Journal of Clinical Psychiatry*, 50, 43-53.

Whiteman, M.C. et al. 1997. Submissiveness and protection from coronary heart disease in the general population: Edinburg Artery Study. Lancet, 350, 541-545.

Whooley, M.A. and Browner W.S. 1998. Association between depressive symptoms and mortality in older women. *Arch. Intern. Med.* 158:2129–35.

Women's Health Initiative (WHI), established by the National Institutes of Health (NIH), and the National Heart, Lung, and Blood Institute (NHLBI) 1991. Published in the August 7, 2003 *New England Journal of Medicine* and the July 2002 and June 25, 2003 *Journal of the American Medical Association*.

Zandbergen, J. et al. 1991. Higher lifetime prevalence of respiratory disease in panic disorder. *American Journal of Psychiatry*, 148, 1583-1585.

Ziegler, J. 1995. Immune system may benefit from the ability to laugh. *J. National Cancer Institute*. 87(5): 342-343.

Zwilling, B.S. et al. 1990. Differential effect on restraint stress on MHC class II expression by murine peritoneal macrophages. *Brain, Behavior, and Immunity*, 4, 330-338.

Wellspring Ministry Resources

How to Minister to Others Seminar

Dr. Mathias provides training for those who desire to minister to others. It is our premise that all believers are ministers of the Gospel. We do not need to be "professionals" to be His ministers. This seminar is designed as a practical, hands-on approach. A workbook is provided to participants. Seminar available on Audio Cassettes with Workbook. $40.00 + shipping.

PERSONAL MINISTRY SESSIONS

Trained staff provides personal and telephone ministry sessions.

Call (907) 563-9033 to schedule appointments.

E-mail: akwellspr@aol.com

Website: akwellspring.com

Please check our website often, as we continually update our ministry and information.

Order Form

To order these books, please use this convenient order form, or call (907) 563-9033 or order from our online store: www.akwellspring.com.

ITEM	QUANTITY	PRICE/EACH	TOTAL
In His Own Image	_____	24.95	_____
Biblical Foundations of Freedom	_____	24.95	_____
Biblical Foundations of Freedom Study Guide	_____	10.00	_____
The Continuing Works of Christ	_____	24.95	_____
Biblical Foundations of Freedom Audio Tapes	_____	30.00	_____
Biblical Foundations of Freedom Video (VHS)	_____	119.95	_____
How to Minister to Others Audio Tapes	_____	30.00	_____
How to Minister to Others Workbook	_____	10.00	_____

SUBTOTAL _____

POSTAGE & HANDLING _____

TOTAL _____

Please print name clearly as it appears on your credit card:

_____
NAME

_____
ADDRESS

_____ _____ _____
CITY   STATE   ZIP

❑ VISA ❑ MC _____
                CARD #   EXP DATE

_____ _____
SIGNATURE   PHONE

POSTAGE & HANDLING CHARGES ON ORDERS:

1-2 Books/Tapes	5.00
3-4 Books/Tapes	10.00
5-6 Books/Tapes	15.00
7-10 Books/Tapes	20.00

Above charges are for domestic orders only. Please call or email for shipping & handling on international orders.

THIS ORDER MAY BE MAILED TO:

Wellspring Ministries of Alaska
PO Box 190084
Anchorage, AK 99519-0084

or faxed to (907) 243-6623